Gifts, Markets and Economies of Desire in Virginia Woolf

Gifts, Markets and Economies of Desire in Virginia Woolf

Kathryn Simpson

© Kathryn Simpson 2009
Softcover reprint of the hardcover 1st edition 2009 978-1-4039-9706-7
All rights reserved. No reproduction, copy or transmission of this
publication may be made without written permission.

No portion of this publication may be reproduced, copied or transmitted
save with written permission or in accordance with the provisions of the
Copyright, Designs and Patents Act 1988, or under the terms of any licence
permitting limited copying issued by the Copyright Licensing Agency,
Saffron House, 6-10 Kirby Street, London EC1N 8TS.

Any person who does any unauthorized act in relation to this publication
may be liable to criminal prosecution and civil claims for damages.

The author has asserted her right to be identified
as the author of this work in accordance with the Copyright, Designs
and Patents Act 1988.

First published 2009 by
PALGRAVE MACMILLAN

Palgrave Macmillan in the UK is an imprint of Macmillan Publishers Limited,
registered in England, company number 785998, of Houndmills, Basingstoke,
Hampshire RG21 6XS.

Palgrave Macmillan in the US is a division of St Martin's Press LLC,
175 Fifth Avenue, New York, NY 10010.

Palgrave Macmillan is the global academic imprint of the above companies
and has companies and representatives throughout the world.

Palgrave® and Macmillan® are registered trademarks in the United States,
the United Kingdom, Europe and other countries.

ISBN 978-1-349-54601-5   ISBN 978-0-230-22843-6 (eBook)
DOI 10.1057/9780230228436

A catalogue record for this book is available from the British Library.

Library of Congress Cataloging-in-Publication Data

Simpson, Kathryn, 1967–
  Gifts, markets and economies of desire in Virginia Woolf/Kathryn
  Simpson.
    p. cm.
  Includes bibliographical references and index.

  1. Woolf, Virginia, 1882–1941—Criticism and interpretation. I.
  Title.
  PR6045.O72Z87647   2008
  823'.912—dc22   2008016182

10 9 8 7 6 5 4 3 2 1
18 17 16 15 14 13 12 11 10 09
Transferred to Digital Printing in 2014

To the birthday of my life, Sarah Burgess, whose love and generosity are without measure.

In memory of my Dad, Allan Gordon Simpson (1925–2003), and my friend and colleague, Dr Mike Davis (1962–2006) – two of the most generous of men.

Contents

Acknowledgements	viii
List of Abbreviations	ix
Introduction	1
1 The Business of Writing: Economies in Woolf's Essays	12
2 Queering the Market: 'Mrs Dalloway in Bond Street', *Mrs Dalloway* and 'The Hours'	50
3 A Gift of Vision: *To the Lighthouse, Orlando* and *Between the Acts*	85
4 Moments of Giving: Generosity and Desire in Woolf's Short Fictions	128
5 Conclusion	163
Notes	165
Bibliography	185
Index	194

Acknowledgements

I thank my family and friends for their love and encouragement, and my friends and colleagues at the University of Birmingham and at the Annual Woolf Conferences over the last eight years for their invaluable and unfailing support and inspiration. I also thank Ruth Hoberman and Alice Staveley for allowing me to have access to unpublished material. I am grateful to the University of Birmingham's School of Education for granting me a sabbatical leave that enabled me to complete this project. For permission to quote from the works of Virginia Woolf I am grateful to the executors of the Virginia Woolf Estate, The Random House Group Ltd., and the Houghton Mifflin Harcourt Publishing Company.

Abbreviations

AROO	*A Room of One's Own*
BTA	*Between the Acts*
CD	*The Crowded Dance of Modern Life (ed. and introd. Rachel Bowlby)*
CSF	*Complete Shorter Fiction*
D	*The Diary of Virginia Woolf (5 volumes)*
JR	*Jacob's Room*
L	*The Letters of Virginia Woolf (6 volumes, ed. Nigel Nicolson and Joanne Trautmann)*
MD	*Mrs Dalloway*
MOB	*Moments of Being*
O	*Orlando*
The Hours	*The Hours: The British Manuscript of Mrs Dalloway (ed. and introd. Helen Wussow)*
TG	*Three Guineas*
TTL	*To the Lighthouse*
TTL Holograph	*Holograph Version of To the Lighthouse*

Introduction

In recent years there has been an increasing critical interest in the relationship between modernist writers and their writing and the marketplace, exploding the myth mapped out in earlier influential studies, such as Andreas Huyssen's *After the Great Divide*, of modernist writers' and artists' absolute disinterest, detachment and contempt for popular and consumer culture. The polarised gendered distinction this myth also assumes between 'high' (masculine) and 'low' (feminine) art is undermined by more recent studies. These have begun to uncover, in Lawrence Rainey's words, 'the growing complexity of cultural exchange and circulation in modern society' (1998, 2) and to explore the contradictory and ambiguous interrelationships between modernist artists, the cultural institutions that produce art, the market, readers and modernist art as a 'commodity of a special sort' (Rainey, 1998, 3). Work in this area focused initially on James Joyce's engagement with advertising. It 'irrevocably opened the modernist canon to consumer theory' (Abbott 194),[1] and there is now a substantial body of work focused on Woolf's writing in relation to these concerns. These important studies elucidate her complex and contradictory engagement with the marketplace and relate this to the sexual and class politics of her work, to her own practice of publication, her personal attitude to the commercial world and to her sense of herself as a modernist writer.[2]

Alongside this exploration of Woolf's often ambivalent relationship to and representation of the marketplace, my study draws attention to the gift economy in operation in her writing and to the importance attributed to the giving of gifts. Focusing on the complex, contradictory and inconsistent interaction of gift and market economies in Woolf's work complicates still further the location of Woolf and her writing in relation to commercial literary production and to the niche-markets in which modernist texts circulated. This focus also expands the critical debate about the feminist and socialist politics of her writing, as well as furthering the interest in Woolf's representations of female sexuality and desire, and in the aesthetics of her writing with which such representations are entwined. The central thesis

2 Gifts, Markets and Economies of Desire

I explore here is that gift-giving in Woolf's writing signifies an alternative feminine libidinal economy. This can destabilise the heteropatriarchal social order that capitalism seems to keep in place, and it can disrupt the ideological values and beliefs these social and economic systems perpetuate. Commodity culture can stimulate and mobilise a profusion of desires that it is unable to contain or control. However, I argue that it is the operation of the gift economy in Woolf's writing that works to realise a subversive economy of desire for and between women so that they can prioritise a different set of values. Contemplating ideas about the 'gift' of creativity and its circulation in the form of books in the literary marketplace also raises broader issues about reading and economies of meaning, which obviously relate to Woolf's preoccupation with the role of her ideal reader – to act like an accomplice reading with generosity.

Gifts and gift-giving have important social, economic and political significance in a wide range of cultures. As Mark Osteen remarks, an interest in them has been a part of the development of Western society itself (1). Most often defined in opposition to monetary economies, and more recently specifically in opposition to capitalist economies, the gift is often perceived as a counter to the ideologies, concepts and moral values such systems endorse. The gift then is seen to represent what is ethically good and resonates with ideals such as altruism, sacrifice and love – a utopian contrast to the calculation, manipulation and corrupting impersonality and self-interest of the market. However, as most theories of the gift demonstrate, this dichotomy is not so clear-cut, nor are the two economies so reliably separate. Rather, there are a wide variety of gifts given for a wide variety of reasons, and motivations for giving and responses on receiving are usually complicated and multi-faceted. In his essay 'Gifts' (1844), one of the earlier theorists of the gift, Ralph Waldo Emerson, defines a true gift as being that which conveys something of the giver, which exemplifies his/her talents: 'The only gift is a portion of thyself' and other gifts are merely 'barbarous . . . apologies for gifts' (1997, 25). However, such a true gift is also problematic in the response it provokes in the recipient, who may feel his/her independence to be compromised by the obligation and gratitude such a gift implies. The importance of gratitude is also key to Georg Simmel's ideas about social bonds and gifts, which similarly works to place upon the recipient an unwelcome state of obligation.

With the expansion of sociology, anthropology and ethnography in the late nineteenth and early twentieth centuries came an intensification of the interest in gifts and gift economies. Since Marcel Mauss' groundbreaking ethnographic study, *The Gift (Essai Sur Le Don)*,[3] was first published in 1925, it is the notion of reciprocity that has been the main focus of theoretical discussions of the gift. It has also been central to the question about whether the gift can be said to exist, 'compromised' as it is by the expectation of a return exchange gift, and so perceived by some as indistinguishable from a

Introduction 3

monetary exchange. Several theorists of the gift argue in different ways that Mauss' theory negates the possibility of the gift, with the system of reciprocity resembling an economic exchange. This view is asserted by Jacques Derrida, for whom the gift is 'the impossible' (1992, 7); for Pierre Bourdieu, gift-giving is a kind of fiction, an 'individual and collective misrecognition' of the economic calculation and self-interest of the exchange masked as a gift (1997, 198). For Hélène Cixous, the obligation to reciprocate is also particularly problematic: she refers to this as 'the paradox of the gift that takes' (1981a, 263). For her a gift given in the hope or expectation of a return gift signals the denial of the gift, and its value is annulled, associated as it is for her with a masculine economy of calculation, thrift and a capitalist ethos focused on making profits. However, for many other theorists, it is precisely the process of reciprocation that seals the social bond so central to the gift economy, and the complex and often ambiguous motivations for giving and receiving are also vital to the social, emotional and erotic bonds that gifts can create. In Mauss' theory, reciprocation is not a paradoxical denial of the gift, nor a smoke-screen masking market exchange, but is rather a fundamental part of gift exchange practices. Indeed, the importance of reciprocity as a means of consolidating social bonds is key to Mauss' analysis of the central significance of exchange practices in the ancient, contemporary, Western and non-Western cultures on which his study focuses. As Osteen claims, the gift 'constitutes perhaps the fullest expression of what it means to be human . . . forges social connections and enacts one's true freedom' (14).

Mauss's theories emerged at a significant historical moment in Europe and, as societies struggled to recover, socially, politically, emotionally and economically from the First World War, debate about ways of managing the economy and criticism of existing economic systems came to the fore (notably, in Britain, where issues of economic adjustment were 'perhaps more prominent than most', (Aldcroft, 1983, 2)). More specifically in the Bloomsbury circle, the ideas of John Maynard Keynes, advocate of deficit spending and credit for the consumer to boost the economy, were to bring about radical changes in the British economy. Mauss draws on the studies of several prominent ethnographers. The key tenets of his study are that gifts are never freely given, and that social bonds are formed and consolidated, and cultural continuity ensured, by the obligation to reciprocate. Gifts exchanged are also never simply material, but inherently spiritual, even magical, imbued as they are with the identity or the soul of the donor – an idea most clearly encapsulated in his understanding of the *hau* of Maori exchange systems. Although Mauss notes the closing down of gift economies in capitalist societies, he also looks hopefully for traces of a gift economy remaining in Western European society of the time, perceiving gift practices and 'the morality of former times' in individual, group and state activities and legislative changes (65).[4] Using his theory of gift economies, Mauss casts a new and critical light on the increasingly commodified, impersonal and anonymous

4   *Gifts, Markets and Economies of Desire*

nature of Western culture, a culture impoverished by capitalist values and practices: 'the mere skimpy life that it is given through the daily wages doled out by employers' (69).[5]

It is not clear whether Woolf knew of Mauss' work, but the general interest in the 'primitive' in modernist circles is clearly an influence in her writing. She would also have been aware of developments in anthropology and the newly emerging area of ethnography through her connection with Cambridge academics, notably her friendship with Jane Harrison, a classical scholar whose radically new interpretations and theories of ancient Greek art and culture were informed by anthropological and ethnographic studies. Harrison was herself influenced by the theories of Emile Durkheim (Mauss' uncle with whom he worked). Sandra J. Peacock notes her praise of work co-written by Durkheim and Mauss, and by Henri Hubert and Mauss in the 1890s (181). Other influences on Harrison and Woolf include George Frazer's work, especially *The Golden Bough*. As Meg Albrink notes, Woolf's 'connections within the Bloomsbury Group would have introduced her to the innovations of the Cambridge School of modern ethnographers, a group that included Malinowski, W. H. R. Rivers, and Alfred Cort Haddon' (197).[6]

In Woolf's writing, it is the broader interest of Mauss' study – to examine what participating in gift practices reveals about people's perception of things and people (Carrier 9) – that is of particular interest. In addition, it is the different perspective on social structures and the organisation of Western culture that understanding gift economies can bring, as they 'throw light upon our morality and help to direct our ideals' (Mauss 71, 78–80), which is also significant. These key aspects of Mauss' work resonate strongly with the effect of gift practices found in Woolf's writing as they illuminate her social critique in new ways through the dynamic interconnection of the social, the economic and representations of desire. Throughout much of her work, Woolf expresses concerns similar to those of Mauss about the (all-pervasive) ethos of capitalism. Her writing also explores the ways in which a gift economy can operate in part as an alternative to capitalist exchange by privileging generosity, social bonds and intimacies, and rendering unimportant the purely monetary value of the objects exchanged. Significantly, the expectation or even obligation to reciprocate does not necessarily annul the spirit of the gift and convert it into a mercantile exchange; rather, it fulfils one function of the gift which is to reinforce social bonds.

Mauss' understanding of a present-day gift economy, in which commodity and gift economies co-exist, also sheds light on the gift economies in Woolf's work which operate in relation, rather than in a simple opposition, to the market. Although expressions of generosity and the literal giving of gifts do work to undermine capitalism's acquisitive ethos and the fixing of value and have a utopian quality, they take place within a capitalist society and so subvert this economic system from within. This does not mean that the gift

Introduction 5

is subsumed in the dominant paradigm of capitalist exchange so that it becomes an impossibility or simply a 'fiction'. Rather, the profound ambiguity of the gift (in terms of motivation, its effect on the relationship between the participants and its value in every sense[7]) has a disruptive effect, suggestively sidestepping the calculation of market exchange. Further, in an increasingly impersonal and rigid economy (especially in the 1920s with the British Government stalwartly adhering to a policy of fiscal and monetary retrenchment in an attempt to return to the stability of the Gold Standard (Aldcroft 1986, 6)), the need to counter the impersonality of commodity culture through the exchange of personal gifts becomes more urgent (as Carrier argues, 11).

However, Woolf's representation of the gift economy is more spontaneous, pleasurable and risky than the seemingly orderly threefold practice of giving, receiving and reciprocating in an ongoing circulation of exchange identified by Mauss (the apparent certainty of which others have criticised). It is also crucially complicated by her central concerns with issues of gender and sexuality. Woolf's questioning of capitalist paradigms, unlike Mauss' challenges, is bound up with her resistance to and subversion of the heterosexual and patriarchal norms and values capitalism seems to reinforce. A focus on the gift and gift economies expands the feminist perspective on the experience of women in a heteropatriarchal capitalist society offered in Woolf's work as it further complicates the negotiation of both capitalist and gift economies. This is partly because, in giving gifts, women run the risk of colluding with hegemonic social and sexual power structures that identify woman *as* a gift to be exchanged between men, even as they pose a more subversive threat by usurping the active role assigned to men in such monetary and heterosexual economies. As active agents, or what cultural anthropologist Gayle Rubin calls 'exchange partners', women defy the role assigned to them in heterocentric cultures as 'sexual semi-objects – gifts' (542, 543). In doing so they subvert the social mechanisms by which 'obligatory heterosexuality' and women's oppression are reinforced and perpetuated in male-dominated societies, through male 'rights of bestowal' (543, 545). These ideas, presented in her influential essay 'The Traffic in Women: Notes on the "Political Economy" of Sex', are in part a response to the work of structural anthropologist Claude Lévi-Strauss whose study of gift exchange in primitive societies, *The Elementary Structures of Kinship*, adds to Mauss' work by focusing on sex, gender and sexuality. Writing from a feminist perspective, Rubin challenges the unquestioning endorsement of the exchange of women as gifts that Lévi-Strauss posits as intrinsic to the consolidation of kinship bonds. She argues that because women are perceived only as 'sexual subjects', they cannot 'realize the [social] benefits of their own circulation' and that '(t)he asymmetry of gender – the difference between exchanger and exchanged – entails the constraint of female sexuality' (543, 548). Importantly, she makes clear that this 'traffic' in women is not 'confined to

6   *Gifts, Markets and Economies of Desire*

the "primitive" world' but is 'more pronounced and commercialized in more "civilized societies" ' (543). These ideas resonate clearly with Woolf's writing. A focus on gift economies brings to the fore the criticisms of the 'sex/gender system' (a term coined by Rubin, 534) of compulsory heterosexuality on which it is based, and of the stifling of women's desires and agency. Gifts in Woolf's work suggest a subversive sexual politics and the articulation of women's homoerotic desires; indeed, gift-giving and gift economies can be seen to realise and articulate subversive desires which threaten to undermine social and sexual norms and systems.

Hélène Cixous and Luce Irigaray also propose theories of the gift that are intrinsically connected to gender and sexuality, and which have potential to disrupt heterosexual and market economies radically. Their discussion of masculine and feminine economies works simultaneously at the level of the material manifestations of such economies (seeing the masculine economy exemplified in capitalist exchange and the feminine economy in the process of gift exchange) and at the level of the psychological, libidinal and emotional experience. Irigaray contemplates the effect of women taking charge of their own desires and their social and political agency by 'going to market' on their own, 'free from the control of the seller-buyer-consumer subjects' (1985, 196). More radically, women's refusal to go to market at all, and the rejection of a market mode of exchange, creates possibilities for 'a certain economy of abundance' denied by capitalist commerce (1985, 197).

Although for Cixous the sense of obligation and the need to respond with a reciprocal gift or gratitude are issues that problematise the gift, her theory of the gift's subversive potential, so that it threatens to undermine the dominant capitalist paradigm and the heteropatriarchal social organisation with which it co-exists, resonates strongly with the representations of gift economies in Woolf's writing. For Cixous, the feminine gift economy privileges fluidity, indeterminacy, a destabilisation of hierarchies and rational systems, bringing about a disturbance of property rights. It does not try to recover its expenses or to recuperate its losses; in fact, giving, excess and overflow are recognised as sources of pleasure and *jouissance*. This concept of the gift economy as feminine, disruptive and resistant to the commodifying impulse of capitalism has a suggestive significance for exploring the experimental modernist forms and aesthetics of Woolf's writing, which similarly privileges ambiguity, indeterminacy and inconclusiveness. It can be said to have a textual generosity in its richness, depth and associative connections, a syntactic fullness, created through the 'highly elliptical [sentence] structures . . . whose phrases and clauses, sutured by semicolons . . . allow an unbroken accretion or amplification of detail within the individual sentence' (Boone, 1998, 179). Joseph Allen Boone's comment on 'the ubiquitous use of present-tense participial phrases [which] generates forward motion' (179) is also in tune with the gift economy in which, as Lewis Hyde remarks, 'The only essential is this: *the gift must always move*', its purpose is not to 'stand

Introduction   7

still . . . mark a boundary or resist momentum' but to 'keep(s) going' to ensure the circulation of gifts and the connections and bonds they create (4, Hyde's emphasis). In this sense, reciprocation of the gift or the passing of the gift to another recipient in a circulation of gift-giving is seen as positive.

The importance of the reciprocation of gifts as a means of creating and cementing social bonds is also evident in Woolf's own gift-giving practice. The social role the gift plays corresponds to the socialist dimension of Woolf's thinking, writing and political involvements. Woolf lived through a period of dramatic change in British history, in which Britain's international position as a political, economic and imperial power declined, especially after the First World War, and was displaced by the newly emerging powers of Germany and America. These international changes coincided with changes in the social, political and economic structures of British society, and with legislative, parliamentary and economic changes and improvements, as well as with the rise of the Labour Party. These caused rigid class and gender hierarchies to begin to shift (as Woolf records in her 1924 essay, 'Mr Bennett and Mrs Brown').[8] Although Woolf was highly conscious of her securely middle-class status, she was at times both uneasily self-conscious and superior about her class privilege – 'an uneasy woman of property' and 'a chameleon writer', as Alex Zwerdling observes (33). Although she criticised the class system in her writing, she was in no doubt that her class privilege and her inherited wealth were the key to her becoming a writer.[9] Honest enough to acknowledge that her lack of knowledge and understanding of working-class life and experience made her unfit to represent it, her unsympathetic and prejudiced views also surface in problematic and sometimes shocking ways. Yet, she was also a woman who throughout her life was engaged with organisations and causes the aims of which were to bring about social and political reforms. She participated in activities that Mauss would characterise as part of a gift economy – her work for the Workers Educational Association and for the Women's Co-operative Guild, for instance, as well as her giving of charity gifts, her letter writing and other support for various political groups at different times of her life.

Although the gift economy is evident in Woolf's earlier fiction, *The Voyage Out* and *Night and Day*, it is in her writing of the 1920s and 1930s that it becomes more prominent and more complexly connected to ideas about the monetary economy, as well as to her own contradictory relationship to the literary marketplace. As others have noted, Woolf's sense of the market economy was in some ways in tune with Keynes' ideas of the economy as a more fluid and shifting entity. There is a sense in her work of the aesthetic and erotic pleasures that commodity culture can engender and release, with the ever-changing flux of commodity spectacle stimulating both the imagination and desires and opening up new opportunities for women. The sense of endless economic flows and the abandonment of fixed reference points (such as the Gold Standard, which Keynes argued limited the economy) also

8 *Gifts, Markets and Economies of Desire*

clearly correspond with Woolf's modernist aesthetics, modes of creativity and the politics of her writing. However, she was also aware of the ruthlessness that underlies this apparent democratisation of consumer pleasure and of the inequality of access to material comforts and luxury; as Leslie Hankins argues, Woolf's criticism is aimed at 'the [capitalist] power brokers behind the market' (Hankins, 2000, 23). Hankins locates Woolf on 'an ideological faultline' between the private sphere of artistic creation and the 'threatening energy of the streets' (2000, 18). This faultline has many manifestations, and usefully encapsulates Woolf's identity as a modernist writer, a businesswoman and a 'reader-consumer' of commodity culture.

Woolf was involved in the business of writing in several ways: as a reviewer and essay writer, as a novelist, and as the co-owner of the Hogarth Press. This participation in the literary market played a vital role in sustaining her materially, imaginatively, intellectually, psychologically and emotionally. As Lee argues, Woolf was 'intensely conscious of her value in the market-place' (1996, 558); her preoccupation with her earnings in her diaries may in part be related to her life-long anxieties about money (not having enough but not wanting too much). These anxieties stemmed, partly at least, from her father's attitude to and manipulative use of money,[10] but also from the close connection she perceived between sales figures and her reputation and success. Sales figures feature prominently in her diaries and seem to be a marker of her artistic, as well as her financial, achievement, so that her earnings act as an affirmation of her identity and success as a writer. Making money and attaining financial independence are also key aspects of her feminist politics. As Jane Garrity argues, '(f)or Woolf, making money is both an act of subversion – precisely because she's a woman – and a form of contamination, because it exposes the economic basis of her literary production' (2000, 197). She also knowingly exploits the literary market in several ways – by commanding increasingly high fees for her journalism as her reputation grew in the late 1920s, by submitting the same piece for publication more than once and so 'making a double income' (Lee, 1996, 559), and by and taking advantage of the opportunity offered to her by Dorothy Todd, the editor of *Vogue* in the early 1920s, not only to make money (her key aim in publishing in such venues), but also to enhance her reputation in a different sphere (Garrity, 2000, 195).[11]

Greater financial independence gave her purchasing power and access to the pleasures of commodity culture. She did learn to use her 'spending muscle', but she was also conscious of her preoccupation with money, and the pleasures of spending it were coloured by concern about her difficulty in spending 'without fuss or anxiety' (*D3* 212). Her diary repeatedly returns to these issues and to the distaste she feels for the commercial world even as she benefits from it.[12] Interestingly, Woolf's fiction represents very limited instances of spending, perhaps revealing this unease. As a highbrow writer, Woolf sustained an idealistic belief in the value of writing as a form of art for its own sake, and she saw the dangers and detrimental effects of the commodification of writing. This ideologically conflicted position of participation in, yet distance from, the market was a tricky balance to sustain for Woolf, as she weighed up her money-making with a resistance to the capitalist ethos in order to maintain a sense of her writing as separate from other commodities. Woolf's co-ownership (with Leonard Woolf) of the Hogarth Press is one of the ways she achieved this balance. Another is her creation of what Hyde calls 'a protected gift-sphere in which the work is created' (275).

In some ways the Hogarth Press seemed to provide an alternative to capitalist enterprise[13] and provided a buffer protecting Woolf to some extent from the pressures and economic exigencies of the commodity market. The Press was a success and expanded. It became 'a serious business', as Woolf records in her diary (D2 307), and developed a significant commercial role that overlapped with the mainstream literary market. As Willison et al. argue, the Press's 'commercial component . . . led inevitably to a rapprochement with the general trade' (xv). However, this expansion was not driven by the capitalist urge to maximise profits[14] and the Press took financial risks to publish work that commercial publishers would not consider. This included material by new and working-class writers, writing that was experimental and politically unorthodox, as well as translations, notably of Freud's writings – a move that entailed a significant risk of prosecution given the shock and offence that Freud's ideas had the potential to create. It also sought to restore, for some of the time at least, a sense of a more holistic process of literary production, as Woolf was involved not only in the writing of her texts, but also in their printing, binding, marketing, packaging and posting – the elements that capitalist mass production isolates in the production of alienable commodities exchanged in an impersonal market.

The Press was also part of the changing literary market in which modernist art was perceived not merely as an object of simple and immediate mass consumption, but rather as 'a rarity' with value as an investment (Rainey, 1999, 43). The Woolfs' decision to reprint 'Kew Gardens' in 1927 in a limited edition format was, according to Staveley (2003), motivated by the temptation of capitalising on Woolf's growing status and maintaining some control over her work, as well as by making a profit in this niche market in which her work, carefully produced to look expensive, was marketed as a collectible. Willison et al. also argue that the Press actually facilitated the entry of modernism into the more general literary marketplace and contributed to 'the eventual reception of modernism in Britain and America in the late 1920s and 1930s which had been initiated by Pound and Ford' (xv). The success of the Hogarth 'Uniform Editions' of Woolf's novels (begun in 1929) not only made her writing more affordable to the common reader, ('reaching that wide public audience of common readers, which she found so necessary', Snaith, 2000, 45), but this publication of inexpensive editions 'staked a claim for Virginia Woolf's commercial value and . . . for the lasting value of

10 *Gifts, Markets and Economies of Desire*

her works' (Lee, 1996, 558). The Hogarth Press, then, was a significant way in which Woolf negotiated the economic pressures of the marketplace as it created space in which Woolf could write and experiment. She records the feeling of being 'the only woman in England free to write what [she] like(s)', and of having 'a queer, & very pleasant sense, of something which I want to write; my own point of view' (*D3* 43; *D2* 107). As Laura Marcus notes, it created a liminal space, 'a space somewhere between the private, the coterie, and the public sphere' (1996, 145). Straddling the boundary between the value of art and market value attributed to her work, it facilitated the sense of freedom, control and security necessary for Woolf to write.

Woolf also negotiated the contradictions of her position by reassuring herself of her integrity as an artist, even as she made money from her writing. For instance, after her success from publishing in *Vogue*, she felt the need to 'atone' and to assert her literary credentials, declaring, 'I am going to write about Stella & Swift for Richmond, as a sign of grace, after sweeping guineas off the Vogue counter' (*D3* 33).[15] Again, having reflected on the good level of pre-publication sales of *To the Lighthouse*, Woolf writes, 'to show I am genuine, I find myself thinking of other things with absorption & forgetting that it will be out on Thursday' (*D3* 134). The profits she makes from this novel are also put at a remove from the market economy by their literal and symbolic transformation into a gift: 'We have a nice little shut up car. . . . The world gave me this for writing The Lighthouse, I reflect, a book which has now sold 3,160 (perhaps) copies' (*D3* 147). She is also at pains to distinguish the writing she produced for money (her reviews, essays and the short stories she sold to magazines) from her creative writing (her novels).

Although it is possible to trace Woolf's discomfort about her commercial success to her sense of superiority and snobbishness, and to see this as a key indication of her contradictory (and possibly hypocritical) attitude to her success, what is also clear is that these earnings enable her to construct a 'gift-sphere' (Hyde 275). In Hyde's terms, like other artists, Woolf 'converts market wealth into gift-wealth: (s)he converts [her] earnings to the support of [her] art' (Hyde 275). In her diaries and letters she repeatedly returns to the importance of making money, not for the sake of hoarding her wealth, but to earn sufficient to be free to write what she likes. As she reflects on her gifts as a writer once the record sales of *Orlando* are assured, 'one has the play side; the gift when it is mere gift, unapplied gift; & the gift when it is serious, going to business. And one relieves the other' – the upshot will be 'books that relieve other books' (*D3* 203). It is this balance that sustains her as an artist and enables her to develop her creative gift; it makes it possible for her to negotiate the market economy without being subsumed by it.

Woolf's writing privileges the gift and a gift economy in its content and form, and indeed gifts of books are at the heart of many of the gift exchanges Woolf records in her diaries, letters and fiction. As with the giving of any gift, the motivations for giving in Woolf's writing are complex and sometimes

Introduction 11

contradictory; gifts can open a utopian space or act as a means of manipulation; they are often ambiguous and problematic, but are always concerned with issues of social relation in a male-dominated capitalist market economy. Zwerdling argues that a 'persistent interest' in Woolf's writing is with 'how people – real and imagined – have negotiated the conflict between what they want and what is expected of them' (1986, 5), and the giving of gifts is an important part of this negotiation and of the fulfilment of desires. With its fluid, ambiguous and generous forms, Woolf's writing creates heterogeneous possibilities for interpretation, inviting a reading practice premised on generosity and an investment of time as well as intellectual and emotional energy. This is not, then, a simple exchange of meaning between text and reader,[16] but rather, an ongoing creative process of generating meaning.

The first chapter, 'The Business of Writing: Economies in Woolf's Essays' focuses on Woolf's non-fiction. It begins with 'Street Haunting: A London Adventure' (1927), then considers her two extended, polemical essays, *A Room of One's Own* (1929) and *Three Guineas* (1938) alongside some of her shorter essays, 'Oxford Street Tide' (1931–2), 'Why Art Today Follows Politics' (1936), 'Reviewing' (1939) and 'Thoughts on Peace in an Air Raid' (1940). These publications throw light especially on Woolf's feminist and pacifist politics, and on her own negotiation of the commercial world as a woman writer, as well as on her modernist aesthetics. Chapter 2, 'Queering the Market: "Mrs Dalloway in Bond Street", *Mrs Dalloway* and "The Hours"' explores the representation of the interrelation of the gift economy and commodity culture as a means of realising women's homoerotic desires. Chapter 3, 'The Gift of Vision: *To the Lighthouse, Orlando* and *Between the Acts*' examines the role of the woman artist, and her homoerotically inspired creativity, as a source of regeneration and renewal in the face of the deadening and deadly effects of the tyrannies of capitalism, patriarchy and war. Chapter 4, 'Moments of Giving: Generosity and Desire in Woolf's Short Fictions' looks in detail at the ways in which Woolf's shorter fictions engage with gift and market economies to realise homoerotic possibilities and to disrupt and challenge dominant norms and imperatives.

1
The Business of Writing: Economies in Woolf's Essays

Although Virginia Woolf wrote over five hundred articles, essays and reviews during her professional career as a writer, this aspect of her *oeuvre* has been critically under-represented in favour of a focus on her novels. Literary journalism was of central importance to Woolf's entry into the literary profession, and she benefited in many ways from her success as a reviewer and essayist in the marketplace, not only in financial rewards (until the late 1920s this writing was Woolf's main source of earned income),[1] but also in developing a wider and more diverse audience for her essays than she achieved for her novels during her lifetime (as Gualtieri notes, 3). This wider recognition and fame also put her in a position to develop what was for her an all-important connection with her common readers. As Beth Carole Rosenberg and Jeanne Dubino indicate in their introduction to the edited collection of articles, *Virginia Woolf and the Essay*, the essays and articles published in Woolf's lifetime[2] attracted critical attention in 'the important British (and sometimes American) literary journals, and in the arts and literature section of journals' (1–2).[3] Lee also attests to the popularity and success of Woolf's essays, 'In her lifetime, she was highly praised and respected as a sensitive, cultured critic of "brilliance and integrity"' (2000, 93, quoting Majumdar and McLaurin). For the most part, as with her short fictions, however, although further editions of selected essays were published after Leonard Woolf's death (Lee, 2000, 94), Woolf's essays have been critically assigned a secondary importance in favour of her fiction.[4]

The huge project to publish all of Woolf's critical writings begun by Andrew McNeillie in 1986 (Lee, 2000, 94) marked a significant turning point, opening access to this important, extensive and diverse body of work and enabling critical assessments of Woolf as a serious essayist. Rachel Bowlby's two volumes of selected essays 'set out to make the essays more available to a larger public, while at the same time attempting to reject the opposition of popular to elitist, low brow to highbrow that has relegated them to the role of minor work' (Gualtieri 14). This increased access to Woolf's non-fictional writing has given rise to a 'reincarnation (or renaissance) ... of

Woolf as an essayist' (Lee, 2000, 91) and a re-evaluation of Woolf's essays as valuable work independent of her fiction. It has also renewed interest in readings across the genres of Woolf's writing, which explore the interconnections of issues and approaches, and illuminated in new ways the concerns, contradictions, questions and anxieties found throughout Woolf's work. These concerns about the effects of the marketplace and the politics of a patriarchal culture on (women's) experience, opportunity and personal and artistic integrity are of crucial importance. This is true not only in the two extended essays that have assumed a central place in Woolf's *oeuvre*, *A Room of One's Own* (1929) and *Three Guineas* (1938), but also in the shorter essays considered here, whose more direct relationship to the literary market perhaps adds greater complexity to the criticisms of capitalist values and commodity culture that they offer.

As part of this criticism of a male-dominated monetary economy, the essays also foreground the importance of the gift in several ways: in relation to artistic/creative gifts, to generosity and the giving of gifts, and to the modernist aesthetics and experimental forms of Woolf's essays, forms that exceed expectations and transgress generic boundaries, as they invite the generosity of the reader in participating in the creation of meaning. However, the essays also involve an interaction of economies. Woolf's ideal common reader, for instance, was brought into being by the emergence of the literary market, opening literature up to readers other than the wealthy patrons of the arts (see Gualtieri, Chapter 2). Further, as in 'Street Haunting: A London Adventure' and especially in her fiction written in the 1920s, Woolf explores the aesthetic pleasures and creative stimulation that commodity culture offers, as well as the sensual and sexually subversive potential that women's engagement, particularly their generous engagement, with market economies suggests. As Woolf's personal circumstances changed, and the escalation of Fascism in Europe led to dramatic changes in the social, political and economic context in which Woolf worked, her essays make clear, in ever more satirical and scathing ways, her view that the increasing intrusion of market forces and political agendas into literary writing has damaging effects (as is evident in 'Reviewing' [1939] and 'Why Art Today Follows Politics' [1936]).

These essays reveal a complex engagement with a range of recurrent and overlapping concerns, notably the changing social, political and economic situation for women. They raise questions about women's negotiation of the marketplace as shoppers, consumers, and wage earners, and also as artists, creatively inspired by commodity culture and with wares to sell, but wares that must refuse commodification if their artistic integrity and independence is to be assured. The energy of commodity culture is inspiring, its spectacle fascinating, and its sensuality potentially subversive. However, the politics and economic logic that drive capitalism, connected as they are for Woolf with patriarchal power structures, are potentially damaging. The crux of Woolf's complex and contradictory attitude to women (herself included) making

14 *Gifts, Markets and Economies of Desire*

money on the literary market is that she not only perceives this as essential to women's financial, emotional and psychological independence and emancipation from a constrained domestic role, but also sees the risks it entails. Earning money from writing is the entry point into the literary profession and is the thing that 'dignifies what is frivolous if unpaid for' (*AROO* 62). However, it means that women run the risk of being seduced and subsumed by the powerfully enforced ideologies and values of the male-dominated capitalist system, and of being entrapped anew by the pressures of the profit motive (as is clearly elucidated in *A Room of One's Own* and *Three Guineas*).

These anxieties are also a product of Woolf's largely antithetical attitude to consumer culture. As a highbrow writer, Woolf sustained an idealistic belief in the value of writing as a form of art for its own sake. She saw the dangers and detrimental effects of the commodification of writing and was keen to shield her writing from contamination. Leila Brosnan teases out possible distinctions between Woolf's critical writing which is 'treated as "journalism" when considered in a commercial context and as "essays" when viewed in a non-commercial one', as published by the Hogarth Press, for instance (6). In 'Reviewing', Woolf tries to preserve the distinction between reviewer and critic in an attempt to solve her dilemma about literature's relationship to the market (Brosnan 6), and as a defence against what Woolf saw as the damaging and distorting effects of the market on literature. However, as noted above, such distinctions are highly unstable, not least because of multiple publications in 'literary' and 'market' outlets,[5] but also because the 'parameters of the essay genre are unclear' (Brosnan 6). Gualtieri also highlights the tension between Woolf 'cherish(ing) the essay as the first of modernist forms in its fragmentary, unresolved and preliminary character' and 'her perception of the modernity of the genre, which she saw as indissolubly linked to the emergence of mass readership, consumer culture and narcissism' (18). It is what Woolf perceived as the detrimental effect of the market exercised through the influence of a mass readership that gave rise to her fears, because this readership was conceived, as Gualtieri suggests, as both a 'tyrannical master whose desires are not easily satisfied' as well as a passive, 'infantilised' mass, 'governed either by its animal instincts or, more ominously, by the wishes and interests of those in authority' and the writer is thus 'enslaved' (62–3).

Woolf's attitude to the market was highly ambivalent and, at times, she derived excitement and satisfaction from her commercial work. She took great pleasure in her earning power, and the importance of women earning their own income is something that recurs in the essays considered here. In attaining economic independence literally from fathers and brothers and symbolically from the traditions, values and power hierarchies of heteropatriarchal society, women can voice their independent opinions. The importance of this freedom from need to charm men is a major focus of *A Room of One's Own* and *Three Guineas*, where it represents the key to a more just,

The Business of Writing   15

egalitarian and humane society. Although Woolf was often defensive about her commercial work, it is sometimes also a marker of her refusal to conform to expectations: as in her retaliation against Logan Pearsall Smith who, 'fastidious and catty', criticised her ethics and accused her of lowering her standards by writing for *Vogue* (Lee, 1996, 470).[6] As Lee remarks, 'Being in *Vogue* was being at the party' (Lee, 1996, 470), experiencing the pleasures and excitements of the fashionable world and being part of a new conjunction of the commercial, the artistic and the literary orchestrated by Dorothy Todd, editor of British *Vogue* 1922–6. Christopher Reed's recent work on the queerness of *Vogue* also confirms the attitude of the magazine which 'delights in destabilizing institutionally sanctioned hierarchies' (Reed 378).

Although Woolf's representation of consumer culture in her essays is tempered always by a firm resistance to capitalist values and activities, and also exposes the exploitative power at work in this consumer (and consuming) activity, her essays also delight in the sensual, erotic pleasures and creative stimulation that commodity culture can offer. Her representation of shopping is of a liberating, stimulating and even sexually subversive experience. Essays such as 'Street Haunting' and 'Oxford Street Tide' engage with the excitements of commodity spectacle in a way that offers insights into the aesthetics of Woolf's writing and exemplifies the ideal processes of reading that other essays also explore ('Modern Fiction' and 'How Should One Read a Book', for instance). The role of the female shopper (or window shopper) is one that has subversive potential because, in giving women licence to participate in the male-dominated world of the marketplace, it presents a feminist challenge to the patriarchal privilege of owning and controlling property, including the sexual 'property' of their own bodies (which forms the core of Woolf's socio-economic criticism of male-dominated culture in *A Room of One's Own* and *Three Guineas*). The focus on the experience of shopping also importantly illuminates the 'unrecorded li(ves)' of women (*AROO* 85) and privileges the new feminised spaces of modernity, marking a significant counter to the prevalent masculine values that find expression in a literary focus on sport or war (*AROO* 70). The literary focus on shopping at once privileges women's difference of experience and perspective, and gives scope for women to articulate and satisfy their desires, to imagine other possibilities and to earn a living. '(T)he everchanging and turning world of gloves and shoes and stuffs' (*AROO* 86) is one in a constant state of flux, its provisionality and shifting nature resonating with Woolf's modernist aesthetics and with the sexually subversive politics of her style. Although Woolf depicts herself often as a somewhat reluctant shopper, her writing asserts the importance of women's economic freedom and participation in this central experience of modernity.

As shoppers, women are subject to the manipulative power of a male-dominated capitalist economy driven only by the profit motive, which sets up a power dynamic in which women are constructed as passive dupes,

16 *Gifts, Markets and Economies of Desire*

tricked into spending money on the basis of an impossible promise of a satisfaction of desires. However, Woolf's representation of shopping serves to expose simultaneously the ruthlessness of capitalist exploitation as it refuses the construction of women, in thrall to this worship of commodities. Negotiating the temptations of insatiable acquisition that the capitalist forces behind commodity spectacle insist on is a key element of resistance to the lures of the market. It is achieved not only by making a minimal investment in sustaining the capitalist economy, but, importantly and somewhat paradoxically, by spending accompanied by acts of generosity which, in excess of the rational transaction of the market, are coded as feminine and subversive. Tratner and Wicke[7] both argue persuasively that Woolf's attitude to the economy was influenced by John Maynard Keynes's radical theories of deficit spending, whereby spending and the stimulation of consumer desires and demands were the key to financial recovery in post-war Britain. They posit interconnections between the monetary economy, libidinal and literary economies, so that spending and indulging consumer desires simultaneously unleash unspoken or repressed desires and help to generate new aesthetic formations in Woolf's writing. Wicke also suggests the influence of Bloomsbury as a 'coterie for and of consumption' that altered ideas about markets and marketing (1994, 10, 5). In relation to *Mrs Dalloway*, Wicke also suggests that gendered consumption, when performed generously, can be 'reformulated as the nature of the gift' so that shopping becomes not only utopian, but can liquefy 'the hierarchies and divisions of the gendered social world' (1994, 18, 19).

This emphasis on generosity (in the sense of gift-giving and creative gifts) and the interconnection of monetary, libidinal and aesthetic economies within Woolf's texts is clearly rich territory to explore. However, these 'generous' aesthetics and the excessive 'textual generosity' of her writing, paradoxically, also work to put up a resistance to the commodification *of* her writing. Woolf's commercial writing as a reviewer and essayist facilitated '(h)er development into the kind of novelist she wanted to be' (Lee, 2000, 92), by bringing her into contact with a wide range of contemporary novels, giving a broader frame of reference for the contemplation of literary issues, and opening up a critical and creative space that enabled her to develop her own modernist aesthetic and modernist forms. However, she fiercely resisted the commodification of her writing in some ways, and highlighting the generosity in and of her writing seems to help distance the economic forces that caused her so much personal anxiety. Importantly, it also indicates a political desire to displace capitalism as the dominant economic and ideological frame of reference, especially given its increasingly influential role in the social regulation and limitation of women's lives. In this sense, the modernist aesthetics and genre-blurring forms of Woolf's essays can be seen as a form of resistance to commodification in that they refuse the experience of easy consumption or reading. Although Woolf sought to make her literary journalism and essays accessible to a wide audience, her critical writing also refused to offer an authoritative consolidation of ideas, a 'nugget of pure truth' to price up for sale or to measure out for consumption (*AROO* 5). As Lee argues, 'The essays' wandering structures, their "speculative and hesitant" refusals to lay down the law, create a form of subversion' (Lee, 2000, 95), and aim to sustain an intellectual and creative connection with the reader that goes beyond a simple transaction of meaning. In the privileging of indeterminacy, provisionality and a sense of dialogue with the reader, Woolf's essays sustain a process of inquiry and discussion, which, often inconsistent and inconclusive, refuses to shape itself into a clearly defined product of her thought or opinion.

Recent attention has been given to the diversity of Woolf's essays, and to the different traditions she draws on and transforms as she experiments with genre, often blurring generic boundaries to create more elastic, hybrid forms. Although Woolf experienced the writing of fiction and non-fiction very differently, and saw the two forms as originating in different parts of her mind, and as an effect of different kinds of artistic gift (as, indeed, they had a different goal), critical studies show how her essays and fiction interconnect, overlap, and cross-fertilise (Lee, 2000, 97). Pamela Caughie suggests that Woolf's essays blend fact and fiction as, 'by playing out a spectrum of possibilities for prose writing, Woolf avoided the need to polarise differences and to choose between the two alternatives' which were between 'playful writing for its own sake and purposeful writing for the sake of an ending' (1991, 20). In fact, as Gualtieri, and Rosenberg and Dubino, argue, Woolf's essays resist a literal, realist exposition of 'truth', diverging from a logical, linear structure that would lead to a clear and definite conclusion or solution to the inquiry made in the essay. Rather, they draw parallels between Woolf's innovative genre-blurring essay forms and theories of the essayistic mode put forward by European Marxist theorists Theodor Adorno and Georg Lukács, stressing the way such a mode privileges process over result, insists on a dialogic form, disrupts distinctions between genres and 'makes problematic any clear-cut opposition between cognition and aesthetic experience', so that 'the essay creates a form where knowledge can be experienced as art' (Gualtieri 5). As emphasised in other modernist forms, the form of the essay is inseparable from the content and is created through the interplay of ideas and language, through chance connections, 'freedom, flux and luck', and gives rein to imaginative speculations and possibilities to allow 'identity to coalesce' (Rosenberg and Dubino, 12). The representation of identity and subjectivity in such essays 'mimics in its very form the experience of a scattered and only loosely connected self' (Gualtieri 5). Although this experience is still mediated through language and the essay's form, the insistence on 'the formlessness of human experience' makes the essay 'the most suitable form with which to combat the homogenisation of individual consciousness by mass culture and the systematic reduction of

18   *Gifts, Markets and Economies of Desire*

that consciousness to an abstract entity in the theories of human sciences' (Gualtieri 6).

These parallels also imply a connection between the form of Woolf's essays and the criticism of capitalist power dynamics Adorno and Lukács put forward. They theorise the negative effects of this dominant ideology on all aspects of experience, cognition and desires, arguing that the focus on commodities, so central to capitalist thinking, distracts from genuine engagement and questioning of social changes and power dynamics. Criticism of the capitalist ethos and its detrimental effects on experience and art is also prominent in the content of many of Woolf's essays and articles, as well as in her personal writings, particularly those written in the 1930s. In these later essays, Woolf found it harder to sustain the playfulness that was part of her critical strategy in her essays of the late 1920s, which dealt with women's relationship to the market. Even by the time she came to write *A Room of One's Own*, however, it would seem that Woolf had to work hard to maintain this balanced performance. Writing to Ethyl Smyth, she explains her strategy of fictionalising circumstances so that her ideas would not simply be dismissed as too personal, and written with her own 'axe to grind' (Lee, 1996, 556). However, this issue does enter *A Room of One's Own* as Woolf's narrator is also keen to see whether the fictional author Mary Carmichael has a 'pen . . . or a pickaxe' in her hand as she writes (*AROO* 77). The slippage between the Marys in the essay and, as the wielding of an axe/pickaxe suggests, with Woolf herself indicates the anger bubbling beneath the surface of this essay.

Woolf's hostility towards dominant institutions and the ideological and economic values they enforce becomes increasingly bitter in the 1930s. She came to see the inseparability of patriarchal tyranny and the capitalist urge to acquire ever more possessions and property as fundamental not only to bringing about war, but also to the fostering of fascist thinking in the minds of everyone, not just the tyrants and dictators rising to power in Europe. 'Thoughts on Peace in an Air Raid' articulates this integral connection between commodity culture and 'subconscious Hitlerism'. It pins its hopes on the belief that women's ideas can induce 'creative feelings' in men so as to counter violence and belligerence. Whereas *A Room of One's Own* privileges the experience of shopping over that of the battlefield (*AROO* 70, 86), 'Thoughts on Peace in an Air Raid' demonstrates how shopping and the power dynamics of capitalism on which commodity culture is premised *leads* to the battlefield. If, as Lee argues (2000, 93), Woolf's 'political reading of the literary marketplace was an essential part of her feminism' (as we see in 'Street Haunting', 'Oxford Street Tide' and *A Room of One's Own*), what becomes clear in her essays and journalism of the 1930s is the way her feminist reading of capitalist, heteropatriarchal economies was essential to her pacificism and her sense of herself as an artist increasingly marginalised by the intensified politicisation and constriction of culture, writing and language itself. In the atmosphere of the mid- to late 1930s, contaminated, 'adulterated' and 'poison(ed)' (*TG* 108, 61) by the greed for property, the lust for power and the display of masculine superiority, Woolf contemplates how to counter war lust through fostering creativity and human feeling. She advocates an acceptance of difference, and challenges the social, political and economic nexus of power from within, not with opposition and conflict, but through generosity. In the face of the all-powerful and all-pervasive 'money motive', and as economic and political forces become more dangerously enmeshed than ever, Woolf explicitly turns to the gift as both a rhetorical strategy and an ethical counter to the mindset focused on war. In *Three Guineas*, her narrator offers three guineas as 'free gift(s), given freely' (*TG* 116), though crucially this money-gift is accompanied by lengthy, generous, challenging yet empathetic considerations of the different situations in which those requesting financial help find themselves. The epistolary form emphasises that this exchange of gifts is crucially about creating bonds and openness, expanding channels of communication and making connections across differences between donor and donee, which are vital in helping to prevent war.

In her 1927 essay, 'Street Haunting: A London Adventure', Woolf explores the pleasures and dangers of commodity culture through the perceptions and experiences of her narrator, whose quest to buy 'a lead pencil' is the pretext for adventuring through the streets of London on a winter's afternoon. The commodity that she seeks suggests that she is a writer or artist, but in any case she responds creatively to the fascinating spectacle of commodity display. Her consciousness is flooded with the beauty she sees, her identity and desires seemingly as fluid as the changing scenes around her. Although such aestheticised responses and modes of perception depend on retaining only a superficial perspective on the operation of this economy, to 'glid(e) smoothly on the surface', 'to be content with surfaces only' (*CD* 71, 72), the repeated emphasis on the importance of sustaining an indifferent trance-like state, where 'the brain sleeps as it looks' (*CD* 71), indicates the difficulty of not engaging intellectually and emotionally with the effects of capitalism on her own and others' lives. The essay scratches beneath the glittering surface of the consumer economy to glimpse the ruthlessness that underlies it, and the effects of an economic ethos based on acquisition and greed rather than on a redistribution of wealth. With a focus also on books as commodities and the relationship of literature to the marketplace, it also contemplates how a woman artist can harness the energy and desires of modernity as experienced through commodity culture without compromising her artistic integrity, or being transformed into a commodity herself by being complicit in the damaging politics of the capitalist system. As Laura Marcus neatly sums it up, 'Aesthetics and commerce are both twinned and opposed' in this essay (2004, 66). However, this relationship is also further complicated by the focus on generosity and, indeed, on shielding the products of an artist's creative gift from the control of market forces through the social bonds that a gift ethos fosters.

The essay begins with the powerful desire to go 'street rambling', the impetus to embark on this 'London adventure' being the urge to escape the

20 *Gifts, Markets and Economies of Desire*

objects in the narrator's home, objects that define and delimit the identity of the narrator. It is significant that the one object singled out for comment is a bowl that was acquired as a result of a hard sell, when a 'sinister old woman' foists it on to the narrator with the pretence of 'quixotic generosity' at an inflated price (*CD* 70, 71). Any pleasure from the beauty of the bowl itself is impossible, signifying as it does the negative emotion of the moment of its transaction (and associated with the subsequent disturbances the narrator experiences: the innkeeper's argument and the revelations of 'the melancholy Englishman' *CD* 71). This moment has become 'stabilized, stamped like a coin indelibly among the million that slipped by imperceptibly'. This metaphor clearly enforces the point that capitalism not only has an impersonal monetary currency, indifferent to the individuals who merely perform the roles of buyer or seller, but also that capitalist economic forces come to have a very personal impact. In this case exchange assumes a negative 'emotional currency' for those involved, fixing aspects of experience and identity at the moment of transaction. From the outset, it is clear that commodities hold far more than simply material or monetary value, and that economic forces impact on even the most private and intimate aspects of identity, a point reinforced later in the essay. At this point the narrator seeks escape from the confines of the domestic sphere. It is the 'pretext' of buying a pencil that legitimates the pursuit of her (unspoken) desires, conferring on her the freedom of anonymity as she joins 'that vast republican army of anonymous trampers' (*CD* 70). Although intent on making only a minimal investment in commodity culture, this role of shopper grants her access to the sensual, sensory and social pleasures of 'rambling the streets of London' and to being the willing recipient of the 'free gifts' of commodity spectacle and the pleasures of window shopping (*CD* 70). This is an intoxicating and creatively stimulating experience – the streets are 'beautiful' with 'islands of light' and the air has a 'champagne brightness' – in which the narrator feels herself to be open and receptive to every sensation, like 'a central oyster of perceptiveness, an enormous eye' (*CD* 71, 70). That this sense of pleasure in the fluidity of commodity culture is in tune with Woolf's response to and gendered appropriation of Keynesian ideas (as discussed above) is suggested by the mention of 'the brown stain on the carpet' that 'Mr Lloyd George [whose economic policies Keynes opposed] made . . . putting the kettle down' and so burning the carpet (*CD* 71). That the stain is a burnt 'brown ring' associates it with the shape of the bowl, the economic transaction of which has also 'stained' the memory of its acquisition and the narrator's feelings about it. It suggests the detrimental long-term and all-pervasive effects economic policies can have on private experience.

Deliberately sustaining a superficial perspective (one she needs to actively resume after her criticism of the 'deforming' effects of capitalist economies, discussed below), the narrator is stimulated and inspired by the 'glossy brilliance' and 'splendour' of the city (*CD* 72), and by the constant flux and activity of 'the tide of trade' which seems to have 'cast up nothing but treasure' 'upon the shores of Oxford Street' (*CD* 75). In Woolf's essay, 'Oxford Street Tide', this sense of continual flux and flow is overwhelming. The modern city itself, its fashions, commodities and physicality, is subject to perpetual change; indeed, this is its 'charm' (*CD* 115). The new currency in this modern city is premised on discovery, invention and creativity, 'ever fresh, ever new', and on an apparently democratic access to the 'unending beauty' on offer (*CD* 116). In both essays, Woolf seems to draw a parallel between certain aspects of commodity culture (its celebration of the new, its privileging of sensual pleasure and imaginative stimulation, and its transitory and provisional nature) and her ideas about modernist writing and reading. Indeed, in 'Oxford Street Tide' it is as if the whole edifice of the city is in tune with modernist creativity's privileging of flux and impermanence, as the department stores themselves seem but 'flimsy abodes – perching grounds rather than [solid and permanent] dwelling places' (*CD* 115).

As the narrator in 'Street Haunting' gazes into a shop window, the objects on display prompt her to imagine a house in which they could be arranged. Crucially, the pleasure of her creativity lies not in the realisation of this fantasy through purchase of its components, but in the lack of 'obligation to possess' them so that her fantasy can be decreated, 'dismantle(d) in the twinkling of an eye' and replaced by another (*CD* 75). This particular fantasy creation of an imaginary house recalls the example used to illustrate the contrast Woolf draws so pointedly in her essay, 'Modern Fiction' (first published as 'Modern Novels' in 1919), between the realism of a writer like Arnold Bennett, who offered 'a shop keepers [*sic*] view of literature', and her own modernist forms and aesthetics (*D4* 16). Bennett, who wrote 'methodically covering his regulation number of pages in his workmanlike beautiful but dull hand' (*D4* 16), 'can make a book so well constructed and solid in its craftsmanship . . . There is not so much as a draught between the frames of the windows, or a crack in the boards', and yet this fiction is unconvincing, 'life . . . refuse(s) to live there', 'Life escapes', thus short-changing the reader (*CD* 6, 7). Rather, fiction should aim to capture the flux of experience, the 'myriad impressions – trivial, fantastic, evanescent, or engraved with the sharpness of steel' (*CD* 8), impressions which resemble those derived from the experience of the flux of commodity spectacle, when 'passing, glimpsing, everything seems accidentally but miraculously sprinkled with beauty' (*CD* 75).

Her criticism of realist forms not only focuses on the aesthetic qualities of this writing, but also makes the connection between the production of such literature and controlling economic forces. Hankins argues that Woolf's revisions to 'Modern Novels' (revised and reprinted in 1925 as 'Modern Fiction') were made to 'strengthen(s) her assertions that capitalist factors control the writers' choices' (2000, 24). In conforming to the dictates of the literary marketplace (obeying the 'powerful and unscrupulous tyrant who has him in thrall', *CD* 8), realist writers like Bennett produce writing for easy

22   *Gifts, Markets and Economies of Desire*

consumption, and accept that art is merely a commodity like any other. One of the revisions Woolf makes to her essay, Hankins indicates, is the introduction of the 'Bond street tailors' to represent the powerful influence of the literary marketplace. They embody, she suggests, the 'capitalist power brokers' (2000, 24) whose influence and economic sway Woolf's writing resists in its refusal to delimit, define and conclude. Woolf's modernist aesthetics may often be inspired by the fluidity of the commercial city, and her modernist creativity may resonate with the flux and excess of commodity culture, but her writing refuses to be a commodity for easy consumption. In contrast to the fixing and finishing of the Bond Street tailors, her writer-narrator's eye in 'Street Haunting' is described as 'sportive and generous: it creates, it adorns, it enhances' (*CD* 75). The imaginary scenes created are transitory, speculative, and retain the energy of flux and fluidity so central to the experience of modernity and to the sense of the modern subject. This creative engagement with commodity aesthetics also confirms the impossibility of absolute self-possession and self-knowledge (a key concern and moral goal in the teleology of realist fiction), given the multiplicity of selves revealed to us through the diversity of fantasies and desires it inspires in us all. We are 'utterly at variance' with our 'main being so that we are streaked, variegated, all of a mixture; the colours have run' (*CD* 76).

As energising, exciting and creatively stimulating as the experience of commodity culture is, its fascination can, however, only hold the imagination for so long. Seeming to anticipate the notion of 'eye candy' in current discourse about the commodity, especially in relation to the objectifiction of women's bodies, Woolf's essay notes how cloying the 'simple, sugary fare' of endless beautiful things soon comes to be (*CD* 72). Beneath the attractive glitter and twinkle (*CD* 113), what drives this economy is the ruthlessness of the profit motive. This is made apparent in the discussion of the 'largesse' of the new merchant-aristocrats. More ephemeral than the gifts of 'gold or . . . loaves' given in the past, this 'takes the form of excitement, of display, of entertainment', and is seemingly given for 'free', but which similarly sets up the expectation of return (*CD* 115). Indeed, the giving of these 'gifts' is more calculated and single-minded than the patronage of the past, 'their object – to entice the shilling and eleven pennies as freely from our pockets as possible' (*CD* 115). Like the 'quixotic generosity' of the woman who sold the bowl to the narrator in 'Street Haunting', the generosity of 'the great Lords of Oxford Street' is false, and their sales pitch a trap (*CD* 71, 114).

The ruthlessness of the capitalist economy and its dangerous gender politics are hinted at in the beginning of the essay. Here, it becomes imperative for the narrator to assume the role of a shopper, even on the flimsy pretext of buying a pencil, in order to walk the streets and to undertake her 'London Adventure' 'safely' (*CD* 70). In other words, she must guard herself from the suspicion of being a street walker with something (her body) to sell. Not only does this draw attention to the fact that in a capitalist economy nothing is beyond the realm of commodification and that trade is ubiquitous, 'ingenious and indefatigable beyond the bounds of imagination' (as Woolf asserts in 'The Docks of London', *CD* 111), but that, as a consequence, women continuously run the risk of the easy and dangerous slippage from consumer to consumed that participation in the commercial world entails (as is evident in the boot shop, discussed below). It also, importantly, draws attention to the range of (sexual and other) desires that commodity culture can stimulate and promise (but ultimately fail to) to satisfy through the purchase of things.

This point is made forcefully in the essay when, stepping into a boot shop, the narrator observes a 'dwarf' woman trying on boots. Here Woolf begins to unpack the operation of commodity culture and its effect on women's psyche, emotions and sense of self. The pleasurable effect of consumption is apparent in the way that the woman's 'peevish yet apologetic expression' becomes 'soothed and satisfied' as, in the process of displaying her beautiful and perfectly formed feet in several different shoes, she becomes 'full of self-confidence' (*CD* 73). In this female space and in front of the mirror, she displays and performs for the pleasure of her own gaze and anyone else who cares to watch. This magical space of capitalist consumption facilitates the creation of an ideal fantasy self through the very processes of fragmentation of women's bodies used in advertisements and shop window displays to maximise the effects and the profits of commodification.[8] What is evident here are the ways that dominant structures of meaning and value are reinforced in consumer culture and, as Felski argues, 'subject(ed) women to norms of eroticized femininity that encourage(s) constant practices of self-surveillance' (90). Focusing only on her feet in the various shoes allows the woman to fantasise about her feminine perfection, the promise of transformation at the heart of commodity culture, and the subsequent romantic possibilities of being loved. Although not well off (she is 'shabbily dressed')[9], so powerful is the promise of transformation and satisfaction of her desires that she is 'ready to lavish money upon her shoes' (*CD* 73). However, the 'ecstasy' created in this capitalist transaction is short-lived. Once outside the sphere of enchantment of the shop, almost immediately the fantasy shatters, 'the ecstasy faded, knowledge returned', and her sense of identity returns, 'she had become a dwarf only' (*CD* 73). The repetition of 'deformed' and 'deformity' emphasises the way that capitalism not only manufactures desires in the consumer, but does so through engendering a powerful sense of lack that is, as reference to the 'grotesque' here suggests, out of all proportion to our needs or to actuality. The impossibility of commodity culture being able to deliver all it promises causes the bubble of illusion, the fantasy of perfection, to burst but, simultaneously, keeps the cycle of desires in motion, shoring up the imperative to buy more.

Tratner argues that Woolf's response to the repressions inherent in hegemonic capitalism was to embrace 'alternative traditions of oppressed

24   *Gifts, Markets and Economies of Desire*

groups: Jews, women, homosexuals, the working class, all the members of Woolf's "outsiders' society"' (1995, 14). Although Woolf's representation of all of these 'outsiders' is inconsistent, their involvement with commodity culture and market exchange tends to open up a space in which the dominant cultural values endorsed by capitalist enterprise are significantly undermined and brought into question, as we see with the dwarf woman and the poor and destitute here. The woman's mood of bitter disappointment is infectious and in the streets it affects how the narrator perceives the people around her: 'the humped, the twisted, the deformed' (*CD* 74). The 'hobbling grotesque dance' her mood seems to set in motion is a significant description in light of the woman's purchase of shoes. It would seem that not only do the shoes disappoint, but that participation in this system is 'hobbling': restrictive, impairing free movement and fettering free will (and potentially leading to destitution). That hobbling is associated with the restraining of horses makes an implicit connection with the description of 'the humped body of an old woman flung abandoned on the step of a public building with a cloak over her like the hasty covering thrown over a dead horse or donkey' (*CD* 74). These associative links broaden and significantly intensify the criticism of the capitalist economy raised here as, juxtaposing the luxury and promise flaunted in commodity display with the reality of the homeless and destitute who 'lie close to those shop windows', the inequalities and injustices this economy exacerbates through its ethos of acquisition at all costs are blatantly exposed. Before 'suddenly' encountering the homeless and desperate, the middle-class narrator is on the point of complacently assuming that the poor 'do not grudge us . . . our prosperity', an attitude that coincides with her perception of the poor women and men she passes in the street earlier whom she assumes are, like the narrator herself, escaping from the realities of their lives, 'bright' and triumphant 'as if they had given life the slip' (*CD* 74, 71). Her new awareness that the poor are not immune to the promise of comfort, which is as unattainable for them as it is untouchable through the transparent yet impenetrable barrier of the shop window (*CD* 74), and of the viciousness with which the commercial world flaunts its excessive riches, amounts to a vehement indictment of this economic system.

In the midst of the conflicting experiences of the city streets – the pleasures and creativity inspired by commodity spectacle, yet the ruthlessness of the capitalist economy that drives the commercial world – the narrator turns to books for a sense of 'anchorage' amid the 'thwarting currents of our being' (*CD* 76). It is only in the variety of books, the 'vast flocks of variegated feather', that our variegated selves can experience a real affinity (*CD* 77). What is important is that, although the books are for sale, they are also described as 'homeless', an identification that aligns them with the homeless people commodity culture excludes. This confirms that these second-hand books are positioned as a different category of commodity from those that fetter and consume, and that they are involved in a different kind of 'commerce'.

The Business of Writing 25

Books are not simply alienable objects generating a short-lived moment of ecstasy. Rather, they fulfil a social and emotional function that can be long-lasting. The narrator's description of the different relation books create with the buyer – an intimate or capricious friendship, an affectionate bond – recalls Woolf's own notion of the ideal reader for her books: a 'fellow worker and accomplice' (*CD* 60). It seems no surprise, then, that the books the writer-narrator specifically singles out are those written by women adventurers, 'indomitable spinsters', some of whom go far beyond the shores of England, and beyond the reach of the tide of commodities on Oxford Street (*CD* 77–8). This 'tide' is also rivalled and supplanted by 'the ancient sea of fiction' that 'washes' 'like a punctual everlasting tide' (*CD* 78). Although this fiction adheres to the Victorian formula of heterosexual romance and a happy ending, with which Woolf's own fiction is deliberately at odds,[10] it is an important part of the varied 'company' books create (*CD* 77).

It is significant that these objects occupy the margins of the literary market: they are relatively cheap and have lost the important commodity asset-value of newness. That the books are second hand – a kind of waste, or recirculation of goods – puts them at a further remove from their commodity value on the market and affords them immunity from the activities associated with marketing and reviews. The books here occupy a position at odds with the excesses of commodity spectacle and economics; they are not lavishly displayed or ordered to maximise profits, nor are buying and selling the key modes of interaction here. Indeed, displacing capitalism's central tenet of maximising profits, the bookseller prices the books on their merits and on their inherent worth, making an independent judgement based on the specific qualities of the book and on a sense of fairness. Although there is no sense that the narrator haggles over prices (nor does she buy a book), the social connection she has fostered with the bookseller may also pay a part in the lowering of the original price. The shop acts as a haven in which the narrator can 'balance [herself] after the splendours and miseries of the streets' (*CD* 76), an image that perhaps offers some relief for Woolf's own dilemma as a highbrow artist with wares to sell on the marketplace. Unlike the tortoise seller in 'Oxford Street Tide', intent only on making a living and staying out of poverty, Woolf, her economic position secure, is 'thinking of educating the mass to a higher standard of aesthetic sensibility' (*CD* 116). 'Street Haunting' locates the vehicle for this, literature, in a different category and mode of commerce.[11] Within this more intimate space of exchange, the centrality of monetary exchange is displaced. Here transactions are performed with generosity, thus opening up possibilities for social connection, and for harmony as the essay moves increasingly towards a more ethical sense of buying and selling.

Finally and ironically, it is in the narrator's actual engagement in a capitalist exchange, the purchase of the pencil, that the opportunity for a genuine expression of generosity arises. Ruth Hoberman argues that the purchase of

26   *Gifts, Markets and Economies of Desire*

the pencil 'reverses the bowl-narrative' (2004, 83), correcting the disturbance this purchase entailed and restoring harmony and social connection.
However, this is perhaps not a simple reversal because the narrator feels
compelled by 'the rod of duty' to participate in this exchange (as the repetition of 'must' indicates), in order to justify her adventure and so maintain a
sense of propriety for her potentially suspect *flânerie*. This 'rod' becomes
manifest in the lengthening shadows, 'a little rod about the length of one's
finger [that] begins to lay its bar across the velocity and abundance of life'
(*CD* 79). It might also indicate the bolting of shop doors, announcing the
end of the commercial day and reinforcing the importance of time in a capitalist economy, a prioritisation in conflict with the narrator's desire to
linger in the contemplation of her past and future selves. However, she acts
on her own compunction – 'the right of the tyrant to insist' – and goes in
search of a shop 'where, even at this hour, they will be ready to sell [us] a
pencil' (*CD* 79).

The consumer space of the stationers' shop is personalised and invaded
by the argument between the married couple who keep it, 'Their anger shot
through the air' (*CD* 80), and the conversation of the shopkeeper who serves
the narrator remains affected by his personal emotions which find an outlet
in his intimate, distracted and effusive conversation. His 'incompetence' as
a capitalist shopkeeper leads to the first stage of restoring the harmony
between him and his wife, as he has to call on her for help. Using her pre-
rogative as consumer to prolong the process of transaction is an act of kindness on the part of the narrator and allows for harmony to be restored
between the couple. However, her purchase complete, she returns to the
streets only to find all the shifting vitality of commodity culture has disap-
peared. This marks not only the end of the commercial day, but suggests
something more: having made her purchase, the narrator too experiences a
sense of disappointment. In contrast to the warmth and generosity of her
experience in these more marginal consumer spaces, the streets, though still
beautiful – 'the road was of hammered silver' – are felt to be sterile – 'the
pavement was dry and hard' (*CD* 80). However, this transaction yields more
than simply an object to own. Rather, the pencil's status as a commodity is
significantly undermined by its designation as a 'spoil' plundered from the
rich treasures of the city, and by its treatment as a kind of gift, imbued as it
is with its harmonising moment of exchange, and it is 'examine(d) . . . ten-
derly, . . . touch(ed) . . . with reverence' (*CD* 81). Further, it is the promise of
artistic creativity to come, especially the narratives that will sustain a fluidity of identity in the imagination, that ensures the vital, life-enhancing qualities of this commodity beyond its value on the market, and beyond the
moment of capitalist transaction which would usually 'stabiliz(e) [and]
stamp(ed)' in a reductive closure of possibility (*CD* 71). What is apparent is
that, although material and economic circumstances shape experience and
consciousness,[12] adopting different systems of value that privilege generosity

over making money or acquiring possessions can also shape our view and our representation of the world and experience differently.

Although the tone describing the reverent attitude to the pencil is ironic, from the outset the purchase of the pencil has meant something more than the simple participation in an economic transaction. As a pretext for adventure and for indulging in unspoken desires, it leads the narrator to the stimulating experience of the spectacle of commodity culture. However, representing only a minimal investment in the capitalist system, it reveals a resistance to the acquisitive ethos of capitalism and the damaging consequences of participating in it. Finally, as a generative tool (for writing/sketching), the pencil has implications for the narrator's creative engagement beyond this consumer experience. This has significance for the dilemma Woolf perceived for the artist, whose work is at once separate from politics and economics yet inherently connected to and dependent on the forces that influence the market. As Hankins suggests, Woolf and Walter Benjamin 'advocate intellectuals rethink-[ing] their roles within commodity culture to invent ways to survive without being absorbed into the system of rewards and the market' (2000, 29). This is a dilemma that Woolf explores more fully in *A Room of One's Own*.

At the end of this essay the narrator returns home, presumably to 'the solitude of one's own room' that she felt the need to escape at the beginning of the essay (*CD* 70). With her pencil, she is equipped to begin to create. The privilege of a room of one's own and the economic comfort the narrator of this essay seems to enjoy are, of course, the material constituents (which also have symbolic significance) vital, as *A Room of One's Own* demonstrates, for women to become artists, to be able to create and especially to write. That this may have particular relevance to women writers is suggested by the parallels drawn by the narrator of 'Street Haunting' as she steps out of the second-hand bookshop and into the street, a movement from the 'glimpse and nod and . . . moment of talk' – the brief encounters with books that her browsing entails – to her chance overhearing of a snippet of conversation between two women talking in the street (*CD* 78). Despite the spatial transition between the shop and the street, the narrator's imagination engages both with books and conversation similarly and creatively. What seems significant in 'Street Haunting' is that the women the narrator overhears are discussing a monetary measure of friendship: the question of whether the friendship is 'worth [the] penny stamp' necessary to sustain it through communication by letters (*CD* 78). Although the narrator avers that the details of the 'crisis in their friendship [to which] the penny stamp refers' will never be known, the important point seems to be that any such monetary measure of a social bond (for women) represents a crisis in itself, a crisis especially exacerbated by the possibility implied here, that financial limitations may prevent women from writing at all. The monetary and material conditions necessary to sustain women as writers who are free to voice their difference of perspective and experience as women is, of course, the central preoccupation in *A Room of One's Own*.

28   *Gifts, Markets and Economies of Desire*

With a more overt focus on 'Women and Fiction',[13] *A Room of One's Own* considers the social, cultural, political and, inseparable from all of these, the economic factors affecting women's ability to write in Woolf's present moment and in the past, factors that work to deny women a financial, intellectual and creative/literary legacy on which to build. Lee's point that '*A Room of One's Own* could be read as her [Woolf's] own disguised economic autobiography' (1996, 556) is apt given that Woolf's narrator is in a similar financial position as Woolf herself, with a legacy from her aunt and the expectation that women can make a living as professional writers. The essay as a whole is permeated with the language of the market and monetary metaphors, seemingly aiming to demonstrate one of the important points underlying Woolf's thinking about economic factors: that they mediate all our experience, shaping our thought processes, our intellectual concepts and our emotional landscape through the very language we use to communicate and to express ourselves. As in 'Street Haunting', *A Room of One's Own* explores the interconnection of politics, economies and aesthetics and, with its teasing, playful form, demonstrates the difference that thinking generously and privileging creative gifts can make. This essay developed out of two lectures Woolf gave to women students at Cambridge University in 1928. It retains an address to an audience the dynamic of which gives scope for a more playful and teasing tone and a more open economy of meaning, as Woolf's narrator approaches her topic as if in conversation with her audience/reader.

The social, political and ideological limitations patriarchal culture places on women also affect women's relationship to the monetary economy, to what they can and cannot earn, own and have access to. The difference in their experience of this economy has helped to form women's intellect, perception, temperament, psychological and emotional states in distinctly different ways from men, leading to a difference in experience and perspective. Personal circumstances, social mores and gendered roles, social hierarchies and power dynamics, and limited opportunities for experience all impede women's writing. However, it is the economic factors – notably women's lack of access to money – that, historically and in Woolf's time, have had the most serious impact in stifling women's 'intellectual freedom' in denying them the time and space in which to write, as well as the experiences and perspectives on the world that monetary resources can enable. It is the formation of women's difference in perspective and experience (felt as 'the sudden splitting off of consciousness' from patriarchal culture, *AROO* 93), however, that is of fundamental importance in countering the profoundly damaging effects of the capitalist ethos which, in conjunction with patriarchal power structures and masculinist thinking and actions, fuels the 'the instinct for possession, the rage for acquisition which drives [men] to desire other people's fields and goods perpetually' (*AROO* 38). As Woolf elaborates in *Three Guineas*, this 'instinct' of greed leads to male rivalry and to war, as

The Business of Writing   29

acquiring money and power is bound up for men with insecurity and a need to constantly assert and prove their superiority.

This difference is manifested in the distinction between a male-dominated capitalist economy and a woman-centred gift economy. This points to a broader significance of the existence of the two kinds of economy at work: a masculine economy, which operates both to hoard its gifts and to amass more wealth, and a feminine economy, which is premised on generosity, indeterminacy, and which acts as a disruptive force (as Cixous characterises a feminine gift economy), destabilising hierarchies and rational systems, and undermining property rights. The distinction between these two economies emerges, for instance, in the narrator's representation of the men's college. In Woolf's exaggerated description, 'money was poured liberally' into the establishment of the physical and cultural edifice of Cambridge University in the form of monetary gifts, 'An unending stream of gold and silver' from 'the coffers of kings and queens and great nobles', and more recently 'from the chests of merchants and manufacturers' (*AROO* 11). The college also hoards the gifts it receives, taking them out of a circulation of generosity by limiting access to its buildings, notably the library 'with all its treasures locked up safe within its breast' (*AROO* 9). For Woolf, books are the common store of wealth to which all should have access, and which are to be shared, not channelled into the male-specific hoard of the college, acquired and possessively guarded as a symbol of wealth, power and authority in accordance with capitalist values.[14] As Woolf argues more vehemently in *Three Guineas* (*TG* 28, 38), these 'gifts' are really investments, and male graduates, having learnt 'the great art of making money' are able, in their turn, to return money and gifts to their college (*AROO* 11).

In what turned out to be Woolf's 'richest year' to date (Lee, 1996, 558),[15] she is keen to insist that her preoccupation with money in *A Room of One's Own* is not for its own sake, but for the necessary material comforts and the power and independence it represents. The significance of financial independence for women, as the narrator illustrates in relation to her own legacy from her aunt, is not only in the material comforts in which to write, but importantly freedom from a dependence on men, which has enabled a less bitter, more impersonal criticism of patriarchal culture. Crucially, it offered her a radically altered perspective, one that was liberating, open, expansive, and 'unveiled the sky' (*AROO* 39). That this legacy is a gift exchanged between women also distinguishes the narrator's economic independence from the male-dominated capitalist economy and its egotistical, acquisitive, possessive ethos. This distinction is confirmed by the fact that until late in the process of redrafting and revision of *A Room of One's Own*, the narrator's legacy came with the proviso forbidding her investment in the capitalist economy. As Rosenbaum notes, 'Nothing can take away the £500 a year as long as the narrator does not gamble in the stock market' (xxv). The publication history of *A Room of One's Own* ironically confirms the aunt's wise caution against

30 *Gifts, Markets and Economies of Desire*

literally and metaphorically buying into the acquisitiveness and greed of capitalist economy: it was published 'just days before the great crash of October 1929' (Rosenbaum xxv).

In contrast, the narrator's aunt's gift, passed on to her because they share the same name, frees the narrator to nurture her 'one gift', her creative gift, which having to write for money caused to 'perish(ing) and with it [her] self, [her] soul . . . like a rust eating away the bloom of the spring, destroying the tree at its heart' (*AROO* 37–8). This feminine gift is fecund, fertile, bringing new life and nourishment. Indeed, as the narrator argues later, this 'renewal of creative power' is unique to women, and it is only 'in the gift' of women 'to bestow' such creativity (*AROO* 82). This gift refers both to women's procreative power and nurture, but also to other aspects of women's creativity that have long been a fertilising source, 'refresh(ing) and invigorat(ing) . . . quicken(ing)' the 'creative power' of great men, 'fertiliz(ing)' their 'dried ideas' (*AROO* 83). At this point in *A Room of One's Own*, the narrator is discussing the new and experimental novel by fictional author Mary Carmichael, *Life's Adventure*, and reflects on the 'intricacy and the power of this highly developed creative faculty among women' which exceeds 'the resources of the English language' (*AROO* 83). Writing like Mary Carmichael's, formed to fit closely 'every hollow and angle' of the female body, to capture the 'extremely complex force of femininity', and offering an empowering perspective, 'as if one had gone to the top of the world and seen it laid out majestically beneath' (*AROO* 84, 83, 89), threatens to disrupt profoundly the values and conventions of not only the male-dominated literary establishment, but patriarchal society as a whole, especially as 'clever girl(s)' like Mary take up other opportunities that post-war changes brought in terms of women's political and professional independence. The energetic potential of women's creativity is evoked in the organic image describing Mary's 'wide, eager and free' sensibility, 'It feasted like a plant newly stood in the air on every sight and sound that came its way' (*AROO* 88). The subversiveness of her writing is implied in the way her fiction 'brought buried things to light', not least the intimacy of women, described 'perhaps for the first time in literature' (*AROO* 78).

The narrator's discussion of the experimental form of *Life's Adventure* suggests a modernist aesthetic that resembles Woolf's own. Mary Carmichael's novel seems, as much as Woolf's fiction does, to disrupt the heterosexual economy with its tantalising suggestion of homoeroticism between the two female characters. The suggestiveness of the relationship between Mary Carmichael's characters, Chloe and Olivia, remains only as a hint in the published version of *A Room of One's Own*, in the naming of the presiding magistrate in the obscenity trial of Radclyffe Hall's overt lesbian novel, *The Well of Loneliness*,[16] and in the narrator's teasing pause with instructions to her audience/readers not to 'start' or 'blush' at the revelation of this affinity between women she is about to make (*AROO* 78). However, the way in which Chloe and Olivia 'like' each other, and what men such as Chartres

Biron attempt to censor, is made more explicit in the manuscript version.[17] Although for some the final revisions amount to 'a telling piece of self-censorship' (Lee, 1996, 526),[18] the form and content of Mary Carmichael's novel have a self-consciousness and teasing playfulness that keeps homo-erotic possibilities in play, not least in the representation of 'those unrecorded gestures, those unsaid or half-said words' of women 'alone, unlit by the capricious and coloured light of the other sex', and the shift from heterosexual 'love [being] the only possible interpreter' of women's experience in writing (*AROO* 81, 80), to a focus on women's professional lives and intimacy beyond the familial and domestic scene. Indeed, Chloe and Olivia shared a laboratory together, and were thus in control of 'experiments', scientific, literary, sexual and, as relatively new professional women, economic, the results of which may challenge the values and beliefs of male-dominated institutions of all kinds.

What seems of equal importance to the writing of this new form of fiction is the process of reading and re-reading it with generosity; that is, not to get to the end and to a feeling of satisfaction, but to take pleasure in the ambiguities and teasing deviations that are in excess of narrative linearity. In doing her 'duty' as a reader, Woolf's narrator embarks on the 'adventure' that Mary's novel represents. This is not only in imaginatively exploring the experiences of women never before recorded in writing, and in stepping into the shadowy spaces and the suggestively erotic 'serpentine caves' of women's unspoken or half-spoken desires and ambitions (*AROO* 80), but in accepting a new and active role as a reader, working as an 'accomplice'. For instance, the narrator includes herself (and possibly her own audience/ reader) – in the 'us all' – with the characters whom Mary Carmichael 'succeeded in getting . . . in a canoe up the river' (*AROO* 78). She is also willing, like Mary herself, to engage with the subtle and ambiguous forms of women's expression ('the shortest of shorthand . . . words that are hardly syllabled yet,' *AROO* 81), to accept the indeterminacy and inconclusiveness of this writing (that 'the important point' is always 'just a little further on', *AROO* 87), and to relinquish the usual responses that create the illusion of a profound engagement with a book, but which are exposed as the results of being 'merely lazy minded and conventional into the bargain' (*AROO* 87). The use of the language of the market here also points to the fact that this new form of women's fiction is not simply a commodity for easy consumption: the 'bargain' of narrative satisfaction is not so easily struck and this more ambiguous, uncertain and disruptive writing refuses the commodifying impulse of capitalism. Rather, the reader must be prepared to speculate and gamble, to accept not only the fluctuation in the current of thought, 'one of the fundamental metaphors by which Woolf organizes her book' (Rosenbaum xxix, referring to *Women & Fiction*), but to engage with new textual and sexual currencies and to invest in new economies of meaning. That the economies of such writing are more fluid, indeterminate and generous

32 *Gifts, Markets and Economies of Desire*

in generating potentially endless possibilities for interpretation is suggested here in the rhetorical strategy of using a discussion of a fictional piece of fiction to discuss women and fiction (what Rosenbaum refers to as 'the double fictive frame', xxix). In particular, the narrator has declared that the frame of her lecture/essay as a whole is also 'making use of the all the liberties and licences of a novelist to tell . . . the story' of arriving at her opinion on the topic 'Women and Fiction' (*AROO* 6).

Indeed, the aspects of Mary Carmichael's narrative explored by the narrator as being unconventional, innovative and subversive are echoed in the structure of her own discussion. The narrator is also Mary, as her invitation to call her 'Mary Beton, Mary Seton, Mary Carmichael' suggests (*AROO* 6), and this sets up a slippage of identity which helps to undermine conventional structures of author/ity. The doubling and tripling of names and the slippage between the Marys compound the indeterminacy and ambiguity of women's writing, emphasising a disruption of boundaries, identities and roles, and highlighting the textual generosity of this essay by this emphasis on the multiplicity of its generative sources. This ambiguity of authorship is also a defiance of systems of literary property, so central to the operation of the literary market; it also enhances the fluidity and impermanence privileged in Mary Carmichael's style, as well as Woolf's, which create the protean qualities of women's fiction that Woolf's essay itself puts into practice.

Such highly self-conscious and disruptive strategies characterise the structure and rhetorical strategies of *A Room of One's Own* as a whole, which operates what Cixous would characterise as a feminine gift economy. Premised on openness, generosity and dialogue, from the outset *A Room of One's Own* resists not only the hierarchy of value that an authoritarian disquisition would assert, but, simultaneously, the operation and values of capitalist exchange. The disruption of the conventional form of the lecture/essay means that, like the readers of *Life's Adventure*, the reader/audience of *A Room of One's Own* must accept a similar change in the economy of meaning and indeed in the role in the exchange of meaning they are invited to play. No longer able to assume a passive acceptance of what they are told, they must play an active role in this more democratic, equitable exchange, assessing what has value to them and what is 'worth keeping' (*AROO* 6). The narrator not only points out the complexities and ambiguities of the topic of 'Women and Fiction', but, subverting the function of an academic exposition, makes clear that she will 'never be able to come to a conclusion' or 'hand' her audience 'a nugget of pure truth to wrap up between the pages of [their] notebooks and keep on the mantelpiece for ever' (*AROO* 5). The metaphor used to convey the impossibility of encapsulating the meaning of women and fiction is one resonant with economic meaning: a 'nugget' is strongly associated with gold in its natural state and suggestive of precious raw material to convert into money, commodities or some valuable object to hoard and use as a display of power and authority (as the men's college does with its 'treasures'), or to trade in the academic world or beyond (*AROO* 11, 22). That this exchange (a nugget of truth in exchange for an hour of the audience's attention) is a capitalist exchange, inherently connected to a masculine economy of value, is demonstrated by the other 'nuggets' found in the essay. These include the 'ingots and rough lumps of gold' given by kings and nobles to found the university (*AROO* 20), as well as the 'pure nuggets of the essential ore' of truth so effortlessly 'extract(ed)' by the male student who, trained to analyse what he reads with a capitalist efficiency, works in the British Museum which is, metaphorically, one of the 'department(s)' of the 'factory' of London (*AROO* 28–9, 27). Woolf's narrator's refusal to provide such a 'nugget' makes clear from the beginning that her words about women and fiction cannot be readily absorbed into a monetary economy; nor can women's creative gifts be measured out and packaged up and a value placed upon them. Rather, she invites her audience/reader to enter a dialogue, to use their own judgement about what is valuable independently of any academic 'gold standard'.[19] She offers her ideas in the hope of their ongoing circulation and transformation in the lives of her female audience/readers, seeking a relationship of mutual co-operation and reciprocation.

The emphasis on narrative and the subjective interpretation invited subverts the masculine linearity and efficiency of traditional forms of the lecture and essay. The inclusion of stories is not a only playful self-referential device, but expands the form beyond the limitations of masculine thinking in generating a different creative mode of engagement with ideas, in accordance with the idea that women's 'creative power differs greatly from the creative power of men' (*AROO* 84). Noticing a Manx cat from the window as she dines at the men's college, the narrator comments, 'It is strange what a difference a tail makes' (*AROO* 14), implicitly referring to the position of women who, without a phallic 'tail', are excluded from the privileges and wealth of the men's college. What Woolf's lecture/essay demonstrates is the immense difference that the generative potential of a tale (or two or three) can make. The narratives included here give rise to the generosity and subversiveness of the text and are concerned with women's creative 'gifts'. The tale of the imaginary Judith Shakespeare is of central importance, not only because it highlights the material and ideological prohibitions on women's creativity and participation in the male-dominated literary sphere, which has incalculably impoverished the literary tradition, but also because this tale acts, like the imaginary novel by Mary Carmichael, to bolster the limited literary tradition that does exist. The ending of *A Room of One's Own* exhorts women to write, and to draw on the 'continuing presences' not only of the actual women writers of the past, but of the potential vitality and creativity that has lain dormant in women and should now be resurrected, given 'the opportunity to walk among us in the flesh' (*AROO* 108). *A Room of One's Own* finally

34 Gifts, Markets and Economies of Desire

concludes that it is this work 'even in poverty and obscurity' that will lead ultimately to women's financial, intellectual and personal independence, and is for this reason and for its own sake, 'worth while' (*AROO* 108).

Towards the end of *A Room of One's Own*, Woolf's narrator elucidates the vital role that the creative writer performs in their ability to capture what is meaningful in everyday experiences but which, because they are part of everyday reality, and indeed because there are many different experiences of 'reality', are not recognised as such by others. The writer's sensitivity and creativity translate this residue of experience, 'what remains over when the skin of the day has been cast into the hedge', for the reader so that they can see 'more intensely' and find 'the world . . . bared of its covering and given an intenser life' (*AROO* 104, 105). Such a role is an 'invigorating' one and is performed 'for the good of the world at large' (*AROO* 105, 104). These ideas about the importance of art and creative writing become increasingly prominent in Woolf's writings of the 1930s when she feared that words themselves seem to be reduced to simply a political tool.

Woolf's concern with the preservation of the integrity of the artist and with sustaining the freedom essential for the creative gift to flourish comes to the fore especially in the mid- to late 1930s. As the economic and political ground began to shift, what Woolf saw as the damaging ramifications of the increasing commodification of writing and the pressures of the literary marketplace come into sharper critical focus in her essays of this period. As Lee suggests, Woolf 'came increasingly to resent the traps and compromises of the literary market-place' (Lee, 1996, 559), not only the force of the market to dictate taste and to exert control over what writers produce, but also its power over reviewer-critics and the readers themselves. Woolf's increasingly bitter and satirical discussion of the corrupting and distorting influence of the marketplace is expressed in the phrase she uses in *Three Guineas*: 'intellectual harlotry' (*TG* 114). This indicates her view that writers themselves had become like commodities for sale, not under a street lamp in Piccadilly, but, as the analogy she draws in 'Reviewing' indicates, in the glare of a metaphorical shop window, subjected to the fiercely critical and public scrutiny of reviewers and, through them, the reading public. Woolf's essays make clear the impossibility of integrity and a genuine assessment of literary worth in the literary marketplace, where writers and reviewers alike are not only subject to 'shop window temptations' (the pressures of the profit motive and the precarious sense of fame and success premised on the reviewer's display of wit or public exhibition of revenge), but must also keep pace with the ever-turning world of commodity culture in which time and column inches equate to money and must be efficiently used (*CD* 160). Writers in such conditions run the risk of injured or inflated reputations, which have an impact either for good or bad on their 'sales', but which crucially, and always detrimentally, have an impact on their 'sensibility', distorting their aesthetic values (*CD* 153).

The Business of Writing 35

In 'Reviewing', Woolf outlines the way that meaningful channels of communication between the writer of 'imaginative literature' and the reader, and between the reader and the reviewer, are destroyed by the distorting effects of the market and mass communications (*CD* 152). As modern reviews become shorter, more quickly produced and increase dramatically in number, this damaging impact is magnified (*CD* 154). The vast number of reviews, all trying to 'measure' the new writing, to complete its 'packaging' for the market, brings out a vast number of opinions so that 'praise cancels blame; and blame praise' (*CD* 155). The result is that reviews are 'worthless' in terms of two of their key functions: 'to sort current literature' and to 'inform the public' (*CD* 154). This leaves only the advertising function in place, though even this is far from effective given 'the present discordant and distracted twitter' that reviewers, forced to 'hedge' their views, rather than offering an expert and considered opinion on the work, produce (*CD* 157, 156). This not only causes such distrust in the public that readers may not buy or read the books reviewed at all (*CD* 155, 157), but it also stifles the potential of the reviewers themselves. Stymied by the imperative 'to write in haste and to write shortly', they have no time to satisfy their 'genuine desire' to tell the authors why they like or dislike the works, nor to develop their own skills as writers, which would not only revive the essay as an art form but in turn 'might make for better criticism' (*CD* 159, 162).

Using the language of the market, Woolf's assessment of the current 'value' of reviewing leads her to consider what changes could be 'profitable'. Her solution is twofold (*CD* 152). To serve the interests of the publisher and the reading public, she proposes 'the Gutter and Stamp' system of reviewing. In this, a brief summary or description of a work is offered and a stamp of approval or otherwise attached, a proposal that is a barely disguised satire summing up Woolf's criticism of the current system of reviewing (*CD* 157). To serve the interests of the reviewer and the author, she proposes a system of private consultation between the two, resembling that of a doctor and patient, in which a full diagnosis of the work could be obtained for a fee. In this scenario, artistic creativity is allowed to retreat to the private realm. Here, shielded from the flash and glare of public exposure and sequestered from the tangible pressures of the marketplace, the writer can again become an 'an obscure workman', honestly producing their best work for a readership which, increasingly respectful of this work, would have their own critical and creative desires satisfied. They in turn would give back their vital energy, 'a ray of pure sunlight', to the ongoing generation of creativity (*CD* 163).

Woolf's imaginary solution is problematic in several ways, not only in its presumption that writers would be in the privileged position of having three guineas to spend on a private consultation, but also in the assumption that paying privately for a consultation would lead to a more 'impersonal and disinterested' critical opinion (*CD* 161). This imagined private retreat is, however, a telling solution that reveals her own anxieties at this time about the

36 *Gifts, Markets and Economies of Desire*

loss of her readership and about her reputation. As Lee remarks, although Woolf 'liked fame, success and money, . . . she hated publicity, especially at a time when the personality of authorship through interviews and publicity was increasing' (1996, 648). The public exposure of every detail of the private, often precarious and painful, process of constructing a piece of art is implied in Woolf's analogy between the writer and seamstress in a shop window. It is the scrutiny of the personality of the author, rather than of the 'finished article' of the book made ready for public view, that repels her (*CD* 152). The prospect of a private consultation resulting in the need for fewer public reviews and so making more space for the art of criticism in commercial publications also attempts to solve Woolf's own anxieties about the commercialisation of her own essays. In this situation, literary criticism would retain its status as art, even as it is published in the commercial sphere. It also obviously accords with Woolf's anger towards the contemporary state of literary journalism, and the distance between this system and her own literary essays that she wishes to emphasise. Anxious about the response to the 'intolerance' of Woolf's views expressed in 'Reviewing', an anxiety perhaps justified by the 'outraged scorn which greeted this satire' (Lee, 1996, 721), Leonard Woolf added a note at the end of the essay to try to balance Woolf's scathing conclusions. As Gualtieri suggests, Leonard Woolf's note also highlights what Woolf tries to downplay: her own professional relationship to the commercial world as a writer of fiction as well as a reviewer and literary essayist (Gualtieri 66).

However, the more productive and harmonious relations Woolf imagines in this essay, in which writers, reviewers and readers co-operate to generate art and to value creativity, are of crucial importance if art is to continue to have a positive impact on society. In 'Why Art Today Follows Politics', Woolf elaborates on 'the relations of the artist to society', demonstrating the important function of art as part of the social and moral fabric (*CD* 133). As a worker, the artist is in a unique position in being dependent on society as 'his paymaster and his patron', suggesting that the artist exists in a liminal position between the monetary and the gift economy (*CD* 134). Although society only rewards the artist materially in a minimal way, it is the intellectual engagement and reward that is crucial: it is the exercise of society's 'critical faculty' that ensures that the artist's work does not 'suffer and . . . perish' from 'work(ing) in a vacuum' (*CD* 134). In return, the artist as a worker repays society not only through the production of 'works of art that have always formed one of its [society's] chief claims to distinction', but through their receptivity to social and political change and their ability to articulate this change in a creative, rather than dictatorial, way, thus nurturing society creatively and intellectually. However, this symbiotic relationship is one that can be distorted and made worthless not only by market forces, but also by political pressures, depicted as voices that 'besiege' the artist, disclaiming the value of art and the artist's role, or 'proclaim(ing) that the artist is the servant of the politician' (*CD* 135).

The Business of Writing   37

In times of peace, a degree of distance/autonomy from politics is accepted as part of the artist's role in order to guard against the mixing of 'art with politics', which would 'adulterate' art, a detrimental effect that would seriously impair the artist's ability to nourish society through it (*CD* 134). Woolf's metaphor of art as bread conveys this effectively: art unadulterated with politics is 'bread made with flour' and will feed not only the society of the time, but, because such bread is malleable and organic, it will sustain and enrich society beyond the moment in which it was produced. On the other hand, art that is highly politicised is 'bread made with plaster' and may not only poison society, but its specific political origins and intention make it inflexible, limiting the meanings and nourishment it can have for future generations (*CD* 134). This idea of art and creative ideas as material staples is echoed in the metaphor that defines the artist's economic relationship with society: the artist receives a minimal financial reward – his/her 'bread and butter' (*CD* 134) – thus emphasising the harmonious, co-operative and mutually-sustaining relationship between art and society that is beneficial to all. Importantly, the bread metaphor also contradicts the idea that art is a 'luxury to be discarded in times of stress': rather, Woolf's metaphor implies that art is a staple more necessary at times of crisis than ever (*CD* 134).

In one of Woolf's last essays, 'Thoughts on Peace in an Air Raid' (1940), she maintains her belief in the power of independent and creative thought to counter the unthinking, 'sterile, unfertile' 'emotion of fear and hate' produced in war, and fostered in the education and upbringing of young men (*CD* 171). As she argues in *A Room of One's Own* and *Three Guineas*, it is specifically women's ideas, born out of their difference of experience and perspective, that are fundamental to 'fighting for freedom ... with the mind', enabling them to 'think peace into existence': the only way to end war in the present and in the future (*CD* 168). It is women who will support men in gaining the 'access to the creative feelings' that will enable them to fight against the powerful imperative, 'cherished by education and tradition', for men to go to war (*CD* 171, 170). However, women can only fight patriarchal tyranny and the fascistic thinking that accompanies it if they are not enslaved themselves by masculinist hegemonic values and methods. As Woolf states, 'If we could free ourselves from slavery we could free men from tyranny. Hitlers are bred by slaves' (*CD* 170). In particular, it is conservative patriarchal gender politics that not only leave women literally 'weaponless', and therefore in need of defending, but which stifle their ideas and intellectual abilities, their weapons of the mind which can replace the weapons of war (*CD* 168).

Woolf's image for the enslavement of women and for their complicity in patriarchal and fascistic tyranny is significantly *the* site of commodity spectacle and allure, the shop window: 'We can see shop windows blazing; and women gazing; painted women; dressed-up women; women with crimson lips and crimson fingernails. They are the slaves who are trying to enslave'

38 *Gifts, Markets and Economies of Desire*

(*CD* 170). Woolf's increasingly vitriolic attacks on the commercial world make clear that the pleasure of commodity spectacle can no longer be enjoyed because the powerful force of the capitalist policies that underlie it can no longer be tolerated. Such a commodity display keeps women in thrall to the glorification of 'eroticised femininity' and channels 'heterogeneous forms of desire' into 'the imperative to buy ever more commodities' (Felski 90). In doing so, it simultaneously disarms women's potentially subversive 'weapons', their 'thinking against the current', collapsing as it does the distinction between the women shoppers and the mannequins on display, and reinforcing the idea that women are objects of desire (and even for sale), not active supporters of the fight for freedom (*CD* 169). What Lady Astor had referred to as 'subconscious Hitlerism', Woolf suggests, is not just in the 'hearts of men', but also in the desires that commodity culture fuels in women (*CD* 169).

Woolf's own political and charitable involvements in the 1930s, especially the mid- to late 1930s, were, for the most part, fluctuating and inconsistent, characterised, as Lee describes, by 'gestures of commitment and withdrawal' and by 'a repeated tendency' of 'joining and quitting', which was partly symptomatic of 'the quarrelsome disunity and splinterism of the Left in the 1930s . . . [and] of the anti-Fascist "front" in Britain' (Lee, 1996, 687, 684).[20] Woolf's engagements with pacifist and anti-fascist organisations (such as For Intellectual Liberty [FIL] and the International Association of Writers in Defence of Culture [IAWDC]), and her differences of view about war and gender issues, fed into *Three Guineas* (Lee, 1996, 684–7). One of her most sustained and consistent commitments was to the London and National Society for Women's Service (LNSWS). It was her 'Professions for Women' talk, addressed to the members of this society, that led to the inspiration for *Three Guineas* and, as is evident in Woolf's fiction, charitable work and gifts often lead to returns in creative gifts. The most significant aspect of Woolf's involvement with this society in relation to *Three Guineas* is her commitment, especially from 1938 until her death, to helping to fund the Women's Library.[21] As Snaith persuasively argues, this library comes to represent the freedom of access to knowledge, specifically to women's history and economic issues, and to books unavailable in public libraries where '(c)ensorship of stock as well as control of access to stock contributed to a subtle policing of the nation's reading tastes by seemingly democratic institutions' (2003, 25). This library, in fact, came to represent for Woolf a utopian and modern space, 'liberated and liberating', in which women could read and research in a communal 'semi-private' room of their own, gaining access to information and ideas that not only allowed them to 'negotiate their difference as they entered the public sphere' and male-dominated professions, but also to attain the freedom of independent thought Woolf saw as so crucial for the prevention of war (Snaith, 2003, 29, 24, 27, 30, 29). Her gifts to this library can be seen not only to correct the hoarding associated with the university library she represents in *Three Guineas*, but also to counter directly the blatant sexism that other libraries enforce in denying women access to the committees that control them, just as women were debarred from being full members of Cambridge University.[22] Woolf's gifts and charity work for this library, Snaith argues, were based not only on her personal connection with Phillipa Strachey (secretary of the library's executive committee), but also on a sense of responsibility, an important motivation at a time when most of her friends, family and acquaintances perceived pacifism as irresponsible (Lee, 1996, 690). It also supports one of the key arguments in *Three Guineas*, which is that women 'can only help [men] to defend culture and intellectual liberty by defending [their] own culture and [their] own intellectual liberty' (*TG* 114). The importance of Woolf's gifts to the library are part of an ongoing gift economy which is so vital in *Three Guineas* and which its publication succeeds in sustaining. This ongoing circulation of the gift takes the form of Woolf's own use of the library as a resource for *Three Guineas*, her incorporation of information she was given by the library into her text puts it into wider circulation, and the active engagement of her readers keeps this gift in motion, potentially circulating the gift wider still.

Most obviously, *Three Guineas* is a satirical attack on the ideological values and beliefs central to heteropatriarchal culture, and on the capitalist economic system that helps to fuel the tyrannies and oppressions of such a culture to the point of inciting war. Whereas the other essays considered here have assumed an unstated middle-class perspective, *Three Guineas* explicitly asserts that its class-specific focus is on the injustice of the political and economic position and experience of the 'daughters of educated men', 'the weakest of all the classes in the state' (*TG* 16), and guineas themselves are notional units of money (worth one pound and a shilling) associated with upper-class transactions (see Black 85). In a lengthy letter, written ostensibly in response to a request for funds to support a society for the prevention of war, *Three Guineas* takes (so-called) civilised society to task, exposing its inequalities, injustices and irrationalities and exploring the violence and destructiveness endemic to it. This response is multiple in that the narrator's letter includes within it letters that she proposes to send to two women who have also asked for financial support. In this way the epistolary form of *Three Guineas* facilitates a widening of the debate, giving scope for considering how the traditional systems of education and the professions underpin the social, political and economic forces driving Britain to war. Importantly, these responses also explore how these influential institutions can be changed by the different perspectives and positive influences that educated middle-class women can bring. However, to do this, women must sustain a precarious balance between 'the devil and the deep sea' (*TG* 86): a pecuniary balance between earning enough to maintain their personal and intellectual independence in order to be free from the need to charm and allure men and to agree with the dominant male point of view (*TG* 19–21), and becoming

40 *Gifts, Markets and Economies of Desire*

ensnared in the capitalist 'money motive' to earn more and perceive everything through a monetary lens. As the social, political and economic history of women attests, economic dependence can enslave physically and intellectually. Women can only counter 'the man's habit' 'to fight' if they have a disinterested 'earned money influence', which is itself free from the seductive influence of money (*TG* 9, 37).

As Caughie suggests, 'Woolf investigates the complex of conditions in which tyranny can function: the psychological, the historical, the economic, and the linguistic' (1991, 115). What seems to be of overwhelming importance in this complex of conditions is the economic: meaning not merely the monetary economy, but implying economies more broadly and metaphorically. The title of Woolf's essay forces the reader to think about money and economic transactions, and the rhetorical device of giving the guineas as gifts disturbs assumptions about the kind of economies at work, and about the principles of these economies. Making reference to Thomas De Quincey, Caughie states that 'the aim of rhetoric is to stimulate thought' (1991, 116) and it is in using the rhetoric of gift-giving that Woolf's essay works towards a viable and ethical way to counter war. The giving of gifts is not only a rhetorical strategy here, however. Rather, it suggests an alternative dimension to the complex of conditions: one in which gift-exchange practices, as Marcel Mauss argues, can enable groups 'to oppose and to give to one another without sacrificing themselves to one another' (82). It is such practices that, Mauss argues, are crucial for the 'so-called civilized world' to learn so that people can 'create mutual interests, giving mutual satisfaction', defending those interests 'without having to resort to arms' (83, 82). However, *Three Guineas* also makes clear what needs to be unlearned to avoid war, as Woolf explores the material and ideological conditions, notably the force of the capitalist economy and the acquisitive, possessive ethos it fosters, that were playing such significant roles in leading Europe to the brink of war.[23]

The resistance to capitalism's insatiable acquisitiveness found throughout Woolf's writing is here more urgent than ever. The greed to possess, to control and to acquire ever more power and force is all-pervasive and central to the social, legal, political and economic structures and processes of her society. Money is both the material manifestation and symbolic representation of this destructive greed. Indeed, money insidiously enslaves those with the opportunity to earn or acquire it, breeding the desire for ever more money to the detriment and distortion of social bonds, the corruption and adulteration of creative and intellectual life, the impoverishment of spiritual and moral values, and the sacrifice of that which is without price: the pleasures and experience that are immeasurable by monetary calculation (*TG* 81–3). With the same deforming effects as the commodity culture seen in 'Street Haunting' and the deadening and deadly effects of the shop window in 'Thoughts on Peace in an Air Raid', achieving too much success in the professions leads to the life-denying obsession with making ever more money,

The Business of Writing   41

stripping life of 'its spiritual, its moral, its intellectual value' and leaving the professional as no more than 'a cripple in a cave' (*TG* 83, 84). This addiction to money is a 'poison' in society, creating the emotions of jealousy and rivalry that predispose men to go to war (*TG* 26). It fuels the market forces that contaminate and corrupt culture and intellectual liberty, leading to what Woolf calls 'brain prostitution': an exchange more pernicious than sexual prostitution because the 'anaemic, vicious and diseased progeny' it creates 'are let loose upon the world to infect and corrupt and sow seeds of disease in others' (*TG* 108). The vituperative attack on the commercialisation of writing signals an intensification of Woolf's lifelong attitude to commercial writing. At this historical moment, the distortion of intellectual and creative integrity commercialisation entails represents signals a new level of danger for Woolf as it feeds the war machine. The development of mass communications means that words can be *mechanically* reproduced as a kind of capital, which can then be invested in propaganda and used for the profit of producing and reproducing certain ideas and ideologies, and influencing collective action. Sonita Sarker explores Woolf's attitude to and participation in the mechanical reproduction and commodification of words, the raw material of her 'trade' as a writer and intellectual, as a form of '"negotiated nostalgia"' (38, 39). She argues that in *Three Guineas* Woolf demonstrates that 'ideologies of liberty, freedom, nation, and peace themselves become commodities in rituals based on quickly proliferating technical inventions and devices' and that 'words themselves have become products of mechanical reproduction in new rituals *of* politics' (49). However, 'the degree, nature and intention of commodification also make a difference' (47). In *Three Guineas* the selling out of independent thought and writing not only for money, but for the mere 'tokens' of fame, 'medals, honours, degrees' is commensurate with the loss of any perspective on the facts and truths of war from outside 'the vicious circle . . . of intellectual harlotry', a 'slavery' inherently connected to war (*TG* 108, 114, 109). However, as Sarker's discussion makes clear, women need to harness the benefits of such reproduction (as it is 'at once help, hindrance, and necessity'), using their own words and engagement with new technologies to earn their independence and 'to remain protected from that ultimate betrayal, "intellectual harlotry"' and to 'protest against inhumanity and gender anonymity' (Sarker 40, 47, 39).

Woolf's narrator argues that money is the currency of men's irrational, unconscious urges to suppress and control women. Noting that 'the public and private worlds are inseparably connected' so that 'the tyrannies and servitudes of one are the tyrannies and servitudes of the other', it is imperative to have freedom in the private realm in order to achieve freedom in the public realm and to prevent war (*TG* 162, 138). To this end, she explores the fears that lead to secrecy, silence and submission in women and the angry denial of women's equal rights in men (to enter the Church as a minister, for example). This investigation leads the narrator to explore further

42 Gifts, Markets and Economies of Desire

connections between the public conscious self and the private unconscious urges as she searches for an explanation for the causes of these fears. She turns, with a mocking approach, to the Freudian idea of 'infantile fixation', which is deemed to 'play(s) a predominant part in determining the strong emotion': the angry protection of male privilege aroused by women entering the male professions (*TG* 144, 146).[24] Turning also to biographical evidence, she explains how men's unconscious urges to exert their control over women are made manifest in the irrational desire of Victorian fathers to possess and control their daughters, socially, sexually and economically, a desire wholly, if implicitly, supported and endorsed by the laws, ideologies, institutions and mores of society (*TG* 155). The stifling of women's abilities and the prevention of women from earning their own income is explained by the fact that money received from other men (earned by daughters) becomes a marker of sexual rivalry unbearable to the Victorian patriarch (*TG* 150–1). Although such attitudes are normalised in a patriarchal and capitalist society, Woolf's essay argues that this obsession with money and men's irrational need to exert control over women are symptomatic of a psychological disorder, an 'affliction', denoting a regression to the primitive, 'savage' urges repressed in the unconscious, urges that become 'rampant' when male privilege is challenged (*TG* 147–8, 155). Women entering professions and earning their own money and independence from their fathers and patriarchs in general is seen as a violation of a 'non-rational sex taboo' infecting male-dominated society (*TG* 158–9, 160–1). This intensified masculinity and the subordination of women are at the heart of the fascism in Europe but also, as Woolf was aware, in the spread of fascism in Britain (Lee, 1996, 685).

Although she eventually gives two of her guineas as 'free gifts, given freely', Woolf's narrator first contemplates imposing conditions on the ways that all the guineas are to be used, making clear the power and potential for control and dominance that gifts carry (*TG* 116). She considers asserting her own views and exercising 'the right of potential givers to impose terms', notes the entitlement of 'the giver of money . . . to dictate terms', and the potential for 'bargain(ing) with' 'honorary treasurers' in need of financial help (*TG* 48, 37, 27). However, all of these possibilities compromise the gift, and the language used to convey these conditions dangerously echoes the fascistic and tyrannical forces seeking to impose views and values, and demanding specific actions. They also allude to the power of the market that helps to create the impetus for war, as well as the forces of reason that make war seem so necessary. Caughie argues that this 'giv(ing) way to the impulse' to exert the power of the wealthy over the poor recipient 'mak(es) the act of charity both gracious and pernicious' (1991, 138, note 5). However, the only terms Woolf's narrator does attach (to the second guinea given to the society to help women into professional work) are, in one sense, empty terms because 'the law of England' has already imposed the social, political and economic limitations on women's position and experience she outlines (*TG* 94–5).

In another sense, though, her 'terms' turn the tables on the historical exclusions, denials and repressions women have experienced, re-evaluating these inequalities positively in terms of the strength this experience gives to women who, now independent and able to earn their own income, can readily resist 'the seductions of the most powerful of all seducers – money', as well as the other lures of distinctions, loyalties and symbols of power that are so dangerously bound up with the impetus towards war (*TG* 95). It is in retaining the experience derived from 'the four great teachers of the daughters of educated men – poverty, chastity, derision and freedom from unreal loyalties' that, with an income sufficient 'for the full development of body and mind. But no more', women can restore humanity to society and use their influence 'to abolish the inhumanity, the beastliness, the horror, the folly of war' (*TG* 92, 96).

As the discussion of donations, gifts and other awards and rewards made in the male-dominated institutions of education and the professions makes clear, such so-called gifts given with the intention to manipulate and control are not gifts at all. Rather, they are bribes (what Carrier calls 'a prostitution of the present', 147), demanding loyalties and duties in and from the recipient which distort and constrain independent thought and action. They create feelings (of pride and rivalry) which both incite belligerence and simultaneously manipulate attitudes and responses that, at this historical moment, feed patriotism and the will to war. Such symbolic gifts are inherent in the masculine economy of value and function, like the 'symbolic splendour' of professional dress, in a way similar to 'the tickets in a grocer's shop' advertising quality and value.[25] Like these forms of dress, they provoke 'emotions which encourag(e) a disposition towards war', as well as distorting attitudes and responses (*TG* 26).

Such gifts are also disguised capitalist investment in both patriarchal tyranny and war. Gifts to men's colleges, for instance, amass return profits and boost the capitalist and the masculine economy by investing in the production of graduates. These graduates will go on to be enterprising and successful in capitalist business, and will design new weapons, shoring up patriarchal social hierarchies and the value of competition and conflict, so reinforcing men's power and authority (*TG* 28, 38). Other so-called gifts, such as rewards, 'medals, symbols, orders and even . . . decorated ink-pots' exert a power over the recipient (as 'the example of the Fascist States . . . instruct(s) us', *TG* 131), having a hypnotising effect that 'paralyses' independent thought and action, and 'inhibits the human power to change and create new wholes', constraining growth and creativity to the well-worn ruts of thought and action imposed by dictators and tyrants (*TG* 131, 132). Woolf's footnote on the 'decorated ink-pots' clarifies that what she refers to is actually a plaque decorated with a Reich eagle which is placed on the desk of those distinguished by the Nazis (*TG* 198, note 19). That she represents this as an ink-pot in the body of her essay emphasises the importance she

44   *Gifts, Markets and Economies of Desire*

places on the freedom to write (especially for women), echoing as it does the necessity, outlined in 'Professions for Women', for women to kill the still-present phantom of the Victorian ideal of femininity, the Angel in the House, in order to win their freedom from overbearing tradition of patriarchal oppression. That the professional woman must fling her ink-pot at the phantom of femininity in 'Professions For Women' parallels the advice the narrator gives to women in *Three Guineas* – to 'fling' the so-called gifts of a masculine economy ('badges, orders or degrees') 'back in the giver's face' (*TG* 93). In these two interconnected essays,[26] the effects of patriarchal oppression and the bribes of a masculine economy have the same effect and are to be resisted, so that women's independence of thought, integrity and psychological and emotional health are not compromised. It is by laughing in the face of the allure of the money and the rewards of a fascistic culture, 'fame and praise' in *Three Guineas*, that women can speak their minds and so help prevent war, women's laughter subversively disturbing property rights and 'the framework of institutions . . . blow(ing) up the law' as Cixous argues ('1981a' 258).

However, the masculine gift economy also 'queers the professions', distorting any sense of a meritocracy through the nepotism that prevails and which, given the 'aroma' or 'odour' of misogyny that the presence of single women in the public office generates, is a gift that particularly queers the professions for women (*TG* 58–9). It is this discriminatory and prejudiced 'atmosphere' that, although 'impalpable', is 'a very mighty power . . . chang(ing) the sizes and shapes of things; it affects solid bodies, like salaries, which might have been thought impervious to atmosphere' (*TG* 61). It is also akin to fascism, dictating how women should live, and which 'if it spreads, may poison both sexes equally' (*TG* 61). Although professional men are able to use their influence in a nepotistic way, 'To have such perquisites in their gift' is poisonous, a point emphasised in the echo of the phrase to describe women's unique vitality and creativity in *A Room of One's Own*, where it is the 'renewal of creative power' that is 'in the gift only' of women (*AROO* 82).

This association of women and the gift of vitality and renewal is both a positive feminist view and a knowingly utopian one, conveying as it does strongly felt hopes and desires for a rejuvenation of society on more democratic lines. It is with such a hope that Woolf's narrator outlines her idealised vision of a women's college of the future as 'a place where society was free', its organisation premised on co-operative, egalitarian and generous principles, and its access wide (*TG* 40). Although this utopian 'dream' is undercut by the economic reality that women students 'must be taught to earn their livings' in order to attain their independence, the emphasis on the 'cheapness' of 'an experimental college, an adventurous college' does bring this dream closer to realisation than it may first seem (*TG* 41, 39). Unlike existing colleges, this one will be more provisional, more receptive to change and indeed will invite and incite change. It will break free of the endlessly repeating cycles of production (of things, money, graduates and citizens),

The Business of Writing   45

and refuse the worship of property that causes society, thinking and creativity to stagnate as it is hoarded out of circulation. The central attribute of the gift is that it must move. In this imaginative gift of a college of the future, Woolf imagines it will be the 'arts of human intercourse' that will be taught, because this can be done cheaply, but also because interaction and communication are essential to the free movement of ideas, a movement facilitated by the removal of barriers, distinctions and hierarchies (*TG* 40).

This cheapness and emphasis on 'human intercourse' are also the attributes of the gifts around which the letter-essay *Three Guineas* is based: the small sum of a guinea to each of the three petitioners, and the lengthy letter that accompanies them. The giving of any gift entails risk, and giving a gift of money increases this risk given its potential for slippage into a purely monetary economy. These monetary gifts then, represent a testing out of the power of the gift that emphasises the positive values and hope Woolf's narrator equates with her final giving of her guineas 'freely', as well as drawing a contrast with the so-called gifts of a masculine economy. As Woolf's discussion makes clear, a woman's monetary gift given to a man 'without fear, without flattery, and without conditions' is a 'momentous . . . occasion', subverting as it does the power hierarchies from within by the very means – money – with which these hierarchies are maintained (*TG* 116). Indeed, it marks a radical point in history and culture in which the potential for 'men and women working together for the same cause', for equality, liberty and justice for all (which are also the goals of the nineteenth-century feminists), is in view. It is only through collective action (like the letter sent to the barrister from 'we') that 'peace and freedom for the whole world' can be achieved (*TG* 125). More than this, though, Woolf's essay brings to the fore not only the necessity of a self-conscious refusal of complicity with powerful ideologies and prejudices that create tyrants and dictators, but also the knowledge that we all have the potential to become tyrants and dictators: 'we cannot dissociate ourselves from that figure [of the fascist dictator], but are ourselves that figure' (*TG* 163). However, it is 'the capacity of the human spirit to overflow boundaries and to make unity out of multiplicity . . . to dream the recurring dream that has haunted the human mind since the beginning of time; the dream of peace, the dream of freedom' that the gifts given in *Three Guineas* move towards (*TG* 163).

The qualities of this dream of peace and freedom – the fluidity of movement, the transgression of boundaries, and the idea of unity composed of difference, indeterminacy and connection – are all qualities of what Cixous would call a feminine gift economy,[27] and are also the qualities of the letters sent to accompany the guineas. Early in *Three Guineas*, the narrator considers that simply to return a guinea in exchange for the letter of request would be 'cheap': an impoverished capitalist exchange, a false measure of the narrator's commitment because it has only a monetary value. This would also not appease the emotional response that the photographs of a Spanish war-zone

46 *Gifts, Markets and Economies of Desire*

generates (*TG* 15). Rather, this requires an emotional engagement, and it is an emotive discussion that is offered in *Three Guineas*. By the end of her letter to the barrister, although Woolf's narrator is still only going to send a guinea, the frame of reference for this donation has been significantly altered. This small sum, although still 'cheap' in a purely monetary economy, is richly invested with the intellectual, emotional and creative responses laid out in the letters. These guineas are no longer susceptible to capitalist reckoning, but their meaning 'overflow(s) boundaries' crossing 'the gulf so deeply cut' between the narrator and the barrister (*TG* 6), not by eliding the differences between them, but by the narrator accepting these differences and entrusting the recipient of her gift to use it well and to keep it in circulation. This reinforces a central notion about the gift, which is that it is not what is given in a gift exchange that is of importance, but the meaning attributed to it at the moment of giving. It is the emphasis repeated at this point on the fact that the guinea is 'a free gift, given freely' that suggests a freeing of this money from an enslavement in a capitalist economy and from all the corresponding fetters (ideological, emotional and material values and desires) that the narrator's letters demonstrate can destroy the 'dream of peace' (*TG* 163).

The letter itself also defies the importance of using time efficiently, which lies at the heart of a capitalist economy. The narrator repeatedly refers to the need for haste and the importance of not wasting time, yet her letter is inefficiently long, and she has delayed her response for three years. However, the detail with which Woolf's essay engages with the issues that giving gifts raises is both an indication of the complexity of the historical moment in which they are to be given and a measure of their importance. Indeed, the lengthy explanation of why conditions imposed on the gifts of guineas would be detrimental is in itself a form of textual generosity, and an example of generous thinking as it keeps ideas in circulation. As with the lecture in *A Room of One's Own*, this letter demonstrates ways of thinking creatively, expansively, generously, and, like the narrator of *A Room of One's Own*, the narrator in *Three Guineas* refuses to confine her response to a single rational line of argument, never offering a single 'nugget of truth'. Rather, it is repetitive in structure and in the ideas it expresses; it sets up provisional arguments only to undo or replace them, and it refuses to give a definitive answer. It gives 'freely' and excessively, relinquishing the control and imposition of 'truths' synonymous with tyranny and fascism. As Caughie notes, 'Woolf refuses to play the game of assertion and denial, or accusation and defence' but rather 'her essay chatters, repeats, digresses, and disperses its argument over three letters, numerous notes, and endless evidence' (1991, 118). In sustaining this generous, indeterminate style, it refuses a final transaction of meaning, a final closure of discussion, and in doing so also evades any final position that would act as a basis for retaliation from an opponent. As Caughie persuasively argues, the strength of Woolf's essay lies in this changed response to the forces of oppression and violence: 'Instead of confrontation and attack, evasion and decampment. Instead of anger, laughter' (1991, 118). This socio-political critique of the structure of opposition is voiced through the style of the letter in other ways too. Woolf's identification of a thread connecting the unconscious, the private realm, the public sphere and the urge to war is not only significant for the argument that she makes about the links between patriarchal tyranny and fascism, but the reading across boundaries and perceiving similarity and connection in what is conceptualised as distinct and in opposition, is an important way in which this essay seeks to find a solution to the seemingly inevitable momentum towards war. Although it maintains and emphasises women's difference of view and difference of experience from those of men as vital to the prevention of war, the form of *Three Guineas* refuses the 'either/or' logic of rational thought, resisting the sense of hard and fast oppositions that simply mimic war. It identifies women as outsiders to the patriarchy (at the fundamental level of denying them 'the full stigma of nationality' and membership to the patria, *TG* 94), but paradoxically returns repeatedly to the need for women to change its institutions (its education systems and professions) from within. This point is reinforced by the incorporation not only of reference to the requests of the women treasurers, but also quotations from their letters, as well as Woolf's narrator's proposed replies and the imagined responses of her interlocutors to what she proposes to say. The inclusiveness this letter encourages is confirmed by the address in the final paragraph to her three correspondents as 'the three of you', suggesting she will send this whole letter to all three (*TG* 164). The giving of three guineas draws attention further to the disruption of binary thinking as it puts into motion a three-way sharing of ideas, rationales and evaluation of needs. The epistolary form of *Three Guineas*, then, engages her addressee in a dialogue that calls for a new frame of reference based on generosity of thought and feeling. The antidote to war, Woolf suggests, lies in the willingness to empathise with the complexity of the difficulties others face, and in both perceiving and tolerating difference.

Snaith's work on the letters Woolf received after the publication of *Three Guineas* and the correspondence she established with many of these readers confirms the success of this work not only in widening Woolf's circle of readers, but importantly in setting in motion ideas that go on circulating beyond the final words of Woolf's essay. This correspondence suggests that *Three Guineas* continues to transgress the boundaries of experience (of class, gender and education) and disturb the distinctions that help to perpetuate acceptance of war (Snaith, 2000b). These letters are both acknowledgements of the gift and 'return' gifts in terms of their praise for *Three Guineas*, as well as in their creative and critical engagements with Woolf and her ideas. As Snaith's research demonstrates, *Three Guineas* continued to keep the gift economy in motion beyond its publication. It acted as the catalyst for further donations to the Fawcett Library Appeal (a campaign that aimed to raise a

48 *Gifts, Markets and Economies of Desire*

£15,000 endowment) from Woolf, whose 'support for the Fawcett campaign coincided with the publication of *Three Guineas'* (Snaith, 2003, 20, 26), and whose commitment to the library was consistent and generous from 1938 onwards. Woolf donated money and the books the library requested each month, often spending time and energy searching out rare books. She also wrote to friends and acquaintances to ask for donations to the campaign fund.[28] Woolf also gave her manuscript of *Three Guineas* to May Sarton so that she could sell it to raise funds for the Refugees Society (*L6* 314), donated signed copies to raise funds for the League of Nations (Snaith, 2000b, 7, and 2003, 16–7) and 'allowed and paid for extracts to be published in the Married Women's Association' (Snaith, 2000b, 7).

The essays considered here address some of the key issues found throughout Woolf's writing, notably the connections between women and writing (the aesthetics of writing as women and the problems of negotiating the literary marketplace), the material circumstances that facilitate creativity but which threaten also to regulate and limit women's lives, the importance of having money enough to be independent intellectually, personally and creatively but not to assume an acquisitive, hoarding capitalist approach to money, and the importance of sustaining a circulation of money, things, ideas and creativity with generosity and political and social awareness. Woolf's ambivalent feelings about her own role in the literary marketplace as a woman writer in some ways account for some of the contradictions and complexities in her representation of these issues, but these personal feelings overlap and interact with her political values and commitments as a feminist, socialist and pacifist. It is this political investment, with its subversion of, and challenges to, established traditions and rigid conventions, that is frequently articulated through the operation of a gift economy, and signalled by generosity and excess in Woolf's writing.

In content and form, her essays place the onus on generosity and superfluity, as they seek to displace the masculinist thinking and hegemonic practices that limit the potential of women, and which ultimately lead to war. However, although at times she extols the virtues of the 'outsider' role for women, this fantasy of existing beyond the social, political, economic and linguistic institutions that compose our world and shape our existence is impossible, and the limitations of dualistic thinking on which such a fantasy is based are exposed. Although the role of outsider can be liberating and stimulating, as the narrator finds in 'Street Haunting' when she 'step(s) out of the house', she finally must return inside her middle-class home: she cannot escape the gendered socio-economic influences that have shaped her and her view of the world. However, she takes into that space her experiences as an observer and the pencil acquired in a context of both monetary exchange and generosity. She will, it is implied, like Woolf herself, look to new ways of assessing experience, making judgements and exploring new systems of value and meaning from within these institutions and cultural

The Business of Writing 49

formations. A commitment to a gift economy is one way Woolf finds to exchange something of value without attaching a price tag, or compromising her status as an artist. Such reassessments and new approaches involving generosity are not only for the benefit of women, but, as *Three Guineas* and her later writing suggest, for the benefit of men and the whole of society if it is to be at peace. Writing in a letter about her essay 'Thoughts on Peace in an Air Raid', Woolf contemplates the 'next task' when the war is over, which she feels must be 'the emancipation of man', freeing men from the 'disabilities' (the urge to fight) incumbent upon their 'sex characteristics' so that they can 'give up glory and develop whats [*sic*] now so stunted . . . the life of natural happiness' (*L6* 379–80). Woolf implies that this will be possible in a period in which men and women will need to work co-operatively, 'pooling' their work, and will bring about an improvement of society and culture for all. As is clear in *Three Guineas* and 'Thoughts on Peace in an Air Raid', Woolf is keen to privilege women's creativity because, as she states in *A Room of One's Own*, it is in the gift of women to renew and revitalise literary and cultural traditions and, her writing of the mid- to late 1930s suggests, to bring about and sustain peace.

2
Queering the Market: 'Mrs Dalloway in Bond Street', *Mrs Dalloway* and 'The Hours'

With their focus on shopping and consumption, the interrelated texts of Woolf's short story 'Mrs Dalloway in Bond Street', *Mrs Dalloway* and 'The Hours' in many ways encapsulate Woolf's ambivalence about consumerism, capitalism and commodity culture. Shopping in these texts is a self-consciously performed activity that puts into question the heteronormative expectations that women's participation in the market economy seems to endorse. The narratives explore the subversive potential of women entering the marketplace with money to buy, and hence to satisfy their own consumer desires, and indeed to satisfy desires that are potentially at odds with social and sexual norms. The gift economy in operation in these texts is key to signalling a libidinal economy that seems resistant to heterosexual imperatives. There is a sense that the interaction of gift and market economies has the potential both to disrupt capitalist market systems and to destabilise dominant heteropatriarchal social structures. The gifts considered and actually given in these texts have the effect of queering the market – of disrupting the seemingly secure notions of gendered identity and sexuality, and of opening up several other possibilities. This applies not only to the gifts exchanged between women, which often have a utopian quality, but also those given within what can be considered to be a masculine economy of 'pseudo-gifts' given with a specific, calculated purpose. However, this is not to say that a specific lesbian or even Sapphic identity emerges. Rather, as Anne Herrmann suggests, recognising queerness or 'queering' an identity is not about revealing a secret or about 'recuperating a stigmatised sexual identity'; rather, it is about putting norms into question through acts of resistance to compulsory heterosexuality and the 'regimes of the normal' (a phrase she borrows from Michael Warner's *Fear of a Queer Planet: Queer Politics and Social Theory*, Herrmann 10, 7). The ambiguous participation of the Clarissa characters in gift and market economies suggests homoerotic desires, but their desires resist a clear definition. In this way, Woolf explores the tricky negotiation of a cultural territory in which sexual, social and monetary economies interconnect, so as to resist the socially ostracised and

Queering the Market 51

economically vulnerable position in which women who resist the heteronormative role can find themselves.

In their representation of the upper class and, particularly in *Mrs Dalloway*, the governing class, these texts also engage with the significant social, political and economic changes taking place in post-war Britain. Notable among these were the rise of the Labour Party as the main opposition to the Conservative Party, and, in 1924 for a brief time, a Labour administration under Ramsay MacDonald. These narratives represent the anxieties felt as traditional bastions of class power and influence came increasingly under attack. Woolf would have been aware of these changes and their significance, especially because during this period Leonard Woolf was increasingly involved with the Labour Party.[1] Woolf's friendship with John Maynard Keynes also engaged her thinking about economic issues. In September 1923 she records in her *Diary* reading 'some pages of his new book' – *A Tract on Monetary Reform*. In this, he argues against the reintroduction of the gold standard after its suspension during the First World War, claiming that this mechanism for regulating the economy no longer functioned effectively or responsively as it did in the nineteenth century (*D2* 266). Although she claims that 'the process of mind there [in *A Tract*] displayed' is 'far ahead' of her, her fiction of this period is in tune with the more fluid concepts about the economy that Keynes pioneered.

To an extent Woolf self-consciously sets out to expose the failings of these systems of class and gender, and the economic traditions to which they are tied, which are so resistant to change: 'I want to criticise the social system, and to show it at work, at its most intense' (*D2* 248), a feeling that seems to grow out of her mixed feelings for her aristocratic friends – Ottoline Morrel and, since December 1922, Vita Sackville-West.[2] One particular gathering leads Woolf to a 'peevish' outburst in her *Diary* and to recording the 'great deal' of interest she 'suddenly' has in writing 'The Hours' and in wanting to 'bring in the despicableness of people like Ott: I want to give the slipperiness of the soul' (*D2* 244). The intimate relationship that developed between Woolf and Sackville-West as Woolf completed her novel complicates the criticism it offers still further, inspiring as it did the homoeroticism that is so central to *Mrs Dalloway*. Woolf's novel is also complicated, as ever, by her contradictory attitude to making money, as her *Diary* entry, in which she responds to Ka Cox's letter about 'In the Orchard', demonstrates. She anticipates that writing 'The Hours' will be 'the devil of a struggle. The design is so queer & masterful' but recognising that she has a 'gift' to 'insubstantise, wilfully' she turns from her artistic integrity to her own role in the marketplace (*D2* 249). This sense of 'exist(ing) simultaneously in two "economies", a market economy and a gift economy', is one that Hyde discusses as typical of works of art, and describes the liminal space that the Clarissas of 'Mrs Dalloway in Bond Street', *Mrs Dalloway* and 'The Hours' occupy. However, it is the 'queer' design of Woolf's narratives that also draws attention to the sexual aspect of the 'social

52   Gifts, Markets and Economies of Desire

system' she sets out to criticise, as her texts demonstrate the complex negotiation and compromise, and/or resistance and rebellion that her would-be queer characters are involved in. Chameleon-like, the Clarissas of these stories move between monetary and gift economies, and expose the interconnections between them, as each, in different ways, offers opportunities for exploring homoerotic desire from the safety of a privileged social position.

At one point intended to be the first chapter of *Mrs Dalloway*, 'Mrs Dalloway in Bond Street', as the title suggests, is located in commercial London, and is premised on Clarissa Dalloway's shopping trip to buy a pair of gloves. It would seem that the cultural anxiety generated by the increased visibility of women in the public realm, 'invading' male spaces and participating in male activities, is ameliorated here by Clarissa's apparent class and gender conformity, summed up in the objects she intends to purchase. However, the commodities Clarissa seeks to buy signify something other than the apparently normative identity and behaviour they might seem to suggest, and a central issue in Woolf's story is a significantly revised connection between libidinal and monetary economies. The street itself, with its history of being 'regarded as a man's street' and 'on the prostitute beat', seems to be a significant location for this story of subversive female desire (Adburgham 254). Although Abbott argues that by the time Woolf was writing 'Mrs Dalloway in Bond Street' and *Mrs Dalloway*, Bond Street 'had succumbed . . . to the democratising rules of the new marketplace' (199, note 8), Clarissa's occupation of this space signals a potentially threatening 'trespass' into and transgression of a site where both male-dominated market and libidinal economies powerfully intersect. No gifts are actually given in this story but, as the interplay of gift and market economies reveals, the libidinal economy in operation here is exclusive of men and resistant to the commodification of female bodies for the sole gratification of male heterosexual desires.

Ruth Hoberman identifies shopping in this story as positive as well as problematic (91). Significantly, she argues, shopping promotes relationships and social exchanges: 'human contact is the story's subject' (92). In particular, though, the subject of this story is *female* contact, of bonds between women that differ from the bonds implied in the street's name. What seems significant in Woolf's story is Clarissa's ability to empathise with other women, to feel admiration for women and possibly attraction to them. What we see in this story is the ways the usual bonds (of exchange, business and personal relationship) can, in Cixous's words, 'function otherwise' to destabilise market and heterosexual economies (1981b, 50). Shopping in Bond Street provides opportunities for Clarissa's 'bonds' with other women to surface in an ambiguous way through what she *almost* purchases, and, importantly, through the gifts she considers giving. At odds with capitalist consumerism and the flow of cash and commodities, Clarissa's actual concerns focus on 'flows' of other kinds as she expresses her wishes to give gifts to women.

In her essay, 'Castration or Decapitation?' Cixous outlines the ways in which a masculine social, psychic and libidinal economy 'decapitates' women, silences the feminine and the female body. However, she also considers how this system could be disrupted through, in her words, 'resistance to a masculine desire conducted by woman as hysteric, as distracted' (1981b, 50). In 'Mrs Dalloway in Bond Street', Clarissa is not exactly an 'hysteric' but she is 'distracted' from her participation in the masculine market economy by a preoccupation with the womb and menstrual flows. Significantly, this preoccupation is what seems to motivate her desire to give gifts to women. Like Clarissa in *Mrs Dalloway*, she seems to want to compensate Milly Whitbread (a parallel character to Evelyn Whitbread in *Mrs Dalloway*) for the difficulties with her menopause (implied by Hugh's explanation of their visit to the city in the short story) and to compensate the shop assistant in the glove shop for the pains and discomfort of her monthly losses. The roots of Clarissa's generosity and sympathy, then, are bodily as well as emotional, and they are exclusive to women. Significantly, the gifts she considers giving are what Hyde would call 'threshold gifts', gifts that not only 'mark the passage from one place or state into another', but that also offer protection during that change and can 'act as the actual agents of [,] individual transformation' (44, 41), suggesting perhaps the altered perspective on desire that Clarissa's gifts signify.

The gifts Clarissa considers giving to Milly and the shop assistant offer an escape from daily life, and involve Clarissa in recollections of her past.[3] Standing outside Hatchard's bookshop, Clarissa contemplates buying a copy of Elizabeth Gaskell's *Cranford* for Milly. For Clarissa, this novel conjures up a simpler, idyllic world and she becomes lost in a nostalgic reverie about her youth – a time of transition, a liminal state in which her desires and mature emotional bonds were emerging and in a state of possibility. Clarissa's choice of novel here signals her conventionality and lack of modern sensibility (as we also see in her attitudes to visual art and fashion). It would be easy to dismiss this proposed gift as something that simply confirms the traditional values Clarissa seems to hold, especially given Woolf's criticism of the limitations of realism and her particular criticisms of Elizabeth Gaskell.[4] However, Woolf's self-consciously ironic description of what Clarissa admires about this realist novel[5], and the implied meanings and suggestive associations this novel acquires in Woolf's more fluid and ambiguous modernist text, seem significant, not least because of *Cranford*'s focus on a community of women from which men are largely excluded and on the 'economy' that maintains their bonds.

At the beginning of Gaskell's novel, we are told that Cranford is 'in the possession of amazons' and that the relationships between the women of this community are sustained by the practising of 'elegant economy' so that even those of 'moderate means' can participate in entertaining their neighbours (*Cranford* 39, 42). This 'economy' acts to bolster the immense class

54   Gifts, Markets and Economies of Desire

snobbery, antagonism and pretension (represented as absurd by the ironic narrator, Mary Smith), but also perpetuates a near exclusively female community. Later in the novel, having lost her investments, one of the characters, Matilda Jenkyns, sets up a shop. This is far from being a capitalist enterprise, however, and only makes a 'profit' because of the generosity of her community. In his analysis of *Cranford*, John Kucich considers this novel's transgressive potential in a way that makes it a highly significant gift in Woolf's story. Having considered both Gaskell's conformity to and divergence from gender norms, he argues that, 'Far from being a nostalgic glance at a provincial backwater, *Cranford* reaffirms a purely female, contemporary cultural authority, based on feminine affiliations with genteel pretension. It is largely about the feminised power of nineteenth-century culture (or "pretence" or "refinement") to ascend the social scale, with or without the assistance of male economic power' (207).

He argues that 'solidarity is accomplished through one of Gaskell's basic signs of social disorder – the lie' (207), and earlier in his essay claims 'lying is defined as a characteristically female transgression' (190). The apparent conformity, set against the economic and 'moral' deviance, of the ladies of Cranford is echoed in the community of women based on transgression in 'Mrs Dalloway in Bond Street'. Woolf's shoppers similarly form a community exclusive of men, practise an 'elegant economy' of glances and gestures, and, it is suggestively implied, that their bonds may well be transgressive in an erotic way. That this gift may have a deeply encoded reminder for Milly of Clarissa's love and desire for her in the past could also be hinted at by this gift, since one narrative strand of the novel is the thwarted love of Matilda Jenkyns and Thomas Holbrook. They have been separated by the force of social expectations in the form of family snobbery years previously and meet again when Thomas goes to town to buy gloves (which are not purchased), bringing to the surface desires not fulfilled, possibilities unexplored and, for a short time, the possibility of love being renewed. The gift Clarissa considers for Milly not only helps to emphasise the female-specific space of Woolf's story, but points to a (utopian) woman-centred monetary, social and erotic economy free of the 'assistance', limitation and proprietary power of 'male economic' and sexual 'power'.

The gift of a holiday for the shop assistant is similarly motivated by Clarissa's sense of empathy, generosity and nostalgia for her past, as well as by her desires. It is in the glove shop that Clarissa considers the gift of a holiday and we see the complexities and erotic possibilities of the interaction of the gift and market economies in this context. Like the parallel scene in *Mrs Dalloway*, which takes place in a florist's shop, the setting for Clarissa's participation in capitalist exchange is also erotically charged. There is also a sense of prior connection between Clarissa and the shop assistant, as there is in *Mrs Dalloway*. Whereas in *Mrs Dalloway* this scene is more central to the network of connections that link the gift economy and homoerotic libidinal desires, the sexually suggestive context of having gloves fitted and drawn off adds greater erotic significance to the idea of gift-giving. Like the florist's shop in *Mrs Dalloway*, the glove shop is a feminine space. The masculine economy, signalled by Bond Street, is marginalised, and is merely a distant hum, a sound that can only intrude in a dulled way, apparently stifled by the atmosphere of expectation and the female-specific commodities (gloves and silk stockings) for sale: 'They [Clarissa and the other shoppers] waited; a clock ticked; Bond Street hummed, dulled, distant' (*CSF* 156). This shop is a space of female intimacy. It has a potentially erotic atmosphere as gloves are fitted and removed by the female shop assistants, and as the women shoppers look at each other, exchanging glances. It is a space in which Clarissa expresses her admiration and implicitly her desire for women as she gazes at them 'through the hanging silk stockings quivering silver', an image vibrating with sexual suggestion (*CSF* 157).

Clarissa's entry to the shop is also suggestive as she makes an instant, possibly flirtatious, connection with the shop woman:

> 'Good morning,' said Clarissa in her charming voice. 'Gloves,' she said with her exquisite friendliness and putting her bag on the counter began, very slowly, to undo the buttons. 'White gloves,' she said. 'Above the elbow,' and she looked straight into the shop woman's face.
>
> (*CSF* 156)

The unnecessary lingering over removing her gloves, her bag on the counter and her direct gaze add a sense of suggestiveness to this exchange. Krystyna Colburn also identifies this moment as one having lesbian potential, suggesting that it is 'nearly a seduction, of the reader if not the shop-woman', and goes on to point out that 'the syntax leaves just what is being unbuttoned ambiguous' (73). Clarissa's actions here can also be read as a self-conscious performance of the usual process of capitalist exchange, a performance that exposes the underlying power structures and puts them into question. Her actions seem deliberate and exaggerated, so as to signal a mocking imitation of the procedure of transaction, just as she seems to subvert the whole (ostensible) purpose, from the a market point of view, of going shopping – not to purchase but to participate in erotic exchanges with other women. In this sense, Clarissa is queering the process of market exchange in her masquerade of heterosexual femininity; the idea of a gift economy foregrounds the queer suggestion of this performance still further. The shop assistant has already remarked admiringly on the slenderness of Clarissa's hands, a compliment given while 'drawing the glove firmly, smoothly, down over her rings' (*CSF* 157). Moreover, it seems significant that the *specific* context in which Clarissa imagines and rules out the gift of a holiday is the physically intimate one of having a glove fitted and drawn off. This context is only implicit in the story – this particular fitting is not 'present' at the textual surface – but in this

56 Gifts, Markets and Economies of Desire

feminine space, in which eroticism is already evoked, this detail makes Clarissa's fantasy of a gift even more subversive.

That Clarissa does not buy *Cranford* and does not pay for a holiday for the shop assistant might suggest her lack of commitment to the feminine gift economy and her lack of investment in such bonds. However, this could also indicate a refusal to participate in a system of property and possessions.[6] The fact that she only considers buying Milly a 'little *cheap* book' could indicate that the gift and the bond it represents are trivial (*CSF* 155, my emphasis). However, it is also significant in representing only a minimal investment in a masculine capitalist economy. Cixous, in a similar way to Derrida, discusses the way in which gifts can be annulled by the necessity of return, calling this 'the paradox of the gift that takes' (1981a, 263). The paradox of the gift in this story is not that it is given with the expectation of a return (unlike many of the gifts in *Mrs Dalloway*), but that that the gift *is not* given at all. The gift economy remains elusive, suggestive, queerly present but is not made tangible. It thereby resists recuperation into dominant economic systems.

Despite the lack of gifts actually given, Clarissa's *imagined* gift-giving still retains a disruptive and resistant potential. On their honeymoon, Clarissa's husband, Dick, dismisses her desire to give impulsively as 'folly' and asserts that trade with China is 'much more important' (*CSF* 157). Dick's economic lesson, presumably forcefully delivered given the long-term impact on Clarissa, hints at a sense of threat and draws attention to the idea that gift-giving has the potential to scupper the economy and trade. It threatens the economic system by undermining the notion of a fixed hierarchy and certain measurement of value, and by disrupting the controlled flows of profit and loss. In a sense, the exchange of gifts between women also scuppers the heterosexual economy in which women are the gifts exchanged between men, not the givers or the receivers. Drawing on anthropological studies, Rubin argues that because women are 'sexual semi-objects – gifts', rather than 'exchange partners' or 'sexual subjects', they cannot 'realize the [social] benefits of their own circulation' (542–3). However, in gift exchange between women, women assume the agency of 'exchange partners' and 'sexual subjects' with the power to negotiate their own pleasures, and to give pleasures to other women. The promise of Clarissa's gifts in both cases is pleasure and escape. As I will discuss later, the gifts given in *Mrs Dalloway* by Clarissa and others are more problematic and far from 'pure', but they are also potentially more threatening to heteropatriarchal and capitalist structures.

Dick's choice of the word 'folly' is quite apt when we consider its meaning in the architectural sense – that is, of a mock building constructed to satisfy someone's fancy or conceit, or as Woolf's story suggests, to satisfy other kinds of longing. In this sense, a folly can function as a mocking imitation and subversion of the 'architecture' of the capitalist economy; the 'folly' of giving impulsively, then, can mockingly undermine the foundations of capitalist

Queering the Market   57

and heterosexual economies. That Dick tries to prohibit Clarissa's impulsive behaviour on their honeymoon seems to be a recognition that such 'impulses' have the potential to bring the disorder of flux and fluidity to market and sexual paradigms. In this story, the flow of people and commodities, the bodily flows of women (their menstrual blood and tears) and the more fluid economy of the gift have the potential to blur and even to dissolve capitalist and heteropatriarchal structures.[7]

'Mrs Dalloway in Bond Street' explicitly puts the market and gift economies into opposition, but Clarissa's negotiation of and participation in the two economies remains ambiguous, as for Clarissa in *Mrs Dalloway*. Dick's system keeps everyone in their place – in terms of class, gender and role in the process of capitalist exchange – and Clarissa seems to agree: 'Of course he was right. And she could feel the girl wouldn't want to be given things. There she was in her place. So was Dick. Selling gloves was her job' (*CSF* 157). In many ways, Clarissa's gift is problematic anyway: it can be read as patronising and motivated by class prejudice, and it is a possible slight on the shop woman's hard-earned independence. It too could be considered a means of maintaining social hierarchies and keeping hierarchies of value in place. Her obvious placing of her bag on the shop counter, far from being a facet of her flirtation, could also function as a sign of her superior status and authority, immediately making blatant the economic power dynamic between these two women and emphasising the shop woman's obligation to satisfy this customer's desires. Similarly, the compliment the shop woman gives to Clarissa about her hands also sustains the class differences between them, since slender and be-ringed hands are markers of Clarissa's upper-class status.

In reneging on her gift, Clarissa seems to comply with a masculine economy that silences the feminine and, in Cixous's theory, denies women's erotic and emotional needs and desires. Clarissa stifles her impulse to give a gift to the shop assistant (and presumably to Milly) and, seeming to favour Dick's economic sense, also becomes more 'business-like' in her attitude to the shop assistant, more 'thrifty' with her time and attentions, and more focused on bringing the transaction to a close:

> At last! Half an inch above the elbow; pearl buttons; five and a quarter. My dear slow coach, thought Clarissa, do you think I can sit here the whole morning? Now you'll take twenty-five minutes to bring me my change!
> (*CSF* 159)

However, the ambiguity and potential for destabilisation of heteropatriarchal systems continues *as part of* the capitalist transaction, as part of the process of purchasing the gloves. Clarissa's impulses towards the shop assistant dissipate, but her serial desires for women continue and her attention is diverted by the entrance of a woman she recognises. This woman's entrance is announced by the roar of traffic as the door opens (a reminder

58 *Gifts, Markets and Economies of Desire*

of the busy city and the operation of the masculine economy), but also by the brightening of the silk stockings in the shop. Immediately this woman 'distracts' Clarissa, a certain 'ring in her voice' triggers emotive memories for Clarissa (*CSF* 158); again she recalls a pre-marital state, a youthful pastoral idyll indicated here by the reference to Sylvia. This could be referring either to Sylvia Hunt, mocked earlier in this story for her dowdiness by a now-deceased friend of Clarissa's youth (*CSF* 154), or to Clarissa's sister, Sylvia Parry, a connection more evocative of a sense of female intimacy.[8] This memory immediately leads to thoughts of an imagined future, after the death of her husband. Although apparently this is Clarissa's fantasy about her own stoicism, both remembered and imagined times are significantly periods when Clarissa is at a remove from heterosexual structures. Following this train of thought, and still immersed in the fantasy of a future free from her marital bonds, the other customer's exclamation as she splits a glove draws Clarissa's attention. Clarissa's homoerotic gaze lingers admiringly on this 'sensual, clever' woman, objectifying her as a 'Sargent drawing', and trying to find the point of connection to capitalise on this momentary meeting (*CSF* 158). The end of the story is Clarissa's recollection of the woman's name, Miss Anstruther, but this is clearly only the beginning of further exchanges between them. The final words of the story affirm her connection with this unmarried woman, and the pleasure this affords Clarissa, as she smilingly speaks this woman's name.[9]

However, the story's attention to the object of Clarissa's venture into the marketplace – the gloves, like the flowers in *Mrs Dalloway* – also maintains a sense of Clarissa as a highly ambiguous figure. In one sense, gloves represent propriety and are firmly coded in the story as a signifier of a specific class, gender and attitude, and reinforce social barriers and differences; they endorse Clarissa's role as Mrs Richard Dalloway, and signal her complicity in the dominant social order. What becomes clear, though, is that this is not their only function in this story: they too 'function otherwise' (Cixous, 1981b, 50).

The gloves Clarissa purchases are French with a pearl button (and so are explicitly feminine and elegant), and the purchase is overlaid with her recollection of her uncle's Victorian measure of femininity, as Clarissa recalls, 'A lady is known by her gloves and shoes, old uncle William used to say' (*CSF* 157).[10] Like the flowers in *Mrs Dalloway* that Abbott refers to as 'aristocratic commodities', the gloves in this story can be read similarly as a 'fixed symbol' of Clarissa's upper-class status, and Clarissa apparently readily colludes in traditional attitudes and systems of value (1992, 201). Indeed, much of the story is preoccupied with the fitting of gloves: getting gloves that fit properly seems to suggest a sense of 'fitting in' socially, of being seen to be 'proper(ty)' in the heterosocial order.[11] For Cixous '(t)he realm of the proper' is both heterosocial and phallocentric, with 'proper' etymologically bound to the concept of 'property' (1981b, 50). Significantly for Woolf's story, Cixous goes on to say that the 'proper may be the opposite of improper, and

Queering the Market   59

also of unfitting' (ibid.). That the customer who cannot get gloves to fit is very sad and mournful seems to signify more than the frustration of not being able to find a pair of gloves in the right size. Indeed this response seems to be more a concern with not fitting in, being appropriate in or complying with heterosocial and heterosexual norms – as both of Clarissa's responses to her suggest. At first, Clarissa's gaze lingers on this 'improper', 'unfitting' woman, whose sideways pose seems to invite an objectifying gaze. She acknowledges this woman's beauty and attraction, likening her to 'a figure on a Japanese fan', an object of the heterosexual male gaze 'some men would adore', but equally here an object of Clarissa's eroticising gaze (*CSF* 156). In her role as upper-class hostess, however, Clarissa conforms to dominant social norms and values and we see the way that this woman prompts Clarissa to think about the 'dowdy women' whom it would be 'intolerable' to have at her party (*CSF* 156–7).

Clarissa's rapid retreat from her erotic gaze on this woman to the safe haven of what is proper and conventional (her party guests and her Uncle William's measurement of ladylike femininity) could also mark a moment of what Patricia Juliana Smith calls 'lesbian panic' (1997, 2). Smith argues that lesbian panic is 'the uncertainty of the female protagonist (or antagonist) about *her* own sexual identity' and 'occurs when a character – or, conceivably, an author – is either unable or unwilling to confront or reveal her own lesbianism or lesbian desire' (1997, 3–4, 2, Smith's emphasis). Significantly, here, Smith argues that lesbian panic stems from a fear of loss of value and identity in a heterocentric social order:

> what is at stake from a woman under such conditions is nothing less than economic survival, as the object of exchange is inevitably dependent on the exchanger for her continued perceived worth. . . . the fear of the loss of identity and value as an object of exchange, often combined with the fear of responsibility for one's own sexuality, is a characteristic response.
> (1997, 6)

Clarissa's retreat from her fantasy of giving gifts to Milly and the shop assistant, of being an active sexual subject rather than an object of exchange, could equally be read in this light.

In many ways, Clarissa's attitude and scopophilia seem to concur with Felski's assessment of the effect of consumer culture which 'made it possible for women to articulate needs and wants in defiance of traditional patriarchal prohibitions', but which simultaneously 'subject(ed) women to norms of eroticized femininity that encouraged constant practices of self-surveillance' and 'provided a conduit through which heterogeneous forms of desire could often be deflected and channelled into the imperative to buy ever more commodities' (90). However, Clarissa is clearly not compelled to purchase and the discourse about gloves continues to articulate Clarissa's erotic longings for

60 *Gifts, Markets and Economies of Desire*

women even as it operates as a screen for these desires. Far from being simply a 'fixed symbol' of Clarissa's class and gender, or as a commodity into which potentially transgressive desires are safely channelled, we can read gloves in this story as having subversive potential. Discussing the increasing public awareness and visibility of lesbian sexuality in the period after the First World War, Laura Doan focuses on fashion: 'The meaning of clothing in the decade after the First World War, a time of unprecedented cultural confusion over constructions of gender and sexual identities, was a good deal more fluid than fixed' (96). Clarissa's gloves, then, do not necessarily construct her gender and sexuality in a fixed and unproblematic way, but can signal other possibilities.[12]

As we have seen, having gloves fitted can be a sensuous, seductive experience. However, Clarissa's desires for women, unconventionally masculine women, are also associated with the fit of the gloves (just as in the later novel Clarissa is attracted to masculine women who also handle roughly the commodity *she* purchases – flowers). Clarissa's admiration for Lady Bexborough, for her superior status, her aloof 'regal' demeanour and her masculine authority ('talking politics like a man') is summed up in the improper fit of her gloves (*CSF* 156). Lady Bexborough's gloves are 'loose at the wrist' (and her dress is 'quite shabby', *CSF* 156). Yet, far from considering her 'dowdy', Clarissa seems to want to imitate her stoicism. As she considers her determination to 'go on' should Dick die, she significantly 'tak(es) the glove in her hand' (*CSF* 158). Similarly, Clarissa's attraction to Miss Anstruther becomes focused on her authoritative tone as she tries on different pairs of gloves.

Although a symbolic (class) barrier and an actual barrier to physical contact – a commodity designed to reduce the tactile sensation of even the most restrained and polite touch – in Miss Anstruther's hands gloves actually split, bursting literal and symbolic barriers.[13] The image of the skin splitting recalls the orgasmic moment in *Mrs Dalloway*, encoded as a thin skin splitting, an overflow of desire, passion and *jouissance* (*MD* 36). This potentially erotic moment of splitting brings about a collusion of libidinal and market economies. Although a comment about price ('"But it's an awful swindle to ask two pound ten!"', *CSF* 158) seems to immediately recuperate this homoerotic suggestion into the market economy, there continues to be a significant exchange of glances between Clarissa and the object of her attention at that point in the story, Miss Anstruther, which maintains a resistance to this market economy and all it signifies. The seductive impact of this moment is signalled by the symmetrical structure of the sentence, which describes and exaggerates the mirroring behaviour of the two women, intensifying the effect of this glance and emphasising the self-consciousness of this moment and its queer potential: 'Clarissa looked at the lady; the lady looked at Clarissa' (*CSF* 158).

Clarissa's attraction to a range of different women in this story repeatedly distracts her from her ostensible mission to make a purchase of gloves, and

Queering the Market 61

therefore to fulfil her 'proper' role as an upper-middle-class heterosexual woman through her participation in a controlled and rational exchange of objects. As in *Mrs Dalloway*, in many ways Clarissa's role as a female shopper seems merely a masquerade of heterosexual femininity to allay cultural anxieties and to screen Clarissa's more disruptive desires. Far from being a passive female consumer 'seduced by the glittering phantasmagoria of an emerging consumer culture' (Felski, 1995, 62), Clarissa's participation in the masculine monetary economy in 'Mrs Dalloway in Bond Street' continues to facilitate her activities in a feminine libidinal economy, beyond the ending of this narrative. Her overacting of her role as female shopper also alerts the reader to something queer and self-conscious at work in this story. Earlier in the story we are told that Clarissa takes great pleasure in the 'endless – endless – endless' stream of people and sights in the city; equally what we see in this story is the endless flow of Clarissa's desires (*CSF* 154). The story ultimately resists closure: the capitalist transaction is incomplete (the gloves are not yet purchased) and a bond with another woman just renewed.

Clarissa's participation in gift and market economies is not fixed and specific; she is not constrained by either a masculine (capitalist and heterosexual) economy, or limited to a feminine, potentially homoerotic, gift economy. Rather, she shifts between the two, playing both the heterosexual and queer markets from the safety of her role as Mrs Dalloway. Indeed, her 'proper' participation in the market economy provides a space for other 'improper' economies to function. She takes erotic pleasure from shopping and window shopping, gazing at women, exchanging glances, bonding with them, and contemplating giving gifts to enhance the pleasure of women, but ultimately she stakes no claim. She neither gives gifts nor makes a purchase, but takes pleasure in the possibility and processes of both. The story provides plenty of scope for 'speculation' and Clarissa's activities in the marketplace give rise to a good deal of 'interest'. What seems to be the case is that whether participating in market or gift economies, Clarissa's bonds with women are invested with desire in a way that has potential to bring disorder to both capitalist and heterosexual economies. However, it is the operation of the gift economy in this story that helps to bring to the surface Clarissa's subversive desires, desires that can queer the markets and offer resistances to the regimes of heteronormativity. Her gift-giving wishes and fantasies are privileged in the story. They signal her deviant desires and an active subjectivity at odds with the implicitly heterosexual circuit of desire that Felski identifies at work in commodity culture, opening up the possibility of erotic bonds with women (65). Clarissa is an active subject, resisting the passive role for the female shopper engineered by masculine marketing as she acts on her own desires in her exchanges (of glances, touches and compliments) with women. It is Clarissa's gift-giving impulse that opens the way (as Still suggests about 'the gift' in general) to 'thinking the heterogeneous' (12). It opens up a range of subversive possibilities, which are explored further in *Mrs Dalloway*. However, whereas in this

62   *Gifts, Markets and Economies of Desire*

short story Clarissa Dalloway's activities in 'playing the markets' and exploiting both commodity and gift exchanges to satisfy her own desires can be read almost playfully, it is only in the later text, *Mrs Dalloway*, that a fuller sense of the cost of such activity becomes apparent.

Much of the narrative of 'Mrs Dalloway in Bond Street' gets recycled as the first part of *Mrs Dalloway*. Both commodity consumption and the gift economy remain important throughout the novel, with similar erotic ambiguities at play alongside an implicit troubling of the ideological imperatives of heteropatriarchal capitalism. The commodities Clarissa Dalloway sets out to buy in the opening sentence of the novel and her participation in capitalist transaction are replete with homoerotic suggestion. The importance of gifts and the gift economy also becomes apparent in the first few pages as Clarissa contemplates buying a gift for her daughter, Elizabeth. Like Clarissa of 'Mrs Dalloway in Bond Street', Clarissa here also restrains herself from acting 'rashly' and reflects, 'one must economise', suggesting that monetary thrift halts her gift-giving impulse (*MD* 7). With this first mention of a gift, the idea of gift-giving is revealed to be problematic, bound up as it clearly is with the interrelated dominant social, sexual and monetary economies in which women have little real power. This is emphasised when later Richard Dalloway has no such compunction about buying gifts for his wife and daughter, making clear that he is in control of the purse strings and so does not have to 'economise'. As in the earlier story, the idea of the gift is ambiguously and variously modulated, though in this longer, richer text, gift-giving is a more prominent activity and gives rise to more complex suggestions about the gift and the broader significance of the gift economy. Most of the gifts given are what may be called 'pseudo-gifts', that is gifts given in the spirit of capitalist exchange with the expectation of a specific and calculated return; these 'thrifty' gifts are part of a masculine economy which, as Cixous suggests, is premised on 'strategy . . . reckoning . . . "how to win" with the least possible loss, at the lowest possible cost' (1981b, 47).

Unlike the earlier story, however, there is a gift at the centre of this narrative that takes on a utopian quality, is of unreckonable value, and seems to resist recuperation into a commodity or market system of exchange. Sally Seton's kiss could be read as an obligatory return for the generosity Clarissa and her family have shown to her. However, given Sally's impulsiveness and unconventionality, this seems unlikely. More importantly, the spontaneity with which she gives Clarissa a flower and kisses her, and Clarissa's coding of this kiss as a gift, free it from any doubts about the integrity and generosity with which it is given. The effects of this double gift pervade the whole text and inform much of Clarissa's psychosexual interiority, her emotional responses and her actions. It is a gift that accords with Georg Simmel's understanding of the giving of a first gift, described as 'a beauty, a spontaneous devotion to the other, an opening up and flowering from the "virgin soil" of the soul' (392–3) and, as such, as Osteen suggests, 'constitutes perhaps the

Queering the Market 63

fullest expression of what it means to be human ... forges social connections and enacts one's true freedom' (14). The gift economy, or a rather more abstract notion of the 'spirit of the gift' that this first gift sets in motion, signals Clarissa's continued commitment to a feminine libidinal economy, and reveals the homoerotic desires that she tries to suppress and channel into an acceptable form in her role as Mrs Richard Dalloway. However, it is not only this double gift of female *jouissance* that threatens to destabilise heteropatriarchal and capitalist structures in this novel. Rather, the way that the 'pseudo-gifts' are represented also seems to call into question and destabilise the normative social, sexual and economic structures these so-called gifts are meant to support. In Woolf's texts it is the exchange of both 'pseudo' and 'genuine' gifts that has the potential to disrupt economic systems and normative sexual paradigms, to defamiliarise and to make odd; in fact, to queer these very structures.

Repeatedly in the present time of this novel we see Clarissa seeking intimacy with a range of women (from Lady Bruton and her daughter, to Doris Kilman, her housekeeper, and a shop assistant) through the giving of material gifts, and through her social gift – 'to combine, to create' (*MD* 135). This gift-giving and Clarissa's social 'gift' have their origins in Clarissa's one and only experience of being in love – her youthful, passionate relationship with Sally. More specifically, Clarissa's impulse to give gifts and to connect with women stems from what Clarissa considers to be 'the most exquisite moment' of her life when Sally kissed her by the flower urn – a moment experienced and remembered as a precious gift, a 'diamond':

> Then came the most exquisite moment of her whole life passing a stone urn with flowers in it. Sally stopped; picked a flower; kissed her on the lips. The whole world might have turned upside down! The others disappeared; there she was alone with Sally. And she felt that she had been given a present, wrapped up, and told just to keep it, not to look at it – a diamond, something infinitely precious, wrapped up, which, as they walked (up and down, up and down), she uncovered, or the radiance burnt through, the revelation, the religious feeling!
>
> (*MD* 40)[14]

This gift has a profound effect on Clarissa as recipient. The potential threat of such gift exchange between women is immediately apparent in the altered vision, and in the transformation and revelation that it effects in Clarissa. In the ecstasy of this moment of homoerotic pleasure, Clarissa becomes startlingly aware of an alternative to her world and its social and sexual structures, an awareness that could indeed turn her heterosexual world upside down. As Hyde explains, gifts can act as agents of transformation, as 'a sort of guardian or marker or catalyst. . . . a gift may be the actual agent of change, the bearer of new life' (Hyde 45). This gift seems to set such

64   *Gifts, Markets and Economies of Desire*

a process in motion. It is consistent with a period of Clarissa's life when, with youthful exuberance and unchecked idealism, she is open to socialistic ideas and can begin to consider a world without private property, and implicitly a world in which she is not proper/ty either. However, as we also see in the moment of this realisation of new possibilities (both social and sexual), this gift exchange between women is brutally cut off by Peter's jealous interruption: 'It was like running one's face against a granite wall in the darkness! It was shocking; it was horrible!' (*MD* 41).

Although this moment is key in many readings that explore the homoeroticism in and of this text, the significance of Clarissa's investment of this kiss, her endowing this moment of intense physical and erotic bliss, with the quality of the gift has not been fully considered. Although critics have commented on the significance of the kiss as a metaphorical diamond, and the way that this image and its associations epitomise Woolf's modernist poetics and narrative methods, redefine female subjectivity and sexuality, and articulate the sexual politics of the text, little attention has been given to the gift economy that this metaphor sets in motion in this narrative. That Woolf chose to figure this ecstatic moment, this impulsive kiss, as a gift is significant in several ways. Clare Hanson usefully suggests that 'Clarissa's sense of self is a "gift" from Sally Seton' and that this gift 'comes from and moves within . . . a "feminine" economy of "depropriation": it is to be kept but not thought of or measured in terms of its "exchange value"' (1994, 67). However, although she also comments that Clarissa's 'disinterested' feeling for Sally is 'unmarked by the appropriative and possessive elements which characterise relations between men and women in patriarchy' (1994, 70), her focus is on the way that female intimacy, particularly the relationship with and memory of the mother, works to redefine female subjectivity in this novel rather than on the interconnected operation of economies and sexuality in this narrative. Her interpretation also suggests that this gift is taken out of circulation, whereas this moment might be seen as key to an ongoing circulation of gifts and desire between women. That Clarissa conceptualises Sally's kiss as a gift suggests her recognition of the possibility of a different economy of desire, a desire in excess of the social and sexual economies, which valorise motherhood, that dominate her world. Joseph Allen Boone, who also considers the idea of love figured as a gift, suggests that 'by representing the gift of love from woman to woman as an infinitely precious diamond, Woolf tempers the less favorable connotations that accrue to the hard, faceted, centred diamond self' that Clarissa must create in order to reflect 'what the world wants to see' (Boone 190). This image of 'the diamond kiss', diffusing light and radiating warmth, emphasises the blurring of boundaries (of desire and subjectivity) and is an important part of Boone's engaging illumination of 'the modernist poetics and the sexual politics of *Mrs Dalloway*' (Boone, 190, 192).

Clearly, this diffusive gift indicates an eroticism that is at odds with the heteropatriarchal social order and the rational calculation and acquisitiveness of the capitalist economy. This moment of passion between women *could* be recuperated into a heterosexual paradigm as merely an immature infatuation, a crush and a rehearsal for heterosexual relations in the future.[15] However, as a gift, this experience and eroticism are placed beyond the reaches of such recuperation. Its value as something 'infinitely precious' (*MD* 40) puts it beyond the bounds of capitalist calculation and market pricing, just as the process of its exchange between women identifies them as active subjects of exchange (Rubin's 'exchange partners' and 'sexual subjects') and thus puts them beyond recuperation into a heteropatriarchal economy as objects, or gifts, to be exchanged and possessed. That women make gifts of their own desires disturbs the heterosexual economy. This is suggested by the way that the radiance of this diamond gift, and the heat of passion between women it stimulates, threatens to permeate, warm through and distort the cold rationality of the capitalist economy.

Further, that this kiss is *metaphorically* a diamond gift renders its meaning even more elusive, provisional and fluid. A metaphor operates by a process of exchange as one thing is seen, experienced and understood in terms of the meaning and experience of another. However, much like the cycle of gift-giving and receiving, this process of exchange is never complete because one thing is never *exactly* the other. Rather, the generation of meanings lies in the liminal space between the two parts of the metaphor, in an ongoing exchange of meanings, associations and possibilities. When exploring the difficulties of theorising and representing lesbian desire and subjectivity, Elizabeth Meese suggests that metaphor is particularly apt for such representation, speaking as it does 'a language of deviation' in which meaning is 'both anchored (materialised in the figure) and adrift (transferring from figure to figure) from some always unknown origin', so that 'the metaphoric language of deviation (of substitution, drift, and transposition) is put in the service of writing what culture has historically regarded as deviation (as aberration and perversion)' (Meese 75–6). The significance of metaphor is, then, not simply in its function as a literary convention. As Lakoff and Johnson argue, 'metaphor is not just a matter of language ... of mere words'; rather, it is key to the way we perceive our world and make sense of our experiences (6). As such, metaphor 'play(s) a central role in defining our everyday realities'; in redefining these realities as new experiences, we require new metaphors to conceptualise them (3). Conceptualising Sally's kiss as a metaphorical diamond gift enables Clarissa to make sense of this new experience in terms of something familiar. It seems to be what Lakoff and Johnson would call an 'ontological metaphor' – a metaphor that enables experiences to be understood in terms of substances, as 'clearly discrete or bounded', and is a way of making something new familiar because our own bodies are discrete and bounded by skin (25). They suggest that such metaphors 'are necessary for even attempting to deal rationally with our experiences' (26). However, this rational explanation is at odds with the

66   *Gifts, Markets and Economies of Desire*

modernist sense of subjectivity Woolf creates in Clarissa who is, as Boone among others has so persuasively argued, decentred, diffuse, and feels connected, even merged, with others and the world around her. Lakoff and Johnson go on to say that because 'the metaphorical structuring . . . is partial, not total' (13) and there is always a discrepancy between the two terms of a metaphor, some aspects of the concepts are hidden or unspoken in metaphorical expressions and concepts (12).

It would seem, then, that rationality and clarity (in Clarissa's attempt at making Sally's kiss familiar) give way to ambiguity, omission and evasion as this kiss/gift conveys also a sense of 'discrepancy', an unspoken element that escapes the normative social, linguistic and, of course, erotic economies of exchange with which it is so much at odds. Doubly transgressive of the dominant market and libidinal economies of Clarissa's society, this gift, with all its variability of substance, intention and response, serves not to pin down or define, but generates a sense of fluidity and indeterminacy of meaning. Clarissa seeks to give some boundary to this new experience (a diamond, after all, has a clear-cut edge) but its multifaceted radiance refuses to be contained and made familiar. A diamond is a material commodity with a specific value in a market economy, but here it is a metaphor that is powerful because it is impossible to classify or quantify. Indeed, what may seem to be a gesture to the conventional metaphor of love as blind in Sally's advice (Clarissa was 'told . . . not to look at it') could also be a caution against any attempt at seeing this moment rationally, of measuring or conceptualising it empirically. That this kiss becomes a metaphorical gift doubles the transgressiveness and immateriality of this moment. As Meese argues, far from offering something concrete, 'a ready-made structure', metaphor is premised in 'resemblance but not identity', and so the sense of something missing, something unspoken or not fully realised also lingers (79–80). Although Clarissa in one way attempts to give her desires some boundary (and her marriage to Richard Dalloway can be seen as a more obvious attempt at limiting what she feels for Sally), the metaphorical structure she uses tellingly remains resistant to exact definition. It is an apt form for representing desires that are difficult to pin down, and which remain queerly resistant to classification.

Several critics have made the case that this kiss and what is experienced as a violent termination of this ecstatic moment is a, if not the, formative moment in Clarissa's psychosexual development and leads to a repression of her desires for women.[16] Smith's theory of lesbian panic is useful here. She reads the interruption of this moment and the subsequent shame Clarissa feels as 'the crucial moment in which the course of her life was set', with the 'discourse of shame' putting a halt to the new erotic and metaphysical possibilities just beginning to be opened up for Clarissa (Smith, 1997, 46). This shame, she suggests, is the catalyst for the quarrels she has with her suitors, Peter and Sally, which in turn precipitate her marriage to Richard Dalloway.

Clarissa 'thus chooses respectability and repression as her mode of living', a life of 'self-closeting' (Smith, 1997, 47) though lesbian desire lies just below the surface of this masquerade and manifests in brief idyllic moments and rages against Doris Kilman. Boone also carefully traces the ways in which Clarissa's homoeroticism continues to suffuse her present-day existence and significantly argues that Sally's gift, 'the diamond wrapped kiss', becomes transposed into Clarissa's parties, conceived 'as her offering to the world' (Boone, 191). However, he too argues that this '"gift" to the world both replaces and represses the loss of the "most exquisite moment" of her life' (Boone, 197–8).

Although both Smith (1997) and Boone see the interruption of the kiss as a 'loss' and as precipitating a closing down or repression of Clarissa's homoeroticism, both argue that Clarissa's repressed desires return in various oblique and associated forms. One of these forms, I will suggest, is that of Clarissa's ongoing investment in the gift economy, which works to counter the trajectory of repression and denial others have identified. However, Clarissa's participation in gift-giving, as in 'Mrs Dalloway in Bond Street', is contradictory and problematic. Sally's double gift – the flower and the kiss – is displaced and dispersed throughout Clarissa's experience. This moment of profound erotic intensity between the women remains in circulation, but often in a compromised form. Her recollection of her kiss is a utopian moment, an impossible state of plenitude and bliss, and her subsequent gifts to women attempt to recapture some semblance of this moment of ecstasy, to keep the gift of intimacy between women alive and in motion. However, the metaphorical gift of Sally's kiss becomes distorted as Clarissa attempts to convert this metaphor into something material and tangible; the 'religious feeling' generated by Sally's kiss, and the faith needed to accept the existence of pure gifts, untarnished by obligation or calculation, seems largely absent from Clarissa's own gift-giving. Having made her choice of heterosexual marriage and the economic security and status this entails, Clarissa's gift-giving seems an attempt to maintain a sense of distance from the heterosexual norm for women and to retain an active subjectivity; simultaneously, it seems an attempt to exert some control over the flow of her homoerotic desires. Her gift-giving (like her marriage) does not completely deny her erotic longings for women, but attempts to channel them into an acceptable form; the gifts she gives, then, are only those that are appropriate to her role as Mrs Dalloway and as such perhaps belie a sense of insecurity, regret and loss.

If Clarissa's motivation is ambiguous in the earlier story, Clarissa's acknowledged motivation in *Mrs Dalloway* is calculating and far more dubious. She gives gifts to effect a specific outcome, 'she did things not simply, not for themselves; but to make people think this or that' (*MD* 12). She gives gifts to elicit a positive response in others, and to break the routine as a diversion for herself, as in the case of a gift for Evelyn. She acknowledges that it is 'perfect idiocy' to act in this way, and her wish for another chance at her life

68   *Gifts, Markets and Economies of Desire*

implies that she may have done things differently: she would have been more masculine, more like Sally and Lady Bexborough in appearance, and implicitly more disinterested in her actions because less dependent on the approval of others (*MD* 13). Although her own judgement of her actions is harsh, because her gifts intend to make both her own life and the lives of others more bearable, the shallowness of this aspect of her gift-giving could be read as an effect of her role as she has either internalised the values of her class, or is adept at performing the behaviour of her class.[17] Such gift-giving echoes the emptiness of her role as Mrs Richard Dalloway as, enmeshed in her marital state, she is 'not even Clarissa anymore' (*MD* 13). Her complicity in this system is indicated by what can be seen as a corruption of Sally's diamond gift of diffusive, radiant, subversive, free flowing and indeterminate woman-centred desire. Clarissa's self-conscious attempts to conform to her role, to centre and assemble herself as the Tory hostess she must be for others, is summed up using an image of a contained, cold, geometric diamond:

> That was herself – pointed; dart-like; definite. That was herself when some effort, some call on her to be herself, drew the parts together, she alone knew how different, how incompatible and composed so for the world only into one centre, one diamond, one woman who sat in her drawing-room and made a meeting point, a radiancy no doubt in some dull lives.
>
> (*MD* 42)

Her role as Mrs Dalloway is one of reduction, of clear and single definition, and of repression of the many aspects of her multi-faceted self; it is a denial of the expansive potential and possibility suggested by Sally's diamond. In place of Sally's gift, Clarissa seems to have erected a sense of herself as proper and property, as a commodifiable diamond fitting for an object of exchange in a heteropatriarchal economy. We see clearly here the way that the private gift of woman-centred desire is made to assume an acceptable public face, a pattern echoed in the way that Clarissa gives pseudo-gifts to imitate intimacy with women and to channel her transgressive homoerotic libidinal urges into acceptable forms.

A further corruption of Sally's gift, and the economy of desire it sets in motion, is seen in the way that Clarissa actually perceives herself to be in debt. Her sense of debt results from the 'secret deposit of exquisite moments', the moments of bliss that she spontaneously experiences, and which, figured as a private revelation and using the imagery of blossoming flowers ('as if some lovely rose had blossomed for her eyes only' *MD* 33), suggestively connect to Sally's kiss (*MD* 33–4). Sally's gift seems to be both a trigger for other 'gifts' of pleasure and vision (as if Sally's gift is in circulation and giving rise to other exquisite moments). However, it is also the cause of Clarissa's sense of debt and the source from which it must be repaid. It is as if Sally's unconditional gift has become subsumed into a capitalist economic paradigm, which is premised on the logic of profit, loss, debt, payment and repayment, and Clarissa feels that she can never quite give enough. Her taboo desires have become guilty pleasures for which she must pay a price, and Sally's gift has become a fund of happiness which has accrued an illicit interest for which Clarissa must offer recompense. It seems, then, that because she has experiences that exceed the heterosexual economy, she feels indebted to those who enable her to keep up her heterosexual masquerade, who shelter and protect her from the ever-present danger of her desires for women: 'servants . . . dogs and canaries, above all . . . Richard her husband who was the foundation of it' (*MD* 33). Clarissa's sense of being indebted and in debt also seems to be an attempt to put some measure on her moments of bliss; like her public pseudo-gift-giving, this is an attempt to exert some control over her desires.

Against this public role and her superficial gift-giving, Clarissa fiercely preserves a privacy, which acts as a defence against total submersion and objectification in heteropatriarchal social and sexual systems. As Boone suggests, 'In contrast to the legibility of this social self, Clarissa constructs for herself an inviolate privacy that no one can read, touch or see' (Boone 185). Although Clarissa attempts to contain and control her homoerotic impulses and desires, the effect of Sally's gift infuses all of Clarissa's life. It is especially in the private space of Clarissa's recurrent memories, fantasies and imagination that the spirit of Sally's homoerotic gift re-emerges, circulates and works to energise a libidinal economy that repeatedly threatens to irrupt uncontrollably and to disturb dominant social, sexual and political structures. The effect of this circulation of Sally's gift is evident in Clarissa's involuntary physiological response as she recalls the emotional intensity of her feeling for Sally in the past. As she evokes richly nuanced memories of Sally, her amazing power, 'her gift, her personality', Clarissa recalls 'going cold with excitement' as she did 'her hair in a kind of ecstasy' (*MD* 38, 39). In her present moment, as her actions of dressing her hair echo this earlier experience, 'the old feeling began to come back to her' (*MD* 39). This passage acts as a prelude to the memory of Sally's kiss, her diamond gift, and it is as if this erotic gift remains circulating physically, bodily (sending a chill through Clarissa's body in present as it did in the past) as well as more materially and symbolically in the novel. The return of this physical sensation and the emotional intensity suggest that this gift economy remains in circulation beyond Clarissa's control.

Clarissa's experience in Miss Pym's shop is another key moment in the novel that suggests the ongoing circulation of Sally's gift as something that cannot be displaced onto material things, nor made manifest in, or satisfied by, a consumer economy. Here it becomes apparent that not all exchanges between Clarissa and other women are self-interested and calculated. Rather, the somewhat ambiguous relationship between Clarissa and Miss Pym is indicative of Clarissa's investment in a gift economy based on generosity

70 Gifts, Markets and Economies of Desire

and kindness, and on a genuine desire to keep the meaning of the most exquisite moment of her life alive.

Although a conventional site of capitalist exchange, Mulberry's florist's shop and Clarissa's experience of acquiring commodities there (the sweet peas she leaves with) is ambiguous. From the outset, it is clear that there is a prior connection between Clarissa and Miss Pym, a bond of intimacy seemingly generated by Clarissa's kindness and generosity to Miss Pym in the past.[18] In 'The Hours' the extent of Clarissa's kindness is more obvious as Miss Pym had been 'put on her feet by Clarissa years ago'; and Miss Pym reflects, 'And indeed she was a kind lady' and 'kind she still was' ('The Hours' 272, 274). What Woolf deletes from this scene is also telling as it suggests that although Clarissa may look like other heterosexual and feminine ladies, her kindness and generosity (her participation in a gift economy we can surmise) sets her apart. Nor is she treated like the other ladies; instead she is treated with greater intimacy, as Miss Pym 'owed her help, & *would therefore always come out of her little box: & come out of* her box always when Mrs Dalloway came in' ('The Hours' 274; italics indicate words crossed through). This could be read as simply implying a sense of debt and obligation on Miss Pym's part, and suggesting the class differential between them. However, the 'return' of Clarissa's gift in the form of Miss Pym's extra courtesy and attention here paves the way for greater physical proximity and intimacy, with Clarissa's consumption blurring boundaries between a monetary and gift transaction, as Wicke's analysis of this novel suggests. The florist's shop is a space replete with feminine sensuality and sexuality, the commodities for sale being entirely appropriate to conventional notions of women's feminine, domestic identity, but also symbolising female sexuality.[19] However, this space also indicates women's increasing economic independence because, as Abbott remarks, the 'profession of the florist' was 'new (in Woolf's time)' (200). Although perhaps not unusual for a woman of Mrs Dalloway's status not to pay in cash for her flowers, there is no sense of a transaction taking place which would normalise Clarissa's experience in this space, which adds further to the ambiguity of this scene. Even more so than for Mrs Dalloway in the Bond Street glove shop of the earlier story, Clarissa ostensibly fulfilling her role as upper-middle-class wife actually occasions the release, experience and articulation of desires and wishes that have the potential to subvert hegemonic sexual and economic structures. The greater prevalence of the gift economy in this scene in *Mrs Dalloway* intensifies this threat.

Talking to Miss Pym amid the variety of flowers,[20] Clarissa is intoxicated by their sensuality. Because they trigger memories of the sensations that Sally's gift of a flower and a kiss produced in her, these flowers generate an experience of physical and emotional plenitude and operate as a symbol of the ongoing circulation of Sally's gift of homoerotic passion and love.[21] Although all of the flowers contribute to this heady atmosphere, it is the sweet peas that mark an involuntary transition for Clarissa as, by evoking

Queering the Market 71

images of her youth at Bourton, they take her back to an idealised recollection of summertime and to the perfect and profound moment of Sally's kiss. Metaphor works to relocate Clarissa suggestively in this half-remembered, half-imagined time and place. The sweet peas are metaphorically women in muslin frocks and Clarissa seems to be one of the women themselves; she is paradoxically both spectator and participant in this idyllic pastoral scenario:

> and all the sweet peas spreading in their bowls, tinged violet, snow white, pale – as if it were the evening and girls in muslin frocks came out to pick sweet peas and roses after the superb summer's day, with its almost blue-black sky, its delphiniums, its carnations, its arum lilies, was over; and it was the moment between six and seven when every flower – roses, carnations, irises, lilac – glows; white, violet, red, deep orange; every flower seems to burn by itself, softly, purely in the misty beds; and how she loved the grey white moths spinning in and out, over the cherry pie, over the evening primroses!
>
> (*MD* 16)

The attenuated image engages the reader in the sense of tantalising suspense and desire that Clarissa both remembers and imaginatively embellishes; as this moment expands beyond expectations we are caught up with Clarissa in the overflow of emotion and physical sensation.[22] As the image overbalances, it is a moment of *jouissance*, of linguistic excess signifying libidinal excess. The reader is alerted to more subversive possibilities of this feminine economy as 'Miss Pym liking her, trusting her' moves with Clarissa 'from jar to jar' of flowers (*MD* 16). Reading both 'The Hours' and 'Mrs Dalloway in Bond Street' as intertexts for *Mrs Dalloway*, the suggestion of homoerotic intimacy between Clarissa and Miss Pym becomes further intensified and more explicitly connected to Sally's gifts given in the garden at Bourton. Making a similar enquiry to that of Clarissa in 'Mrs Dalloway in Bond Street', Mrs Dalloway in 'The Hours' asks Miss Pym when she has her holiday; in addition, however, she also asks when Miss Pym finds time to go into the garden ('*The Hours*' 273). Coupled with Clarissa's sense that 'shadowy shop girls, pursued her . . . down the garden paths' ('*The Hours*' 275), the garden is both a site of homoerotic pleasure in the past and a metaphor for lesbian possibility in Clarissa's present – a possibility that is both exciting and a source of anxiety. The question about Miss Pym's holiday recalls the gift Clarissa contemplates offering the shop assistant in 'Mrs Dalloway in Bond Street'. It again implies the homoeroticism associated with a gift economy.

As Clarissa is about to give herself over to the moment of exhilaration, to the overwhelming wave of sensual and nostalgic pleasure that promises to obliterate her complex anxieties about Doris Kilman (and in '*The Hours*', a more general sense of uneasiness which made 'everything seem(ed)

72 *Gifts, Markets and Economies of Desire*

treacherous and insecure' '*The Hours*' 275), a noise from the street outside violently intrudes and interrupts this suggestively orgasmic moment. As in 'Mrs Dalloway in Bond Street', the spell of eroticised female intimacy is interrupted by the intrusion of the dominant social order in the form of a noise from a car outside. In the short story not even the 'violent explosion in the street outside' (possibly a 'Bond Street' protest against such female intimacy) can distract Clarissa from her flirtation with Miss Anstruther, but seems only to compound Clarissa's transgressive behaviour in triggering her memory of Miss Anstruther's name (*CSF* 159). In *Mrs Dalloway*, however, this noise does interrupt the moment of a near climax of overwhelming pleasure, an effect that Miss Pym's apology for the noise seems to acknowledge. Stimulated by the fragrance and colour of the flowers, this wave of pleasure is associated with the physical effect of Sally's kiss, but in both past and present it is violently interrupted by an intrusion of some masculine agency.

It seems, then, that in *Mrs Dalloway* the threatening intrusion of hegemonic forces does stifle the eroticism and subversive intimacy of this moment; the noise of a car (possibly containing royalty or the prime minister) backfiring puts a halt to Clarissa's erotic reverie. The effect of this suggests that such forces restrain the gift economy that gives rise to this moment in seemingly insisting that Clarissa resume her function as a consumer of commodities.[23] However, what can be read as an attempt to channel potentially transgressive desires into commodity consumption also seems to backfire here. This is not only because of the thrill that the 'throb of the motor engines' that had been forced to 'come to a standstill' creates (which has the effect of seeming to intensify the heat of the sun), but also because this distraction creates an ambiguity around the moment of transaction in the shop that allows for the possibility of the continued circulation of the gift economy already set in motion. In *Mrs Dalloway*, Woolf reworks some of the narrative elements from the short story (the noise from outside, the uncertainty about the monetary transaction and a mirroring effect) to create an equally suggestively ambiguous outcome to this scene.

As noted above, it is the sweet peas that create the link back to Clarissa's youth and, by extension, to the moment of Sally's kiss. The figurative doubleness of metaphor used to evoke this earlier connection continues in a mirroring gesture in which the sweet peas are central. Miss Pym 'go(es) to the window to look, and com(es) back' to Clarissa 'with her hands full of sweet peas' (*MD* 16); a page or so later (after some speculation about who may be inside the car and the effects of this), Clarissa also goes to the window 'with her arms full of sweet peas', 'her little pink face pursed in inquiry' (*MD* 18) resembling Miss Pym's 'button-face(d)' (*MD* 15). However, by the time Clarissa approaches the window, the narrative has shifted to a view of the florist's window from the outside – 'Mrs Dalloway, coming to the window' (*MD* 18). With this subtle shift, the narrative perspective has jumped to the

Queering the Market   73

outside, to a full focus on the car and the effect on the spectators. With this shift of perspective from the feminine sphere and from the libidinal intensities evoked in the shop, Woolf effects a narrative sleight of hand which means that the moment of transaction – the exchange of the sweet peas (and the homoeroticism they signify) for some kind of payment – is lost to the reader, effaced or repressed in the text. The nature of the exchange of this highly evocative commodity remains unknown and unknowable, and puts the nature of this exchange into question. Clarissa's guess as she emerges from the shop 'with her flowers' that the car is most likely to be carrying the queen going about her charitable duties suggests a continuation of her focus on women and on their gestures of giving.[24] However, by this time Clarissa is once again Mrs Richard Dalloway, wearing 'a look of extreme dignity', 'very upright' and proper, with her erotic impulses and excesses of emotion firmly reined in (*MD* 20, 15).

However, although Clarissa leaves with her commodities, and is apparently satisfied, we know that commodities are not an end in themselves for Clarissa. The gratifications that commodities offer should displace and obviate other more deviant and problematic desires. Instead these commodities set in motion a network of memories, sensations, fantasies and desires, which have their source and expression in the operation of a subversive gift economy in this novel. The extent to which this gift economy is compromised and distorted in Clarissa's re-interpretation leads to the giving of ambiguous and highly problematic gifts. One of these is the floral gift that Clarissa makes to Doris Kilman. These are flowers from Bourton, no less, and are therefore a highly charged, if highly ambiguous, gift indeed. It is only to Doris that Clarissa makes such a gift: a gift that is not only a direct echo of Sally's gift, but which seems also an attempt to keep the profound emotions and physical intensity that this originary, pure gift represents in circulation in Clarissa's present time. Given her extreme and intensely conflicting feelings for and about Doris Kilman,[25] however, her gift and her motivation for giving are hard to interpret. With Clarissa's tendency to use gifts in a manipulative way, it could be that this is again very dubious, motivated by shallow, even cruel, intentions. This is how Boone reads this gift. For him, Clarissa 'forces' the flowers from Bourton onto Miss Kilman, 'creating an unflattering juxtaposition between Kilman and the physical site and primary emblem of Clarissa's "pure" love for Sally (whose "way with flowers" was legendary at Bourton)' and thus provoking 'Kilman's agitated, awkward response' (Boone, 195). The subconscious motivation, he argues, is 'to embarrass Miss Kilman in front of Elizabeth, and she counts on the fact that her ladylike graciousness will only make Miss Kilman look all the more unfemininely disagreeable' (ibid.).

However, Clarissa's motivation for giving this gift is absent from the text. Although demonstrating Doris's unfeminine clumsiness may be part of Clarissa's motivation, it is worth remembering that for women to be

74   *Gifts, Markets and Economies of Desire*

unfeminine is not necessarily to be disagreeable or unattractive to Clarissa. Unfeminine clumsiness with flowers is also a noted characteristic of another masculine woman whom Clarissa admires and is attracted to: Lady Bruton. Similarly, Clarissa in 'Mrs Dalloway in Bond Street' is drawn to Miss Anstruther, who is also clumsy with the feminine gloves she tries on. Like the exchange of sweet peas in Mulberry's florist's shop, what inspires Clarissa's gift of flowers is unknown and unknowable. Like Sally's kiss, the meaning of this gift is impossible to articulate except ambiguously through metaphors of gifts and symbolic flowers.

It is clear that Clarissa initially takes refuge in Mulberry's from her anxieties and intense and highly ambivalent feelings about Doris Kilman ('She hated her: she loved her' *MD* 193). Clarissa resents the influence Doris seems to have over Elizabeth and envies what she thinks is their 'falling in love' (*MD*14). She is apparently offended at Doris's sense of her moral and intellectual superiority, and her determined independence (symbolised by her mackintosh, which is equally offensive to Clarissa's sense of elegant fashion); and her German origins and her spinsterhood stir both hatred and pity. However, Clarissa also recognises that it is the ideological constraints of the privileged and highly conventional role that she has chosen that generate these negative feelings toward Doris and which have the most damaging effect. She reflects that had the world been as she glimpsed it at the point of Sally's kiss, 'turned upside down', with the 'black . . . uppermost and not the white, she would have loved Miss Kilman!'. However, her life, the world she has chosen, forbids this, 'But not in this world. No' (*MD* 40, 15). Her complex feelings for Doris also stem from her recognition of her complicity in the socio-economic and sexual systems that produce and reinforce the brutal homophobia that so impoverishes and embitters Doris.

As Boone suggests, 'the rhapsodic paean to nature's beauty that fills her [Clarissa's] mind as she enters the florist's shop' is intended to 'block the(se) surfacing thoughts of the hateful Kilman'; this is 'a telling act of repression' in which 'this celebration of natural connection creates within Clarissa a "wave" of fluidity that "she let(s) flow over her and surmount that hatred, that monster"' (Boone 194). However, this is not the 'lesbian panic' it may seem to be; rather, the operation of the gift economy suggests something other than this need to *escape* her intense feelings about and generated by Doris. The florist's shop becomes a space where Clarissa's repressed desires can surface – the sensuality of the flowers triggers erotic memories which take Clarissa back to Bourton and to her youthful self, the self in love with Sally. In fact the flowers recall the moment of intensity and pleasure which has defined her libidinal desires ever since – Sally's kiss and her gift of a flower, but also the specific setting beside an urn full of flowers. It is this gift of the flower and the experience of lesbian eroticism and of lavish sensuality (which Doris's poverty and her angry self-righteousness deprive her of), that Clarissa seemingly tries to pass onto Doris in her gift of flowers from Bourton.

Queering the Market   75

However, the way in which this gift is made known in the narrative makes it even more resistant to clear and unproblematic interpretation. The revelation of Clarissa's gift to Doris is narrated from Elizabeth's perspective when, in a scene fraught with tension, she and Doris have tea in the Army and Navy Stores after Doris's purchase of a petticoat. It emerges in the context of Elizabeth reflecting on the incompatibility of her mother and her teacher. There is a suggestion that Elizabeth perceives a calculated and unpleasant intention behind Clarissa's being 'very, very nice' to Doris (*MD* 145). However, just as we never really know whether Clarissa has judged her daughter's feelings for Doris correctly,[26] Elizabeth's understanding of the relationship between her mother and Doris is only partial and her judgement about Clarissa's motivation (complicated and paradoxical as it is), evidently, may be equally flawed and inaccurate.

That this gift reaches the narrative surface in a department store is also significant and brings to light some of the problems with Clarissa's gift. This context suggests again that Sally's diamond gift of lesbian passion becomes distorted when filtered through a monetary economy.[27] It also emphasises the way that Doris's experience mirrors, but in a distorted way, Clarissa's experience of participation in commodity culture in the florist's shop, where flowers trigger the memories and sensations of Clarissa's youthful pleasures and erotic impulses at Bourton.[28] The objects of consumption are not satisfying in themselves, but in her privileged position and in the context of Miss Pym's intimacy, sympathy and generosity, Clarissa has access to a rich seam of pleasure through the flower commodities. In contrast, Doris is alienated by and an alien in the feminine context of commodity display in the department store.[29] She purchases a garment that denotes femininity, but chooses one so outrageous or inappropriate as to provoke a reaction – the shop assistant thinks her 'mad' – and neither the commodity itself nor the process of buying it bring her any satisfaction (*MD* 144). Doris cannot take advantage of the 'range of new opportunities and pleasures – for independence, fantasy, unsupervised social encounters, even transgression' that the 'anonymous yet acceptable public space [of the department store] . . . opened up for women' (Nava 53). These spaces were also sites for women to display their 'rationality, expertise and financial control', but Doris displays none of these (Nava 53). For her, the anonymity and desire such spaces create can be read more negatively as loneliness and dissatisfaction. Even the cake she so greedily consumes does not bring satisfaction, nor does it displace her physical longings for Elizabeth. She is a female consumer, but one for whom the experience of consumption leaves her 'stunned, disorientated, and defeated' (Abbott 205); commodities do not fulfil her desires, and their purchase is entirely without pleasure. Nor does her shopping experience facilitate the articulation and experience of flirtatious and subversive homoerotic possibilities, a point made more clearly in 'The Hours', where she finds herself alone, stumbling through the underwear department after the departure of Elizabeth, with not a hint of erotic possibility for her.

76 *Gifts, Markets and Economies of Desire*

Whereas Clarissa can flirt and indulge in transgressive, homoerotic fantasies from the safety of her position as a feminine, respectably married upper-class woman, Doris has no such protective mask behind which to hide. Doris's class (she is, after all, a shopkeeper's daughter), lack of money and lack of a reserve of happiness on which to draw give her no protection against the censure, prejudice and the economic and emotional deprivation and disadvantage she risks in pursuing her lesbian desires. Although at some level there is a sense that Doris reciprocates Clarissa's intensely ambivalent feelings for her, and that such reciprocation forges a connection between them,[30] Doris's social position, her sense of her own integrity (moral and sexual) and her assumptions about Clarissa's 'escape' from all that torments her (Doris) mean that she is unreceptive to Clarissa's gift. The flowers and the lesbian love and desire they signify for Clarissa are thwarted by the unbridgeable social and political distance between them,[31] and by the polarised responses to their homoerotic desires. As Clarissa has already acknowledged, it is the 'world' as it is that makes it impossible for love to blossom between this queer couple. For Doris in 'The Hours', all the resentment she feels about Clarissa's privilege and the inequalities of this 'world' becomes crystallised in the watercolour picture on the wall, which she assumes is of Bourton: '*She* [Clarissa] *had everything she wanted. Probably that was her home – that watercolour picture of a house in a park. rich, with a smattering of culture. They bought pictures'* (all crossed through, '*The Hours*' 199). It is little wonder, then, that Bourton and everything with which it is associated for Clarissa can never have the same resonance or meaning for Doris. Clarissa's apparent ease in negotiating the social and sexual structures of her world is a key factor preventing her gift from being meaningful for Doris. Thus the gift of flowers from Bourton cannot transcend the differences between Clarissa's and Doris's experience: differences of class, status, politics, perspective, nationality and, crucially, an absence of a shared past.

Although this moment of generosity may be a token of love on Clarissa's part, as well as an attempt to recapture the youthful optimism of her past and to create an opening into the other utopian world where Clarissa could love Doris, it is also a gift that is severely limited by Clarissa's class assumption that what the flowers signify for her will also be of value to Doris. As is said of Millicent Bruton's (implicitly lesbian) companion, Milly Brush, 'life had not offered her a trinket of the slightest value' (*MD* 119). Neither Milly nor Doris have the wealth or privilege that enable Clarissa to experience intimacy with women in relative safety; however, as the choice of 'trinket' suggests, nor would they wish for such trivial things. Clarissa's snobbishness and ambition also hinder this gift's positive significance: her prioritising of her need for success in her role as society hostess leads her to exclude guests she considers unfashionable, dowdy and not having social cachet. This compromises the meaningful circulation of Sally's gift. In their youth, Sally's gift with flowers is one of combining and creating, and seems informed by her socialist ideas; in the present, Clarissa's similar gift with people is devoid of such political force and rather conforms to established norms. Clarissa's gift may for a moment suggest an opening between her world and Doris's; however, as Doris is only too aware, she is never invited to parties (*MD* 146).

Although the gifts Doris gives are different in many ways, her charitable donations are equally complex in their motivation. They enable her to sidestep the status of object of exchange in a heteropatriarchal economy, and to assert her sense of her superior values. However, rather than the sense of settling a debt that motivates some of Clarissa's giving, Doris gives, ironically, because she feels cheated. This enables her to rise self-righteously above the material pleasures she feels have been denied her. Both Clarissa and Doris recognise that they are marginal to the heterosexual economy and their gifts, in radically different ways, indicate this experience of difference. However, gift-giving brings neither Clarissa nor Doris closer to the fulfilment of their desires. It also, in many ways, emphasises the unbridgeable differences between them. These ultimately have an economic source, even to the extent that the hostility in Britain towards Germany as a rival economic power has caused Miss Kilman (who, with her German origins, refused to denigrate everything German) to lose her post and accept employment as Elizabeth's teacher, employment that she finds in many ways degrading.

Although there is a gulf between these women (Doris finding Clarissa to be not kind but 'merely condescending', and Clarissa's intensely conflicted feelings about Doris), the gift Clarissa gives does have an energising function, stirring powerful, if dangerous and threatening, emotions. This is particularly obvious compared with other floral gifts, which take on a more functional role, and which are seemingly part of a system of exchange that resembles a capitalist system governed by profit and loss. Hugh Whitbread's carnations given to Lady Bruton epitomise such a pseudo-gift: he gives them in exchange for a 'free' lunch, but this lunch is also 'given' so that the strategist Lady Bruton gets help from him with her letter to *The Times*. Both characters operate within a 'masculine' economy of exchange, one that always requires a return of equal value. Lady Bruton's ungraceful and unfeminine treatment of the carnations emphasises this: she 'raised the carnations, holding them rather stiffly with much the same attitude as the General held the scroll in the picture behind her' (*MD* 116). Later, in triumph over Hugh's rewriting of her letter and promise of influence in getting it printed, she 'stuffed all Hugh's carnations into the front of her dress' (*MD* 122), a significantly heterosexual gesture which contrasts with the association of flowers for Clarissa. Richard's gift to Clarissa of a 'vast bunch of roses' is a more complex gift but one that can also be read as a pseudo-gift – one given with the expectation of a return and to mark possession. Woolf's treatment of this gift, however, radically problematises such economies and calls into question the heteronormativity such a gift is meant to uphold.

78   Gifts, Markets and Economies of Desire

Roses are the only flower that Clarissa 'could bear to see cut' (*MD* 133) – the only flower she can bear to see commodified – and, given their centrality as a heterosexual romantic cliché, roses seem an apt symbol for the problematising of heterosexual and capitalist economies. Richard chooses roses in the hope that they will signify the declaration of love he is unable to voice. Such a gift is, however, defunct in this novel; not only are roses revealed to be an empty, exhausted signifier of love and romance, but the opening line of the novel makes clear that 'Mrs Dalloway . . . would buy the flowers *herself*' (*MD* 5, emphasis mine). Although Richard glosses his gift as a loving gesture motivated by a generous impulse, he is motivated to give such a gift seemingly out of a sense of rivalry with Peter Walsh. The need to 'celebrate' what he 'reckon(s)' is 'an event' – the urge to tell Clarissa that he loves her – is prompted 'when they [Lady Bruton, Hugh and Richard] spoke about Peter Walsh at luncheon' (*MD* 127).[32] Thirty years after he has claimed Clarissa as his wife, she remains an object with exchange value in the heterosexual economy, the possession of which can be threatened. In contrast to the feminine gift economy as Cixous imagines it, which effects a disturbance of property rights, this gift of flowers (like other gifts in *Mrs Dalloway*) aims to reinforce property rights. His roses, then, are an attempt to secure his investment, and Clarissa's acceptance of them as a commodity (and her ability to see the loveliness in them) can be read as a recognition and acceptance of her own status as a lovely commodity – an object of exchange over which Richard and Peter are still in competition.

That Richard's roses are embedded in dominant social, sexual and economic systems is underscored by the narration of Richard's interaction with the female vagrant on his walk home with his flowers: 'having championed the down-trodden and followed his instincts in the House of Commons' and having an understanding that it is the 'detestable social system' that is to blame for prostitution, he '(b)ear(s) his flowers like a weapon' when he needs to pass the homeless woman (*MD* 128, 129). He is made to seem not only slightly ridiculous, but hypocritical as his roses are used to guard himself from contact with too blatant an effect of capitalist and heteropatriarchal economies on women who must turn to prostitution to survive. However, they also serve to generate 'a spark between them [Richard and the woman]' (*MD* 129). Thus the connections between heterosexual lust, male manipulation of romance, pseudo-gifts as markers of possession, and the capitalist economy are made clear.

Like any object of exchange in a commodity economy, what Clarissa signifies for others is a result of the economy in which she circulates; like the roses, for Richard and Peter she signifies heterosexual love and desire, but she does not actively feel these emotions. She may participate in the heterosexual economy (and reassure herself of her value within this economy), but like the cut roses she is no longer fully alive and her marriage is a metaphorical death (as Jensen has argued in another way). Although she may enact her conventional role as Mrs Dalloway successfully, 'looking at his [Richard's] roses . . . she loved her roses' (*MD* 133), her thoughts immediately turn to the compromise she has had to make over her party; her satisfaction with her roses and her marriage is superficial, and the pretence is barely sustainable once she is alone. In her marriage she is well aware of what she has lost ('some grain of pearl or diamond', *MD* 133), the gem image recalling the integrity of her feeling for Sally, but also her creative potential, the 'radiance' of such gems, which is compromised by Richard's authority and economic control. The image of someone searching for and 'spying' only fragments of pearl and diamond[33] conveys Clarissa's desperate search to recover a sense of happiness and fulfilment she feels she has forfeited by marrying. This seems to be not only a quest for an explanation of her unhappiness, but also an attempt to recover even a tiny amount of the 'something precious' of lesbian desire and the source of her creative inspiration and fulfilment.

Possibly this is also a search for the feeling of 'being in league together' with women, and especially with the unconventional artist Sally who would have earlier been an appreciative audience for Clarissa's artistic expression (*MD* 39). In her public role, Clarissa has to settle for the 'stiff little roses' (like those that adorned the tables at Bourton in '*The Hours*', 44) rather than Sally's unorthodox arrangements of flowers which 'swim on the top of water in bowls', and which comprise an unconventional diversity of flowers, 'all sorts of flowers that had never been seen together' (*MD* 38), and even more suggestively in the earlier draft of this novel, 'all sorts of flowers that couldn't possibly go together' ('*The Hours*' 44). Given the association of flowers and female sexuality, Sally's highly unconventional and liberating 'way with flowers', and indeed her disregard for romantic roses, as Peter recalls 'Sally tearing off a rose, and stopping to exclaim at the beauty of cabbages' (*MD* 84), is a telling counter to the flowers Richard gives to Clarissa. It also seems significant that at the point at which Richard gives his gift, Clarissa's thoughts are also focused on the erotic possibilities of Elizabeth's relationship with Doris, a relationship that reminds Clarissa of the intimacy with women that she has lost. Indeed, her fears that Doris 'had taken her daughter from her!' is a focus for this loss and the verbalised cause of Clarissa's antagonism for Doris, (*MD* 139).

The disruption of the rose as the central symbol of heterosexual love and romance is echoed in other parts of the narrative. For instance, roses, and all they signify, are a profound sense of disappointment for Mrs Dempster, who is one of the crowd watching the aeroplane's advertising stunt. She reflects on the hardship and waste of marriage, and on what she has lost to it, 'Roses; figure; her feet too' (*MD* 31); for her, roses are an emotionally deadened symbol that also lead to her exhaustion. She sums up her feeling about roses and the romantic illusions of happiness they so duplicitously signify by way of a warning to the young woman, Maisie Johnson, 'Roses . . . All trash, m'dear' (*MD* 31). Roses are also associated with disappointments in

80 *Gifts, Markets and Economies of Desire*

love and life for Peter Walsh. In his dream/fantasy as he dozes on the park bench, his sense of disappointment is summed up with the image of 'bunches of roses' being 'dashed in his face' (*MD* 64). As he continues to muse on his relationship with Clarissa in the past, he vividly recalls the devastating moment when Clarissa ended their romantic relationship as feeling 'as if she had hit him in the face' (*MD* 72). A clichéd symbol of heterosexual romance, roses repeatedly recur in this text as commodities and signifiers of a range of desires and emotions. Whether thrown at the prince by a poor woman in defiance of her poverty and in the joyful exuberance of the moment, given as a love token to Clarissa by her husband to stave off his long-term rival, or as a metaphor for the waste, the 'trash', of a married woman's life, roses function repeatedly to open up criticisms of social and sexual hegemonic structures.

Richard cannot finally speak his declaration of love and, although he is brimming over with happiness at the 'miracle' of his love for Clarissa, the roses seem to have a contrary function (*MD* 128). Not only does Clarissa comment on the loveliness of the roses to deflect a more painful question about Doris and Elizabeth, but the roses, this symbol of heterosexual security and possession, themselves spread out 'now of their own accord starting apart' as Clarissa relates Doris and Elizabeth's actions (*MD* 132). In 'The Hours' the movement of the roses, or one of them, seems more telling as a sign of the fragility of Richard's romantic gesture. Its aim of securing his relationship with Clarissa seems not to have worked, '*As they looked* at the roses, one moved apart from the other, suddenly; what's this about Elizabeth? Richard asked' ('*The Hours*' 187; italics indicate words crossed through).[34] As the discussion of roses in other parts of the novel suggests, the heterosexual norms and economies that roses signify are constantly called into question and problematised by the homoerotic currents that pervade the text. Even supposedly secure and definite signs of heteronormativity – such as Richard's gift of roses to his wife – are undermined; here his gift is too clichéd, too overt, too blatant a gesture to be convincing. Instead of confirming the validity of the heterosexual economy, Richard's roses serve only to queer it: this gift, paradoxically, becomes, like other gifts in this text, part of the resistance to heterosexual norms and imperatives.

Although Clarissa is careful not to risk the social and economic dangers that an overt rejection of her status as a possession in the heteropatriarchal system would entail, she does repeatedly stage resistances to this system. The opening words of the novel concern Clarissa's intention to 'buy the flowers herself', indicating her resistance to the sexual and economic position Richard's roses later try to reinforce; her shopping experience is interwoven with the gift economy and homoeroticism, which magnifies the subversiveness of her resistance. That the purchase of these flowers is a contribution to Clarissa's party also confirms the association of these flowers with Clarissa's homoerotic desires and the idea of the gift. Clarissa's party is both a product of Clarissa's social gift 'to combine, to create' and an 'offering' in itself (*MD* 135); not only is it an attempt to keep Sally's gift in circulation, but it actually seems to draw Sally back into Clarissa's social circle. As Boone also suggests, 'if the diamond-wrapped kiss was once Sally's "present" to Clarissa, now Clarissa conceives her parties as her "offering" to the world. Clarissa's libidinally charged past thus continues to flow into the present' (191). Like other manifestations of the gift in this novel, however, the party-gift has potential for disruption but is also subject to the powerful influence of other economies at work. It is as the party unfolds, as this particular gift is unwrapped, that Clarissa realises what she holds in her hands is not a radiant diamond of lesbian desire and possibility, but something defaced and worthless.

Clarissa's party does, momentarily at least, seem to keep the energising force of Sally's gift alive and to renew a sense of social connection and creativity. Initially in doubt about the success of her party, Clarissa watches her guests apprehensively and reassures herself that she can detect signs of life, 'But it was still touch and go' (*MD* 188). This party, like other gifts, involves an element of risk as to how it will be received. It is only when Sally unexpectedly bursts into the room, her exuberance disrupting the orderly rhythm of Clarissa's perfunctory greetings of and interaction with her guests, that Clarissa is freed from her feeling of detachment and apprehension (feeling like 'a stake driven in at the top of the stairs' *MD* 189). She is herself jolted into life and into physical and emotional contact with Sally: 'All on top of each other, embarrassed, laughing, words tumbled out' (*MD* 189).

Despite the fact that Sally has also compromised her socialist politics and seems to have forfeited her diamond gift of lesbian love in marrying a wealthy industrialist, her presence reassures Clarissa that the risk of her party-gift was worth taking. Now Sally is older, conventional and self-satisfied, Clarissa reflects, '(t)he lustre had left her' (*MD* 189). Although the lust for Sally has also left Clarissa, she and Sally share a moment of intimacy as 'with Sally's hand in hers' Clarissa surveys the party she has created, seemingly entranced by the vitality of her offering (*MD* 190). Although their heteronormative choices are to the fore (Richard's roses and Sally's marital product, 'five enormous boys'), their bond has remained central to them both (*MD* 190); for Sally too, Bourton and their youthful, passionate relationship is still precious and 'when she counted up her blessings, she put that friendship first' (*MD* 212). As they stand on the threshold of the room, it is as if the warmth and radiance of diamond gift of the past still suffuses the scene: Clarissa is ecstatic with disbelief at Sally's presence and is 'kindling all over with pleasure at the thought of the past' (*MD* 190). It is still Sally's ability to surprise, if not to shock, that has so unexpectedly brought life to the party and to Clarissa herself. This location is significant not only because it is a threshold, and so a liminal space of possibility, but this particular doorway is where Clarissa stood earlier in the day, contemplating the depletion of her

82 *Gifts, Markets and Economies of Desire*

treasure. Holding Sally's hand, she again has a sense of plenitude and vitality; it is as if, for a moment, the promise of Sally's earlier threshold gift, the radiance and burning passion of the flower and the kiss, can be fulfilled.

It would seem that the ongoing circulation of Sally's gift, signalled in the pleasure of Clarissa and Sally once again engrossed in one another, retains its potential for disruption and as such must be interrupted. This renewed intimacy and revitalised energy is dismissed as 'frivolity' and Clarissa 'reclaimed' from her potentially threatening interaction with Sally by the arrival of the prime minister (*MD* 190). As with the earlier interruption of Clarissa's reverie about her homoerotic past in Miss Pym's shop, there is a danger in the operation of a feminine gift economy which the nexus of heteropatriarchal and capitalist forces, embodied in the figure of the prime minister, must quash. However, although the 'one name' of the prime minister and the traditional dress he is 'rigged up' in still symbolise power, the illusion of this authority is punctured by the effort of his performance: 'He tried to look somebody' (*MD* 189). As Natania Rosenfeld argues, the phrase to describe the prime minister's movement through the party, 'this majesty passing', 'bears a double meaning, for majesty is also passing away, to be superseded by new forms of government', specifically the Labour Government (2000, 103). As she points out, this novel is set 'only months before Labour was to take power' (2000, 107). That he looks so 'ordinary' and could be mistaken for a shop assistant continues to undermine the sense of his authority, but also indicates the *real* source of power and influence as being commercial and monetary. It is this context of increasing capitalist forces, and Clarissa's and Sally's complicity in this economic system premised on property and profit, that renders precarious the ongoing circulation of the gift that Clarissa and Sally's renewed bond represents. This is in stark contrast to the context of youthful idealism and socialist principles in which Sally gave her gift. The motivation of Clarissa's 'offering' is far more complex as well. The party has been read as occasioning yet further demonstrations of Clarissa's snobbery and shallowness: it upholds her normative and conventional role as upper-middle-class wife, mother and hostess for her husband, a member of parliament. Although Sally's gift remains a utopian moment replete with homoerotic and creative possibility in the past, it seems that it cannot be made to translate into an acceptable social or sexual framework; nor can it retain its essential qualities of purity and intensity when channelled into an economy based on possession and profit.

Clarissa attempts to keep this gift in circulation, but the essential qualities of Sally's gift are diluted and corrupted when they are channelled into conventional social and sexual structures. It takes the other uninvited reminder of what Clarissa has 'pilfered' in her quest for social success to bring her a full realisation of the gift she risks losing completely. Septimus, Clarissa recognises, has risked all and has plunged to his death to preserve his homoerotic 'treasure', whereas Clarissa 'had once thrown a shilling into the

Serpentine, never anything more' (*MD* 204, 203).[35] Her 'infinitely precious' gift has become 'defaced' and eroded beyond recognition, its value depleted as it is made to enter, and be absorbed into, the monetary economy, as these associations of her desire with coins emphasise. Her party, her gift, is similarly assimilated into heteropatriarchal and dominant social value systems and becomes 'wreathed about with chatter' and corrupted (*MD* 204). The social prestige she has sought and won is merely hollow. It is only her intense feeling for Doris Kilman that remains satisfying and an outlet for Clarissa's erotic energy.

The ending of the novel, with its shift to the desiring gaze of Peter Walsh focused on Clarissa, seems to confirm her status as an object within the heterosexual economy. However, in a novel in which economies of all kinds have been shown to be so interrelated and perspectives constantly shifting, this final perspective must also be judged as just one of many and one that may very readily be displaced, combined or created anew. This is shown, for instance, by the suggestiveness of Sally's conversation with Peter as she sits next to him awaiting Clarissa's promised return.[36] That this final moment of the novel is one of return includes within it the promise of ongoing connection as, reunited with her would-be lovers of the past, Clarissa returns to her party awakened to the importance of her own 'treasure' in the past and its transformation into love and desire for her future. The representation of the gift in Woolf sometimes takes on a utopian quality. This fantasy projection of Clarissa's future perhaps shares this quality, though it is also one that is both energised and problematised by the frisson of rivalry between Peter and Sally as they contemplate their relationships with Clarissa. Cixous argues that an open-ended text ('always endless, without ending' and determined by a 'female libidinal economy') such as *Mrs Dalloway* and 'Mrs Dalloway in Bond Street', rather than providing a point of closure, instead gives a 'send-off . . . making a gift of departure' (1981b, 53). Such writing passes on 'an endless circulation of desire', which cuts across sexual and relational social norms (ibid.). For Woolf, too, it seems that Clarissa's stories and those relating to her party remain in circulation beyond the ending of this novel, these intertextually related texts and '(t)he lack of closure, the open-endedness of the ever-constructing work' suggesting '(t)he ambiguity surrounding the finality of *Mrs Dalloway*' (Wussow, 1997, ix). That Woolf wrote a further eight stories that focus on the party guests, suggests that she was perhaps 'reluctant to leave it [Clarissa's party]' (Dick, 2004, xvii) and perhaps reluctant to leave the gift economy of which this social creation is a manifestation.

The central Clarissa Dalloway characters of these texts are, like the other Clarissas that appear in Woolf's other writing (in *The Voyage Out* and other short fictions), ambiguous in many ways. These characters are in flux – split between their social role as Mrs Richard Dalloway and, as especially evident in *Mrs Dalloway*, the rich interior life of intense and contradictory emotions

84 *Gifts, Markets and Economies of Desire*

and desires, articulated and encoded in her memories and fantasies. The (social, monetary and libidinal) economic fluctuations explored here are only one way to read these highly ambiguous characters. It is clear that they resist a fixed location in one or other economy, moving between gift and market economies, between homoerotic possibility and heterosexual conformity. The gifts given or proposed by the Clarissas in these narratives can be seen to uphold normative, conventional and class-bound roles and values, and sometimes demonstrate the characters' snobbery and shallowness. However, the gifts given to women in these narratives are imbued with a utopian quality. The gifts in *Mrs Dalloway* serve as Clarissa's one creative outlet and she makes her offerings for the sake of offering what she can to life, feeling she has nothing else of importance to give (*MD* 135). Her party is a gift to draw people together and to forge connections, though admittedly only within a very narrow class spectrum. Woolf's worries in her early construction of Clarissa that she is 'too glittering and tinsely' are offset by the 'innumerable other characters' she will introduce, but later she notes that she has saved Clarissa from being 'too tinselly' by 'inventing her memories' (*D2* 272, *D3* 32). It seems that what Woolf saves Clarissa from is the designation of her as merely an object for display and exchange, the focus on 'glitter' recalling Woolf's description of the commodities in 'Oxford Street Tide'. It also seems significant that the memories she invents to 'save' her character are largely composed of recollections of her gift from Sally. The imagery of radiance, illumination, heat, and kindling associated with Sally's first gift pervades the novel, and indicates how women's generosity can energise and renew a culture in decline. For all the doubts and superficiality associated with the gift-giving of the Clarissa characters, the narratives maintain that women's gifts and generosity have the potential to critique, transform and revitalise an ossified, prejudiced and oppressive social system. They privilege the active role of women as subjects not objects of exchange and forge homoerotic bonds between women which threaten to subvert dominant cultural, sexual and economic norms.

3
A Gift of Vision: *To the Lighthouse, Orlando* and *Between the Acts*

In *The Gift: Imagination and the Erotic Life of Property*, Lewis Hyde discusses the role of the artist in terms of the gift economy in some detail. Emphasising the point that '(t)he true commerce of art is a gift exchange' (158), he claims the part played by art and the artist is of fundamental importance to the social, emotional and spiritual survival of a culture. The creative gift generates a sense of community, continuity and future plenitude and immortality: 'In the realized gifts of the gifted we may taste that *zoë*-life which shall not perish even though each of us, and each generation, shall perish' (152). As is evident throughout Woolf's writings, she clearly saw the role of the artist and art itself as of great importance, recognising also its inherent connections with personal experiences as well as with wider economic social and political systems. The representation of the artist and artistic production in Woolf's writing facilitates and inspires transformations. As it records and acts as the impetus for several different kinds of transition, it also poses a challenge to accepted beliefs and norms and simultaneously offers a sense of renewal and hope. Indeed, as Hyde argues, artistic vision is a gift which has regenerative and transformative potential (158–9), suggesting that it is 'when art acts as an agent of transformation that we may correctly speak of it as a "gift"' (47).

The three novels considered here have a woman artist as a central figure playing a key role in giving of material and metaphorical gifts, and keeping creative and other gifts in circulation. The symbolic value of the giving of creative gifts and the gift of creativity itself is of vital importance. In these three novels there is an increasingly fierce resistance to the all-pervasive capitalist economy and heteropatriarchal ideologies, especially as these forces become manifest in an extreme form in war. In place of a worship of empire and capitalist rationality, Woolf's texts seem to offer an alternative stance premised on generosity and community, where creative gifts act as the focal points for realising a different economy of desire and human connection. In contrast to a market exchange, in which the exchange partner is alien, separate and kept at a distance (Hyde 201), at the heart of a gift exchange is the

86 *Gifts, Markets and Economies of Desire*

desire to forge bonds, to envisage the giver and recipient as part of one another, and to privilege similarity over difference. The artistic gift in these texts acts as a counter to the destruction of war (a kind of impersonal transaction gone mad in which lives are exchanged for power), exposing the tyranny that lies behind it. Creativity and imagination, on the other hand, act as sources of social and cultural renewal and replenishment in the aftermath of war and offer a means of resisting the powerful ideological forces that lead to war. In *To the Lighthouse* and *Between the Acts* in particular, allusions to ancient fertility myths suggest ideas of circulation and fruitful increase. This is also in accord with Hyde's idea of gifts as being 'the agents of that organic cohesion we perceive as liveliness', growing, alive and with 'the products of the imagination . . . ensur(ing) the fertility of the imagination' (150, 148). Woolf's novels, in a similar way to Mauss's theory of the gift, offer a criticism of Western civilisation and look with hope to the gift to bring about cultural renewal. Each novel posits artistic vision as a gift that has regenerative and transformative potential, which can offer a counter to the tyrannies of capitalism, patriarchy and war.

The women artists of these novels present a challenge to the dominant heterosexual economy and the alternative libidinal economy their desires generate helps to precipitate a revisionary framework for seeing and conceptualising relationships at a personal and political level. These texts locate a regenerative energy in the figure of the (sexually deviant) woman artist and her creative gifts, while running the risk of consolidating damaging gender ideals of woman as self-sacrificing and the powerless gift-object. Although the representation of the gift economy remains in some ways ambiguous and is still stifled by hegemonic forces to an extent, there seems to be a positive investment in the energising movement of the gift economy in all three texts which serves to counter the inertia created by social and financial constraints, and to challenge the masculine economy so intent on acquiring and hoarding. It is the connections of the gift and homoerotic economies that facilitate the transformation and continuity of the gift of creativity in these novels.

The temporal frame of *To the Lighthouse* spans a highly significant ten-year period of dramatic change and trauma, from the pre-war period to the early post-war years, from the point of view of civilian experience. This is informed by the period of great social, political and economic transition in the post-war period in which the novel was written. In the aftermath of war, the economic situation and the decline of the British Empire brought significant hardships, and several reforms were introduced that began to transform the social fabric in relation to class and gender.[1] The 1920s was also a period in which class tensions came to the fore in strikes and trades union actions, most notably the General Strike of 1926. This was an event that had a particular impact on Woolf, partly because of her support for the workers on strike, but also because, as Levenback argues, it recalled memories of the

First World War (Levenback 88).[2] Woolf's class prejudices combine problematically in this novel with the socialist and feminist impetus she felt to support the working classes and, Tratner argues, to 'credit' them, especially working-class women 'with saving England from destruction' (1995, 56). The novel also acknowledges Woolf's sense that her own position as a woman artist is closely bound up not only with the breakdown of class barriers, but specifically with the changed experience of working-class women and the disruption of traditional gender ideologies they bring about (Tratner, 1995, 53–5; Emery 226). Her awareness of how social, political and economic forces shape our sense of ourselves and our consciousness, and about 'the hidden connections between individuals' (Whitworth, 2005, 38), is apparent in the interconnections her novel suggests as it traces the impact of the war and the changes it brought alongside the development of the woman artist at the heart of it.

Lily's development also in many ways parallels that of Woolf herself; both intend to create new artistic forms appropriate for a post-war period, yet both acknowledge the profound sense of loss that this entails. In her diary, Woolf records her 'idea' to 'invent a new name for [her] books to supplant "novel". A new – by Virginia Woolf. But what? Elegy?' (*D3* 34). This novel is also Woolf's most overtly autobiographical novel written, as she explains in letters, her diary and in her memoir, 'A Sketch of the Past', as a way of coming to terms with the loss of her parents, especially her mother (with whom she had been 'obsessed' since she died when Woolf was thirteen), and expressing 'some very long felt and deeply felt emotion. And in expressing it I explained it and laid it to rest' (*MOB* 90). Woolf's writing of this novel is a way of making visible her feeling of loss, of transforming this emotion into art, in a way that resembles a threshold gift: she uses her creative gifts to mark her own experience of transition on a personal and artistic level.

This sense of transition is emphasised by the novel's tripartite structure in which the middle section acts as a 'corridor' (as Woolf refers to it, 'Notes for Writing', *TTL Holograph*, Appendix A, 48) between the 1909 section, with its exaggerated gender polarisation tightly bound to a heterosexual and patriarchal paradigm and repeated reference to the heroism of war (through Mr Ramsay's reciting of Tennyson's 'The Charge of the Light Brigade'), and the 1919 section in which gender norms are subject to change and the heroism of war profoundly challenged.[3] The gendered identities and relations between the sexes are also economically defined, and an important dichotomy in the novel is that of the masculine monetary economy (closely tied to the heterosexual economy) and the feminine (homoerotic) gift economy. However, the novel also demonstrates the interconnection and complexity of apparently simple binary oppositions. It also exposes the dangers of the gift for women when the generosity so closely associated with the feminine and with women's position in a patriarchal society (so that they are themselves gifts exchanged between men) is so fundamental to sustaining the operation

88 Gifts, Markets and Economies of Desire

of the heteropatriarchal sexual economy, an economy in which women are treated as objects of exchange and consumption.

The prevalent capitalist perspective is powerfully endorsed and reinforced in the attitudes, beliefs and actions of the male characters who see the world and their relationships in terms of a market economy. Their attitudes to, and feelings for, women are viewed in monetary terms, whereby women are conceived as possessions which can be paid for, owned and, like commodities, consumed. Mr Ramsay's constant demands on Mrs Ramsay, it is implied, lead to her exhaustion and in the holograph draft he sees his children as his possessions to bestow, as 'the best token he could give' to the world (*TTL Holograph* 115). Charles Tansley's class insecurities make him cling more fiercely to a sense of his gender superiority and, like Mr Ramsay but on a far smaller scale, he too takes advantage of Mrs Ramsay's generosity. Significantly at the end of Mrs Ramsay's charitable visit to a poor family, Charles Tansley romanticises her as a goddess, implicitly likens her to Queen Victoria, and 'took her bag' – in doing so laying claim to her as a sexual object and taking control of the potential for her economic independence that her bag signifies.[4] Paul Rayley also sees his relationships with women in monetary terms and, faced with the loss of Minta's brooch at the point at which he has had his marriage proposal accepted, he decides he will buy her another, a purchase he feels will confirm his role as hero and provider and which will, in some way, buy Minta's love. In the holograph draft his acquisitiveness is more pronounced and his thoughts about what marriage will mean for his future are metaphorically described: 'he began fingering *those* astonishing possessions' (*TTL Holograph* 126; italics indicate word crossed through).

However, in operation in the novel is also the sense of the feminine gift, a disruptive force, excessive, erotic, energetic, vital, creative and transformative. The novel shows the importance of this idea of the gift as an agent and a sign of transformation as it passes from one woman to another, and in doing so comes to more forcefully act as a counter to the forces of oppression which result in the destruction of war. This feminine gift is suggestively a productive, creative energy, a metaphorical gift of fruitful increase passed on between the women characters, which resists incorporation into a materialist system and, as this gift moves and changes, undoes any sense of the eternal feminine, premised on self-sacrifice and sympathy. It is essential that the gift moves, and its circulation in this novel is the touchstone of change and transformation.

From the outset, *To the Lighthouse* foregrounds the gift. The perception of objects and the narrative as a whole can be read as a cycle of gift-giving and bestowal and of the increase that comes when a gift is passed on. The literal gift cycle that is completed in the novel is that initiated by Mrs Ramsay. Her plan to send gifts to the lighthouse is motivated in part by her obedience to conventional social norms whereby her philanthropy is an aspect of her proper middle-class role and an indicator of her obedience to class and gender norms. Like other gifts, these are also complex and double-edged, aiming to seal bonds with others and to exert her power.[5] However, although she also harbours a secret ambition to take her philanthropy to a professional level[6] (and thereby transgress these gender norms), and despite the fact that (inevitably) her empathy and concerns for others stem from her middle-class perspective, her gift-giving is also motivated by a genuine sense of generosity. In particular, the gift of the stocking that she is knitting is, like her other creative gifts, what Emerson would call a true 'token(s) of compliment and love', making a gift of one's talent being '(t)he only gift . . . a portion of thyself' (25).[7] Her knitting together of threads is also a metaphor for a genuine desire to make and maintain connections and to consolidate a sense of community that her other gifts of food and socialisation aim to bring about.

The excess commodities, the clutter and waste, of the Ramsay family that she plans to send to the lighthouse are specifically chosen to 'amuse' and give pleasure to the men who work there (this recycling might be seen now as a stand against capitalism). The trip itself is also, of course, a 'gift' to her son, to fulfil James' long-held wish and hope, and to bring him pleasure and amusement. In this early part of the narrative, however, this trip is postponed because, as the dominant narrative perspective of Mrs Ramsay and James makes clear, male rationality triumphs and the refusal to take risks prevents the gifts from being given. This gift is blocked until the final pages when Mr Ramsay, Cam and James fulfil this wish and arrive at the lighthouse to bestow gifts. By this point, of course, Mrs Ramsay's gift, her 'portion' of herself (if it ever makes it to the lighthouse), will be completely redundant and the little boy for whom it was intended will no longer be there, just as the 'gift' of the trip itself for James has lost its magic. However, her creativity and generosity remain alive for Lily for whom the promise of the bestowal of Mrs Ramsay's gifts is key to the completion of her own creative act.

In fact, the circulation of the gifts associated with the trip to the lighthouse is 'unblocked' (in what Woolf conceived of as the second 'block' of her narrative structure, which is the final section 'The Lighthouse'), by a process in which the metaphorical spirit of the gift, originating in Mrs Ramsay's creative, erotic and life-giving gifts (which Lily recognises as artistic and akin with her own) and reinforced by the reiterated association of Mrs Ramsay with a kind of mythic fertility, is seemingly inherited by Lily. Because Lily is less embedded in and compromised by middle-class, heteropatriarchal and capitalist systems of value (as is evident, for example, in her distance from Mrs Ramsay's devotion to matchmaking and marriage), she acts as an agent of transformation, revising this creative, metaphorical and spiritual gift in the post-war period. This results in the literal giving of gifts to the lighthouse men (though it is not clear that this has happened when the novel ends), but also in the completion of Lily's painting, with Woolf's temporal manipulation suggesting the gifts are given at the exact moment of the completion

90   *Gifts, Markets and Economies of Desire*

of Lily's painting. For Lily, this is a moment of vision richly imbued with her memories and the spirit of Mrs Ramsay, but it is also at odds with the values Mrs Ramsay endorsed. Underlying both gifts is the sense of their sustaining social bonds, across class and gender divides. However, there is a tension at the end of the novel between the apparent completion of the cycle and the openness of the narrative's ending. There is a powerful sense of being poised, balanced on a new social, political, economic and aesthetic threshold. This, plus the ambiguity about whether the gift has been given to the lighthouse men, creates a narrative suspension rather than closure.[8]

At this threshold, the abundance, generosity and fertility that Mrs Ramsay represents (and that Lily has inherited) is put to use in a positive and creative way, inspiring a sense of hope and possibility for the future. Indeed, the novel itself draws on season myths and archetypes in its representation of Mrs Ramsay as a goddess to worship and as the inexhaustible source of plenty, increase and growth. With reference to ancient fertility myths and rituals, critics have explored the life-giving energy attributed to her as well as her complicity with patriarchal law.[9] However, although the novel does allude positively to these powerful myths, it also clearly demonstrates the danger of complicity with such myths of the eternal, fruitful and all-giving feminine for women. As others have made clear,[10] the influence of Jane Harrison's feminist interpretations of ancient myths and rituals (in which Harrison demonstrates how matriarchal social structures, rituals and art were supplanted by patriarchal structures and 'heroic' sagas, which privilege the masculine and the individual) complicates and politicises the allusions to myths and rituals in Woolf's work. In many ways, both Harrison and Woolf are engaged in a similar revisionary interpretation of such powerful narratives of gender and gender relations in order to recover a sense of the feminine as powerful, rather than as appropriated and exploited in a heteropatriarchal market economy. Such revisionary politics are crucial in *To the Lighthouse* (in both form and content), a work in which Woolf is also highly conscious of creating a new literary form, but which is, as an elegy, closely tied to the past. It treads a 'razor edge of balance' between the a disempowered conception of the feminine as gift to be exploited and/or sacrificed, and an exploration of the power of the gift when women are themselves the agents, the donors, giving gifts in their own right (Rubin 542).

Crucially, the novel offers a warning about the proper use and abuse of the gift, and about how to preserve the feminine spirit of the gift rather than exhaust and entirely consume it (as if a possession or commodity). In accordance with her reactionary values, Mrs Ramsay disparages her own life-sustaining gifts. Having given him the encouragement that Mr Ramsay demands, she feels an 'exquisite abandonment to exhaustion', 'the rapture of successful creation' 'throbbed through her' (*TTL* 36). However, this 'goddess' does not exalt in her power, nor in the life-giving eroticism of her creative gift. Rather, her deeply ingrained patriarchal thought leads her to be

A Gift of Vision 91

self-effacing and to disparage her gifts; she considers what she 'gave' to the world is 'negligible' compared with what Mr Ramsay gave (*TTL* 36). Significantly, her feelings of inferiority in relation to Mr Ramsay here are bound up with monetary worries, notably about the greenhouse. Her role as a bountiful goddess, and source of fertility and nurture (as the associations of a greenhouse confirm) is restricted by the lack of money to mend the greenhouse roof. She is disempowered in the monetary economy because she cannot earn her own money. Her anxiety about insufficient funds is compounded by the implied criticism of Mr Ramsay's role as a breadwinner. Her predicament is premised on the highly conservative patriarchal ideologies she readily buys into, her worship of masculine logic and rationality and, importantly, her endorsement of capitalist institutions like the Bank of England, which are antithetical to her gifts.[11] In the holograph draft this is clearer as she attributes her fierce sense of duty to men to her grandmother's time and to the fact that men 'created & controlled the Bank of England' (*TTL Holograph* 7), not a more general control of 'finance' as in the novel (*TTL* 5).

Like Clarissa in *Mrs Dalloway*, Mrs Ramsay also questions her own motives for her generous acts, which include her vanity, ego and to make people like her (*TTL* 39). Significantly, she has these doubts in response to Augustus Carmichael's indifference to her gifts and as she reads 'The Fisherman and His Wife', a story about a woman's subversive greed and over-reaching, and about the exploitation of a magical gift of increase. She also recognises that she has no time to enjoy or appreciate the gifts that she has been given (a fact she finds 'disgraceful', *TTL* 25). Identified as a goddess because of her beauty and generosity (components of her role as self-sacrificing angel), she does not participate fully in the gift cycle by being a recipient and allowing gifts to revive and renew her. Her gifts, books inscribed to her as a powerful goddess '"whose wishes must be obeyed" ... "the happier Helen of our days"' remain neglected and in a kind of limbo state because they have been given but not fully recognised as possessions by Mrs Ramsay. As this reference to Helen of Troy suggests, Mrs Ramsay, like the beautiful woman of myth, is perceived by men to be an object or gift exchanged between them rather than having an active role in a gift exchange.[12] One of the books given to her is an anthropological study, 'Bates on the Savage Customs of Polynesia', from which, had she read it, Mrs Ramsay would undoubtedly have learned about the importance of receiving as well as giving gifts in the process of gift *exchange*, since the gift economies at work in 'primitive' cultures were one of the key areas of anthropological and ethnographic studies at this time (*TTL* 25).[13] Reading about 'primitive' cultures may also have opened her eyes to other ways of being as a woman, beyond Western gender norms, a key element of the emergence of Lily (already marked as a different kind of woman by the description of her Chinese eyes) as a modern woman.[14]

However, Mrs Ramsay's gifts and creativity also hint at the disruptive potential of the gift. It is in this respect that the similarities and connections

92   *Gifts, Markets and Economies of Desire*

between Lily and Mrs Ramsay become apparent despite their more obvious differences. A glimpse of Mrs Ramsay's potential to be subversive and its connection with her gift-giving is seen in the early pages of the novel, when her angry defiance of her husband's masculine authority is expressed in her 'little twist of the reddish-brown stocking' as she contradicts his opinion about the weather as his prediction would compromise both her gift of the stocking and the experience she wants to give to James (*TTL* 4). Although at one point she is prepared to 'sacrifice' working-class Charles Tansley at the altar of her husband's ego (*TTL* 15), Mrs Ramsay's gifts to those of a lower class (the lighthouse men, and her material and emotional charity towards Tansley, whose near relation works on a lighthouse) also threaten to disturb hierarchies in forging new connections across class divides, connecting, as Tratner reads the Ramsays' house and the lighthouse, two domestic communities, one middle-class and one working-class, respectively (1995, 56). Mrs Ramsay's sense of urgency about the need to reform the dairy industry (which grows out of her charitable work) reciprocates Tansley's working-class views, so explosively expressed, calling for reform of the fishing industry. However, her attack on 'the prejudices of the British Public' only provokes laughter from everyone around the table (although only Andrew and Mr Ramsay are specifically named). This laughter politely suppresses the threat her views and the independence of mind that such views indicate, a threat made clear by the allusion to the persecution of more overtly defiant and deviant women in the past: the laughter of her family spread 'like a fire leaping from tuft to tuft of furze . . . fire encircled her' and she is forced to relinquish her stand (*TTL* 96). This leads to her contemplation of Lily and to her connection with the independence, deviance and disruptive creativity she admires in her. Although Mrs Ramsay tries to overcome the 'fearful' position for Lily of not being married with her matchmaking schemes, thus indicating the severe limitations on her subversive tendencies, the word chosen to describe the qualities she admires in Lily is 'flare', which recalls the fire imagery that denotes the danger that Mrs Ramsay's views imply just a few lines above and indicates a strong affinity between them.

Like Mrs Ramsay, Lily is subject to dominant value judgements which deprecate and ridicule women's gifts. Unlike Mrs Ramsay, however, Lily sees her vocation as an artist as an escape from these norms. Although Charles Tansley's assertion that 'women can't write, women can't paint' haunts her as she battles to produce her painting, her sense of identity as an artist coalesces in the knowledge that in her experience of her artistic gifts she had 'found a treasure' so that she need never succumb to the social, sexual and economic pressure to marry (*TTL* 79). In the holograph draft, the experience of finding this precious treasure is emphasised further: 'She was aware of some *profound small* trophy retrieved . . . ; some talisman she would sew to the inside of her dress' (*TTL Holograph* 138; italics indicate words crossed through). This is an image that is transposed to describe Mrs Ramsay's artistic conceptualisation of the arrangement of fruit later, suggesting that her imagination is also a treasure, again reinforcing a connection between the creative gifts of these two women. As with other mentions of treasure in Woolf's writing,[15] Lily's treasure has homoerotic resonances. Here, solving the problem of space in her painting becomes synonymous with solving the problem of not wanting to marry. In filling the space at the centre of her painting (and her life) with a tree (an emblem of the vitality and security associated with Mrs Ramsay, and later an image used to represent her), she substitutes what should be the key aim of women to marry, with 'a woman's representation of another woman in art' (Hanson, 1994, 79). Her passion for her art, which she finds difficult and terrifying, but which is also the focus of her desire (she can barely take her eyes off her painting, *TTL* 17), is clearly bound up with her intense and suggestively homoerotic feelings for Mrs Ramsay, which are also experienced as a 'treasure'.

Although Lily maintains a critical distance from Mrs Ramsay's social and sexual conventionality and conformity, she recognises some of the contradictions and complexities of Mrs Ramsay and her gift. Loving Mrs Ramsay and half in love with her, she sees beyond her angelic beauty and goddesslike fecundity to the twisted finger of her glove and all that it signifies; indeed she is privy, as a woman, to Mrs Ramsay's private mockery of men, to the way she can 'maliciously twist' the words and mannerisms of her male guests (*TTL* 46). Lily longs to know her both intimately and intricately, to gain access to the hidden 'treasures' of her heart and mind, to find a sense of 'unity' in the 'intimacy . . . which is knowledge' inexpressible in 'any language known to men', and to represent her through her creative gift, drawing on the insight she has gained from her unconventional and marginal perspective (*TTL* 47). That she is a woman enables Lily to see Mrs Ramsay differently from how men see her, as is evident as she and William Bankes look at Mrs Ramsay posing with James for Lily's painting. Lily's connection with Mrs Ramsay as a woman enables her to add to the 'beam' of his gaze, 'her different ray' – one that gives her access to the more complex, contradictory and less reverential side of Mrs Ramsay, and one that leads Lily to reveal the intensity of her desire for Mrs Ramsay, expressed in her urge to 'becom(e), like waters poured into one jar, inextricably the same, one with the object one adored' (*TTL* 47). The sacrilege of wanting to metaphorically plunder 'treasures in the tombs of kings' – the gifts of passage for the dead – indicates both the intensity of Lily's feeling, but also the acquisitive urge to possess Mrs Ramsay's 'treasures', which is so fundamentally at odds with the generosity and depropriative approach this novel posits as necessary for artistic gifts to flourish (*TTL* 47). As mention of these gifts for the dead suggests, Lily must experience a physical separation from Mrs Ramsay to re-form her desire and her creative gift so as to fully achieve her own gift of vision. This is what happens as the novel progresses. Lily inherits Mrs Ramsay's generosity and creative gift, but it must be transformed through more unconventional and marginal perspectives so that it can continue to circulate in a post-war world.

94 *Gifts, Markets and Economies of Desire*

At this point in the novel, Lily begins to realise the importance of resisting the acquisitive urge that is central to the masculine libidinal economy and to capitalist thinking as she recognises in William Bankes' gaze on Mrs Ramsay a 'rapture' that is impersonal and non-possessive. This gives rise to Lily's spontaneous experience of a 'heavenly gift' for which she feels 'intense gratitude' as it 'solaced her, eased her of the perplexity of life' (*TTL* 44) and 'was exalting' (*TTL* 45). Despite his conventionality (he is a widower and scientist, who values art for its sentimental and monetary value, *TTL* 49) and his name, suggestive of a double allegiance with capitalism ('Bill', banks), as the holograph draft makes clear, William's love 'was love that had never attempted to clutch its object' (*TTL Holograph* 86), and his implicitly suggested homoerotic desire for Mr Ramsay[16] marks a significant allegiance between him and Lily. His interest in her art and his attempt to understand her modernist vision is crucial in the fostering of Lily's gift.[17] As Lily 'subdue(s) all her impressions as a woman' to explain to William the 'relations of the masses' in her painting and the connections she wants to make between them in a 'much more general' way (*TTL* 49), it could be argued that she compromises her art in responding specifically to a man's demands (especially as William 'tapped the canvas with the bone handle' of his penknife, *TTL* 48). However, the sealing of the bond between them as they share 'something profoundly intimate' is suggested as Lily 'nicked the catch of her paint-box to', creating a sound that 'seemed to surround in a circle for ever the paint-box, the lawn, Mr. Bankes, and that wild villain, Cam, dashing past' (*TTL* 50). This sense that creative gifts can expand possibilities for connection in a homoerotic economy of desire suggests a powerful sense of hope for the future, a hope energised here by the presence of the youngest child, the disruptive and disobedient 'Cam the Wicked' (*TTL* 20). Lily feels, with relief, that William had 'taken' her painting 'from her' not as a stolen possession, but by bringing a sense of a collective experience which she can share (*TTL* 50).

This sense of connection, harmony and peace is also what Mrs Ramsay aims to create at the dinner to which everyone comes. Despite her initial weariness and self-doubt, she embarks on her 'business' like 'a sailor' at the mercy of the winds (*TTL* 78). Despite her guests' various emotional vacillations, her offering of food restores a positive feeling. A bountiful goddess, she ensures that there is plenty for everyone' (*TTL* 97). Her daughter Rose's artistic arrangement of the fruit is also associated with the excess of some mythic feast and celebration, reminding her of 'Neptune's banquet' or of 'the bunch [of grapes] that hangs with vine leaves over the shoulder of Bacchus' (*TTL* 90). Appreciating it with her artist's eye and escaping into the fantasy world it represents for her, this fruitful creation gives Mrs Ramsay an imaginative, visual and sensual pleasure, a 'depropriative' pleasure which contrasts, as Hanson argues, with 'Mr Carmichael's appropriative approach to the fruit' as he breaks of pieces of fruit for his own consumption (1994, 88). However, this unity is only an illusion created by the sheer force of Mrs Ramsay's

A Gift of Vision 95

will to give, her ability to enchant everyone with her 'irresistible' beauty and 'abundance', and to 'put a spell on them all' by 'wishing' and willing it (*TTL* 94). Despite her ability to smooth over the fractures of this group, to temporarily halt the vacillation of emotions and create a sense of harmony and positive feeling, she knows that this is only a fleeting moment. As 'she hovered like a hawk suspended' (*TTL* 97, with a near repetition of this phrase, *TTL* 99) over the scene she has created – her own artistic 'treasure', which is metaphorically a radiant 'ruby' – she knows that as a memory this experience of connection will remain precious, but that, like the food itself, the plenitude she has created is not permanent but is 'vanishing' even before she has left the room (*TTL* 103).

The unity that Mrs Ramsay seems to create is also an illusion because, as Tratner argues, 'the beautiful unity of the dinner party and of upper-class consciousness has actually been created by those who have been excluded from it' – 'Mildred the cook [and] Mrs McNab . . . washing the dishes' hidden away in the kitchen (1995, 53). This novel suggests that the changes that must take place to enable art as a gift to remain a life-giving force are bound up with political changes in class and gender. Although the class politics in Woolf's writings are by no means radical (or straightforward), there is a sense in this novel of a questioning and disruption of class prejudices as the connections between Mrs Ramsay, Mrs McNab and Lily serve to offer a feminist as well as a socialist challenge to the forces that fuel war.[18] These forces are both the large-scale politics and economics of European countries as well as the 'repressions and tensions within European families', as Tratner argues, which give rise to violent outbursts (1995, 50). The focus on the creative gifts of these women attempts to offer a counter to the destructiveness of war, as well as to register the social and political changes the war brings to a head. Tratner notes that there was also a dramatic change in modernist attitudes to the masses from the anxiety in the pre-war period about being 'drowned by the masses' to the post-war necessity of being part of 'the mass movements changing society' (1995, 15). He argues that modernists, like Woolf and Joyce, 'were seeking to bring high culture to serve socialist mass movements', as well as to acknowledge the positive transformations that mass movements brought about (1995, 32).

As Mrs Ramsay's party breaks up, there is a sense of political change in the air and, foreshadowing 'Time Passes', as soon as Mrs Ramsay leaves (presumably to discuss Paul's proposal with Minta) 'a sort of disintegration set in' (*TTL* 104). Charles Tansley and William Bankes go to the terrace to discuss 'the policy of the Labour Party' thus altering 'the whole poise of the evening, making the weight fall in a different direction' as if going to 'the bridge of the ship and . . . taking their bearings' (*TTL* 104). 'The Window' is set in a socialist Liberal period in which, as Whitworth notes, benefits and support were extended to the working classes (2005, 36–9). Lily's art is implicitly in tune with this political change, as well as more obviously with the changes

96   *Gifts, Markets and Economies of Desire*

for women that came after the war. Her ongoing battle with conventions in art and with prevalent gender expectations (which tell her she cannot paint as a woman), and with her own personal struggles to realise her creative gift, find palpable expression in her struggles with her painting, and in her attempts to solve the dilemma of how to be a professional painter and a woman. This is figured specifically in terms of finding a way to balance the 'weight' of her representation of the masses on the left and right by somehow connecting them. Tratner suggests that the 'technical aesthetic issues' raised by Lily's discussion of the 'masses' of colour have 'an unusual political resonance' (1995, 68, 67). Seeing Lily's 'painting as a political map of society' (1995, 68), he suggests that her plan to move the tree to the middle to 'avoid that awkward space' (*TTL* 79) indicates a reconceptualising of relationships at a personal and political level. Her revision of the spaces in her painting indicates a bringing together of values and qualities that will enable her to 'legitimately' be a working woman, resisting middle-class models of marriage: 'In such a space Lily could be a working, unmarried, culturally upper-class woman. Being in the middle, she could take on the task of connecting the masses' (1995, 68).

The idea of shifting weight and thereby creating movement also resonates with the idea of gift exchange in which, unlike the 'equilibrium and stasis' of market exchange in which 'you pay to balance the scale', 'there is momentum, and the weight shifts from body to body' (Hyde 9). It would seem, then, that the success of Lily's role as a woman artist, her more marginal homoerotic perspective and the particular political sympathy with and representation of the 'masses' (with making more space for them in her art) are in a symbiotic relationship. However, just as war interrupts Lily's inspiration, temporarily putting a halt to her painting, the novel's focus shifts to the working-class characters Mrs McNab and Mrs Bast. It is as if the 'weight' of the narrative itself is given momentum as the gift of vitality and creativity passes to different hands to be sustained. This results in new forms of fertility and art (a hybrid of 'the carnation mate(d) with the cabbage', perhaps [*TTL* 132]), and Mrs Ramsay's gift is transformed for a new post-war era that Lily will inherit.

'Time Passes' metaphorically charts the political sea-change from the period of liberal reform and the rise of the Labour Party in the pre-war period, through the devastation and dramatic changes of war, to the immediate post-war period from the perspective of the mid-1920s when the longer-term economic consequences of the war were manifested in trade union actions. It also displaces middle-class concerns and authority and suggests, as Levenback argues, that the only meaningful voices are those able to convey the changes brought about by the war 'in the concrete, non-literary terms of lived experience' (Levenback 107–8). Indeed, as philosophical discourse fails to explain the experience of war, Mrs McNab does become a touchstone of sanity in an increasingly mad world. She may know herself to be 'witless' and

A Gift of Vision 97

feels herself to be '(b)owed down . . . with weariness', yet she is able to sail and survive this sea-change – 'she rolled like a ship at sea' (*TTL* 124). This nautical imagery is linked in general terms to political and social change, as in the description of William Bankes and Charles Tansley metaphorically 'taking their bearings' as if 'on the bridge of a ship' (*TTL* 104). However, it also signals a specific connection between Mrs McNab, Mrs Ramsay and Lily as it also emphasises the importance of the gift economy and the movement and transformation of the creative gift. For instance, Mrs Ramsay's sense of her world changing is symbolised by 'the superb upward rise (like the beak of a ship) of the elm branches' in the wind (*TTL* 105), and, as she summons up the energy she needs to give her gift of her dinner party, she is likened to a sailor at the mercy of the winds. Such imagery also depicts Lily's uncharacteristic expression of passion in her urge to find Minta Doyle's lost brooch, 'she would be the one to pounce on the brooch half-hidden by some stone, and thus herself be included among the sailors and adventurers', an urge that suggests Lily's homoerotic desire and emphasises her commitment to a woman-centred gift economy (*TTL* 94).[19] Later, an image of shaking 'one's sails' suggests Lily's ease of thought and creative vision as she looks across the bay to where Mr Ramsay, James and Cam are sailing to the lighthouse on the boat journey, which completes the gift cycle Mrs Ramsay puts in motion at the beginning of the novel.

Importantly, Mrs McNab's reflections on war-time experience in her juxtaposition of the mournful fact that 'every one had lost some one these years' with the injustice of economic inflation astutely connects the economic core of war with its devastating impact on the lived experience of civilians (*TTL* 130). Indeed, what is crucial to Mrs McNab's sense of defeat in the face of the decay of the house is economic. She feels an increased sense of economic powerlessness in this intensely masculine culture of wartime ('Prices had gone up shamefully'), and that her relationship with the Ramsays has been stripped down solely to its economic base: the family now 'just sent her money' (*TTL* 130). Without the generosity and life-giving force of Mrs Ramsay's care and creativity, Mrs McNab temporarily gives up, and the life-sustaining forces of nurture, creativity and increase lie dormant. It is clear, however, that her 'sidelong', marginal perspective on events is crucial in bringing about and recording this changed situation. Woolf's representation of Maggie McNab as leering and lurching accords with Woolf's 'volatile mixture of class feelings' (Zwerdling 87),[20] which gives rise to prejudiced views of working-class women as being uncouth and inane, as well as being a vital and powerful force. It is this energy that is obviously seen to be crucial in literally sustaining the life of this house (a microcosm for the nation). In not only privileging a working-class woman's voice, thoughts and experiences, but also her view – the Ramsays' house is seen through *her* eyes and their mirror reflects *her* (*TTL* 124–5) – Woolf's novel indicates the increasing power and influence of the working classes and women during this period. It is Mrs

98   *Gifts, Markets and Economies of Desire*

McNab's voice and vision that offer hope, and her energy and resilience that are necessary to sustain and transform the creative, life-giving gift. Tratner views Mrs McNab positively as 'a model of the artist' and as 'an alternative to Mrs Ramsay' that Lily can imitate as she completes her painting of Mrs Ramsay (1995, 65). As he and Emery argue, it is possible to see that the novel works to recuperate what Mrs McNab produces and represents into a middle-class frame of reference and representation of the world. When the dynamics of the relationship between these three women are seen in relation to the gift economy, however, the sense of laying claim is not important; a stronger connection between the three creators emerges so that Mrs McNab seems more than simply a model or conduit for the creative gift of vision. As Hyde remarks, 'The gift and its bearers share a spirit which is kept alive by its motion among them, and which in turn keeps them both alive' (36). That Mrs McNab is a gift-giving agent in her own right is apparent from the changes Woolf made between the holograph draft and published versions. Although Mrs McNab has a more prominent and obviously impressive role in the holograph draft as an ancient, mystic seer with a clear message of hope and forgiveness,[21] the narrator is curious about the source of her 'incorrigible hope', 'with no gift to bestow & no gift to take' (*TTL Holograph* 215). In the published novel she is a life force, keeping in motion the generosity and creative fertility she has received from Mrs Ramsay, and imbuing this with her own physical energy so that it is transformed as it is passed on to Lily.

Maggie McNab's spiritual connection to Mrs Ramsay is made apparent in the fact that although reports of Mrs Ramsay's death are not certain, Mrs McNab has a ghostly vision of her. A recipient of Mrs Ramsay's generosity and care before the war, she keeps this gift alive with her memories of Mrs Ramsay. She recalls her gifts of nurture and creativity (giving Mrs McNab milk soup, planting and tending her garden, caring for her children) as she fingers Mrs Ramsay's gardening cloak (now moth eaten); she picks her flowers (to avoid 'waste' and to save the creative life they represent from the marketplace as she fears the house will be 'sold'); and, importantly (as Lily will later do), she 'sees' her. She both remembers seeing her but also projects her vision of Mrs Ramsay 'like a yellow beam or the circle at the end of a telescope', sending it 'wandering over the bedroom wall, up the dressing-table, across the washstand', accompanying her as she cleans the house (*TTL* 130).[22] Although in many ways it is unlikely that Woolf consciously intended Mrs McNab to be viewed as an artist, her vision and the energy that she summons up to revive the house resonates strongly with Lily's and Woolf's modernist artistry; her work seems to intervene, her perspective bringing a disruption to traditional ideas of art necessary for new art forms to emerge in the post-war period. Laura Marcus discusses 'the cinematic aesthetic' that Woolf uses in 'Time Passes,' giving as an example the appearance of Mrs Ramsay 'as in a film or slide projection on a wall' (2004, 103, 104). Marcus focuses on the ideas about memory that this moment explores, rather than on the idea of Mrs McNab's creatively imagining this vision of Mrs Ramsay. However, there is the suggestion of a connection between Mrs McNab's vision of Mrs Ramsay, new art forms and Woolf's transformation of these as part of her modernist form here. Tratner also remarks on Mrs McNab's 'painting those memories [of Mrs Ramsay] all over the house' (1995, 65) as she cleans, conflating her cleaning (her work) with her imagination/creative vision. Tratner makes the point that when Lily later looks at the house for inspiration, it is 'Mrs McNab's re-creation of Mrs Ramsay in the cleaned up house' that she sees (1995, 65). This seems to confirm that it is not simply Mrs McNab's role as caretaker of Mrs Ramsay's gift (enabling it, like the space with which she is associated, to survive), but also indicates the importance of her imagination and her vision in its own right and as an influence on Lily.

Though Mrs McNab can be seen to play an important connecting role, the most obvious sense of passage of the fertile gift of creativity is between the two middle-class women artist/creators, Mrs Ramsay and Lily. As Lily experiences an anguished sense of loss about the death of Mrs Ramsay as she struggles to revise and complete her painting, it is only Mrs Ramsay to whom she refers overtly as a source of inspiration. However, that Lily's glimpse of Mrs McNab occurs as she completes her painting highlights a key moment of continuity between all three. Her presence in this moment inserts a view that disturbs the sense of a simple exchange of the creative gift between two participants, just as her different class perspective and her own vision of Mrs Ramsay triangulates the perspective on them and the relationship between them. This triangulation of vision also resonates with Lily's own altered vision of Mrs Ramsay, from a dome shape to the purple triangle that finally represents her in Lily's modernist painting, a shape that corresponds to Mrs Ramsay's most intimate understanding of herself. The impact of Mrs McNab's perspective and vision works to transform the form of Lily's painting and seemingly the process and experience of producing such art.

Lily's experience of the process of painting is the major preoccupation of 'The Lighthouse'. It she who asserts that the value of her painting (like the value of the gift that lies in the experience of giving and/or receiving) lies in what she has attempted and the process, rather than in the finished product (*TTL* 170). Echoing Mrs Ramsay's joy and erotic pleasure as she contemplates the strokes of the lighthouse beam earlier in the novel, Lily's experience of inspiration is similarly an orgasmic overflow of female pleasure, an experience of *jouissance* as she creates: initially she feels the 'squirt(ing)' of 'some juice necessary for the lubrication of her faculties', then her 'hand quivered with life', the rhythm of her painting 'strong enough to bear her along with it on its current', as she continues to paint (*TTL* 152). Others have commented on the connections created between Lily and Mrs Ramsay by this suggestive, excessive and erotic imagery, specifically in relation to Lily's continuation in

100   *Gifts, Markets and Economies of Desire*

her art of 'Mrs Ramsay's creativity in life' (Hanson, 1994, 89). As Hanson continues, 'The metaphor of orgasm . . . closely connects the two women: it is as though Mrs Ramsay's sexual creativity provides an origin and sponsoring analogy for Lily's particular kind of (female) artistic creativity', a creativity that 'unsettles the phallogocentric symbolic order' and which brings to the fore ideas about '"feminine" creativity in a period of a "sexualisation" of aesthetics' (Hanson 1994, 91, 89).

Although this continuity between Lily and Mrs Ramsay is of key importance, so too is the transformation that the female-centred creative gift has undergone in the hands of Mrs McNab and Mrs Bast. Lily also recognises that the pool of life and time is 'full to the brim' with 'so many lives' (*TTL* 183). Although perhaps her own class prejudice leads Lily to include Mrs McNab as an unnamed 'washerwoman with her basket' amid the 'waifs and strays . . . a rook; a red-hot poker; the purples and grey-greens of flowers', she recognises that 'some common feeling . . . held the whole together' in which Mrs McNab plays an important part (*TTL* 183). Although this momentary feeling of completeness is likened to a lovers' gift 'to choose out the elements of things and place them together and so, giving them wholeness', the natural imagery used to suggest communal feeling is also associated with the notion of gifts as agents of change, as organic and capable of growth and transformation. 'Love' she realises 'has a thousand shapes' and, like her view across the bay, is not fixed (*TTL* 183). Bonnie Kime Scott suggests that this image reveals that Lily 'sees unity and permanence in love as no more than a remote possibility, and largely a fabrication' (1995, 25). However, as the importance attributed to moments of being and transitory experiences of perfection and wholeness in the novel suggests, love and creativity can make powerful bonds and connections, although these are always shifting and in motion, like the gift itself.

As Lily continues to gaze across the bay, her sense of flux in terms of gender and creative forms is reinforced; as she has realised earlier in relation to mythic images of the apparently eternal feminine, such 'vision(s) must be perpetually remade' in this post-war era (*TTL* 173). Here Lily's view, 'which a moment before had seemed miraculously fixed', shifts so that the 'harmony in her own mind' is 'upset' (*TTL* 183). She resolves to 'start afresh' in her struggle to attain the 'razor edge of balance' between Mr Ramsay and her painting. She seeks inspiration, 'that very jar on the nerves, the thing itself before it has been made anything', in her quest to reach the 'something' in Mrs Ramsay and in her painting 'that evaded her' (*TTL* 184). This 'something' in Mrs Ramsay has evaded Lily in the past too, in the image of the jar into which she wanted to merge with Mrs Ramsay. What was a desire for permanent unity in the past is now a jar of disjunction. What is significant in Lily's development as an artist is her realisation that the 'globed compacted thing(s)' are only transitory – it is movement, change and disruption that are most important (*TTL* 183).

A Gift of Vision 101

The most dramatic change for Lily has been the death of Mrs Ramsay but, as the ancient vegetation myths and rituals to which Woolf's novel alludes make clear, the gift of fertility (and creativity) must perish and be cast out in order to be born anew at a personal, political and symbolic level. Lily's response to Mrs Ramsay's death echoes the sense of loss and disintegration of 'Time Passes' but also, similarly, brings new life. Lily has a powerful emotional, but also a painfully visceral, response to the loss of Mrs Ramsay. The shocking and brutal parenthetical description of Macalister's boy mutilating a live fish (by cutting a piece out of its side for bait), occurring simultaneously with Lily's lamentation for Mrs Ramsay, demonstrates the extent of Lily's suffering. Indeed, after this, her 'pain increased' (*TTL* 172). Although she feels that this excess of emotion is ignominious, lost as she is in 'the waters of annihilation' (*TTL* 172), this loss is also a necessary stage in the mythical cycle of increase in which Mrs Ramsay, a conflation of Demeter and Persephone, is imagined wreathed with flowers and crossing the fields, going presumably into the underworld (*TTL* 172). The casting out of death and the bringing in of new life has already been enacted by the collective action of Mrs McNab and Mrs Bast, who perform not quite 'a leaping inspired dance' of the *dithyramb*,[23] but whose actions nevertheless bring about the experience of 'passing from one social state to another' (Harrison 111) as they tip the balance from utter death and destruction and bring about the 'laborious birth' of a society drastically 'changed' in the post-war period (*TTL* 133, 134). Their cleaning is vigorous – they 'slapped and slammed, upstairs now now down in the cellars' – but also has a sense of a ritual dance 'stooping, rising, groaning, singing' (*TTL* 133). Their work symbolically expels death and the masculine heroic (confirmed by the elimination of direct references to the war in the published version).[24] This leads to a resurrection of female power as the force of creativity.

In a repetition and intensification of the patterns in 'Time Passes', Lily takes on from Mrs McNab the 'laborious' role of giving 'birth' to new forms of connection and creativity. This is made clear as her experience of 'the concentration of painting' is also that of a second birth: 'she had a few moments of nakedness when she seemed like an unborn soul, a soul reft of body, hesitating on some windy pinnacle and exposed without protection to the blasts of doubt' (*TTL* 151). The imagery of the *dithyramb* connected with Mrs McNab's and Mrs Bast's work is suggested in the 'dancing rhythmical movement' Lily attains as she paints, 'as if the pauses were one part of the rhythm and the strokes were another and all were related' (*TTL* 151). Casting out old, dead opinions, she engages in 'perpetual combat' and a struggle against 'those habitual currents' of opinion that belittle and deny women's artistic abilities. The newness and innovation of Lily's painting seems to be inspired by the riot and confusion of a new kind of disorderly fertility, of new connections and new seeds for the future that the work of Mrs McNab and Mrs Bast gives rise to. As Hyde says, the gift is 'a property

102 *Gifts, Markets and Economies of Desire*

that both perishes and increases' (182), and the embodiment of this is Mrs McNab with 'her dirge' 'twined about' with 'some incorrigible hope' (*TTL* 125). However, it is only when she joins with Mrs Bast to create a collective 'force working' that there is the impetus for action (*TTL* 132). That it is Lily who will perpetuate this disruption and continue to incorporate the different perspectives that working-class women suggest is confirmed by the fact that, although it is the two artists (Mr Carmichael and Lily) who arrive at the house first, it is the modernist artist Lily who is 'awake(ned)' at the end of 'Time Passes' (*TTL* 136). It is she who will be the bringer of new life, and she who is eager to work out what all the changes mean (despite a temptation to see the war as simply a dream)[25] and to relate what seems unrelated, to forge new connections through her art and gifts (*TTL* 139).

For the gift to flow through her creativity she must acquire self-confidence and express both sympathy for and receptivity to others (Hyde 182), yet not allow herself to be a sacrifice consumed, 'lavished and spent' like Mrs Ramsay (*TTL* 34). Lily has to wait for 'the frame of mind which nourishes the *hau*' (Hyde 149), for new bonds to form, and for new ways of relating to others to develop; she needs to be able to both connect to the past and to re-vision it. Importantly, she has to come to terms with her feelings for Mrs Ramsay – to feel gratitude and so identify with the spirit of the gift, and yet to allow it to 'increase' and to be more meaningful, transformed in this new context and at this different stage of the gift cycle. The work of 'The Lighthouse' is to bring this state about. It is concerned with the reforming and reformulation of the gift of love, creativity and erotic, fruitful increase. Although for Woolf art is a crucial aspect of human experience and relations, gifts and generosity work not only to nurture Lily's specific gift of creativity, but also to inspire new and renewed bonds and relationships.

'The Lighthouse' begins, as does 'The Window', with the proposed trip to the lighthouse and a contemplation of what to send as gifts. Nancy's anxiety and lack of knowledge about what to send makes a mockery of this kind of gift-giving role as a natural one for women. The hints of her possible homoerotic desires in the holograph draft add further to a sense of disruption of the heterosexual economy as she asks 'in *that* a queer half dazed half desperate way *she had* as if she were forcing herself to do what she had no sort of gift for doing' (*TTL Holograph* 238; italics indicate words crossed through). Lily is also faced with the assumptions Mr Ramsay makes about her emotional generosity, and she must resist the pressure of Mr Ramsay's 'insatiable hunger for sympathy' which she experiences as a 'flood' in which she is in danger of being swept away (*TTL* 144, 145). His overly dramatic expression of grief and loss is designed to manipulate Lily's response. The 'veil of crape' his sorrow casts over everything has the effect of deadening the vibrant colours (notably the green of 'the sunny grass') that Lily depends on for her creative inspiration (*TTL* 145). This reference to Victorian mourning rituals makes clear the values he insists on and which were the basis of the emotional and sexual economy of his marriage; it is this economy (summed up in Lily's earlier angry reflection that 'that man took' and Mrs Ramsay was 'forced to give', *TTL* 143) that Lily must resist. This resistance is complicated not only by her knowledge that in constantly '(g)iving, giving, giving' Mrs Ramsay exhausted herself, but also that in doing so Mrs Ramsay had confirmed a powerful expectation that women will always succumb to men's demands and give up all of themselves for very little, if anything, in return: she had 'left all this', meaning not only her family and home, but this legacy of women's self sacrifice (*TTL* 143).

The struggle not to acquiesce in this sexual economy, and the powerful effects of this economy on identity and a sense of self-worth, are seen in the conflict of feeling Lily experiences. In not giving in to Mr Ramsay's demands, or responding to what could be his sexual advances, Lily feels herself to be, and to be perceived as, desexed; partly self-critical and partly echoing the criticisms of others, she chastises herself, 'girding at herself bitterly', thinking herself 'not a woman, but a peevish, ill-tempered, dried-up old maid presumably' (*TTL* 145). However, being an 'old maid' is also a defence against the role assumed for her in the heterosexual economy. She can thus resist the obligation to give of herself, to make herself a (sexual) 'gift' to be consumed by men's demands. Ironically, this 'unwomanly' response is necessary precisely because she is a woman: that she needs to guard herself from being subsumed into this all-consuming sexual and emotional economy is suggested as she 'draws her *skirts* a little closer round her ankles' to prevent contact with Mr Ramsay's pools of self-pity (*TTL* 146, my emphasis). It is, then, Lily's gift as a woman modernist artist and her homoerotic desires that enable her to resist dominant social and sexual norms and the economic relations that underlie them.

Unwilling to concur with the false gift economy that *forces* women's generosity, Lily finds herself momentarily at an *impasse* with her painting ('she remained stuck', *TTL* 144), her creative gift seemingly temporarily blocked by her refusal to give. This *impasse* is soon broken, however, by Lily's spontaneously given compliment to Mr Ramsay about his boots. As with all gifts, this one is a risk – Lily risks an explosion of anger at the inappropriateness of this gift in the face of Mr Ramsay's grief and demands for sympathy. It is, however, a genuine gift ('of compliment and love'), generated from Lily's own artistic passion. It represents what Emerson would call 'a portion' of her own emotional and aesthetic values (Emerson 25). This point is evident in the fact that she appreciates the aesthetic 'sculptured' qualities of Mr Ramsay's boots, an appreciation true to her own preferences for well-made shoes (*TTL* 146).[26] Boots are also a topic of conversation at the dinner party, Mrs Ramsay noting husband's obsession with his boots as she reflects on Lily's 'flare' and independent spirit (*TTL* 96). Lily's gift unconsciously, perhaps, recalls the social bonds Mrs Ramsay created. In this new era, however, Lily's generosity can similarly include Mr Ramsay 'within the circle of

104 *Gifts, Markets and Economies of Desire*

life' but she will not allow his 'beak of brass' to suck her dry (*TTL* 35); she gives a gift but does not give herself as a gift.

Her compliment-gift marks a significant turning point, a dramatic shift in mood, allowing Mr Ramsay to move from egotistical self-pity to a sense of pride, human connection and even (briefly) genuine pleasure in his own generosity. Although still in a position of authority, in instructing Lily (at the age of forty-four) in how to properly tie a boot lace (!), he is no longer completely the domineering patriarch who only takes;[27] for a short while at least, he is a more benign paternal figure and source of a fatherly gift of instruction and advice. This creates a positive feeling, a utopian moment, represented with light comic undertones as 'a sunny island where peace dwelt, sanity reigned and the sun forever shone, the blessed island of good boots' (*TTL* 147). This action on his part causes Lily to again recall his past and present oppressiveness, and Mrs Ramsay's consequent exhaustion (and again to protectively 'pull her skirts about her'). It also causes her to reflect on Mr Ramsay's energy, and to admire 'that other phase' of mood 'which was new to her', a revelation of his vitality and potential for human connection that results from her compliment: 'there was that sudden revivification, that sudden flare . . . that sudden recovery of vitality and interest in ordinary human things' (*TTL* 149).[28] His gift of tying a knot that 'never came undone' is positive as a metaphor for human relations, but, like all gifts, also potentially threatens to enmesh, constrain and bind (*TTL* 147). As with his motivation for taking gifts to the lighthouse (to satisfy his own sense of ritual mourning, to fulfil Mrs Ramsay's conventional philanthropic duty, and to keep her genuine generosity in motion), his gift is also problematic because it grows out of his own pride and authority as well as out of his genuine desire to share his pleasure in good boots, satisfactorily tied.

Mr Ramsay's reciprocating gift also enables Lily to have a genuine feeling of sympathy for him ('she felt her eyes swell and tingle with tears', *TTL* 147), which is not the complete surrender to his needs that he earlier demanded, but is an appropriate feeling of compassion fitting the situation in which '(t)here was no helping Mr Ramsay on the journey he was going' (*TTL* 147). The action of knotting and unknotting, of metaphorically finding a way of sustaining connection without restriction, of keeping a connection with the past yet loosening its hold, and, for Lily, of giving gifts without *becoming* the gift, in many ways anticipates the emotional vacillation evident in the split action of this last section of the novel (most obviously seen in Cam's ambivalent feelings for her father and Lily's for Mrs Ramsay). Indeed, it would seem that the utopian moment of genuine gift exchange between Lily and Mr Ramsay soon vanishes, as 'he no longer needed' her sympathy and, assuming the role of gift-giver as he dispenses the gifts to be taken to the lighthouse to Cam and James, with 'the appearance of a leader making ready for an expedition' he marches off to the boat 'with his firm military tread', the image of the stoic hero he has always assumed for himself (*TTL* 148).

A Gift of Vision 105

The arrival of Cam and James interrupts Lily's opportunity to give sympathy to Mr Ramsay (*TTL* 140). Because the gift must move, this hiatus is painful: 'Her sympathy seemed to fly back in her face, like a bramble sprung' (*TTL* 149). It creates a sense of suspension – a feeling of 'emptiness' that seems to echo her blank canvas (*TTL* 150) – though, equally, it creates the necessary time and space (the 'distance' that Lily comes to recognise as crucial) in which she can attain the frame of mind necessary to create and to nourish the *hau* of the life-bringing and life-sustaining gifts of Mrs Ramsay and Mrs McNab. Lily's vacillation of emotion as she struggles to find inspiration is connected to the shifts in emotion that occur on the journey to the lighthouse. These are closely bound up with the ongoing circulation of gifts and related in part through knotting images. As they journey to the lighthouse, Cam resolves to take no pleasure in the expedition, partly because she resents her forced participation in gift-giving that is not motivated by generosity – 'those rites [Mr Ramsay] went through for his own pleasure in memory of dead people' (*TTL* 157) – but also to resist, like Lily, the pressure on her as a woman to yield to the power and influence her father has over her. Recognising that James is in many ways similar to his father, Cam steers a course between staying loyal to James and their pact to fight their father's tyranny together, and expressing her sense of gratitude and love, her compromise being in silently 'passing on to her father . . . a private token of the love she felt for him' (*TTL* 161).

In the relationship between James and his father there does seem to be a significant change brought about by Mr Ramsay's giving a compliment to his son, a gift echoing Lily's compliment to Mr Ramsay and suggesting that he has been positively affected by it. For most of the journey, James' bitterness and fear of his father's impatience and criticism leave him feeling bound to the tiller by a metaphorical rope 'knotted' by his father, for which the 'only escape' he can imagine recalls the violent Oedipal urges of his childhood: 'taking a knife and plunging it . . . ' (*TTL* 178). However, for what may be the first time, his father compliments him, praising his steering (*TTL* 196), and for a short while at least this gift unknots the fraught relationship between them. This compliment is genuine and comes from his sense of pleasure and pride in his son; however, this too is a specifically masculine gift (he gives the compliment 'triumphantly') and as such it is somehow contained and limited in its effects as it also lays claim to James's success (*TTL* 196). A cynical reading might consider this as a manipulative strategy on Mr Ramsay's part to ensure all of his needs are met, since the effect of this gift is to inspire the wish in James and Cam to give him anything he asks for in return (*TTL* 197). However, when they land it would seem that Mr Ramsay's gift-giving has had a life-enhancing effect and, 'as if he were leaping into space . . . he sprang, lightly like a young man, holding his parcel, on to the rock' (*TTL* 197) to deliver his gifts with energy and imbued with the temporary harmony created on the boat.

106 *Gifts, Markets and Economies of Desire*

Watching the boat from the shore, Lily experiences a feeling of 'untying the knot in her imagination', which suggests the necessary process of unknotting her feelings about the past, specifically her mixed and complicated feelings about Mrs Ramsay (*TTL* 150). Her ungiven gift to Mr Ramsay ensures, through her attention to both her painting and to Mr Ramsay as he makes the journey to the lighthouse, that her new artistic gift retains an all-important connection with the boat, its passengers and its purpose. This connects with her own more profound and complex artistic, emotional and erotic experience in which her newly formed creative gifts reach fruition. At the point at which the boat lands, Lily realises that the gift of sympathy she has been wanting to give to Mr Ramsay 'she had given him at last' (*TTL* 197). It would seem that she has passed onto him the ability to give, to be revitalised by the gift, and to recognise the importance of Mrs Ramsay's generosity and charity, something Lily herself has re-evaluated by this point as being in excess of her middle-class role, and as being an instinct, a natural gift to give and care (*TTL* 186–7).

The completion of this journey closes the circle of this narrative: the gift-giving proposed at the beginning is completed and the trip to the lighthouse finally made – '"It is finished."' says Lily (*TTL* 197). In being able to give her gift of sympathy, Lily is able to complete her painting with an assured brush stroke. The process of reaching this point, of encapsulating great emotional complexity and newness of vision, and, indeed, of sustaining the energy and vitality of her picture, is a painful and convoluted process for her. Lily has struggled to come to terms with Mrs Ramsay's death, to re-evaluate Mrs Ramsay's gifts and values, and to realise what has and what has not been lost. Finally, Lily is able to combine the creative fecundity she inherits from Mrs Ramsay with the vitality, energy and resilience of Mrs McNab.

Lily sees Mrs Ramsay as a key to her composition, and as an organising principle. What Lily feels as Mrs Ramsay's ability to capture a moment, moments which 'stayed in the mind almost like a work of art' (*TTL* 153), is paralleled with Lily's composing shape out of chaos and making something permanent with her art (*TTL* 154). However, such moments, like art itself, have a life of their own and are central to life, as a marginal note in the holograph draft emphasises, 'all things at once came together – like an organic compound' (*TTL Holograph* 294). Mrs Ramsay's gifts are 'the agents of that organic cohesion we perceive as liveliness', which 'ensure(s) the fertility of the imagination' (Hyde 150, 148). As Lily paints she feels Mrs Ramsay's presence, 'she seemed to be sitting beside Mrs Ramsay on the beach', the moment of silence between them being 'extraordinarily fertile' (*TTL* 163). However, Lily's profound sense of loss is experienced as something intense and bodily, which suggests the incorporation of Mrs McNab's bodily vitality. Although Lily distances herself from passionate love, likened to 'a fire sent up in token of some celebration by savages on a distant beach', it is clear that she realises the power of such gifts and the fierce emotion and desire

A Gift of Vision 107

they represent, 'emotions of the body ... one's body's feeling, not one's mind' (*TTL* 169). In the holograph draft, Lily has a 'wild idea that if she & Mr Carmichael made some violent display', a 'savage' offering of a gift to the gods, that 'Mrs Ramsay would come back' (*TTL Holograph* 303).[29]

Lily's painting is, finally, not only a tribute to Mrs Ramsay, but a visible representation of what Lily has lost and gained. Her painting is a kind of death-gift, a threshold gift and a gift of passage that is a means of 'mak(ing) visible the giving up we do invisibly' (Hyde 41, 44). It is not just compensation for what is lost, but a guide for the future. Her painting is simultaneously a defiance of Mrs Ramsay's conservatism and an expression of love for her generosity and creativity. Mrs Ramsay is inscribed there as 'an odd-shaped triangular shadow' (*TTL* 191) – a three-sided shape – in what could be read as a representation of the three sources of creativity in this novel (herself, Mrs McNab and Lily). Her painting represents a precarious balance for Lily, to sustain the generosity and life-giving force of her creative gift and, without exhausting the gift, to balance on the razor edge without cutting through the thread of life. Importantly, she completes this representation of Mrs Ramsay with a vivid image of Mrs Ramsay's presence as a creative force, literally knitting her gift of the stocking in the past, but seemingly part of the present too: 'There she sat' – 'part of her perfect goodness to Lily' (*TTL* 192). The gift she is making for the working-class boy is not simply absorbed into a highbrow art form and cut off from the working-class women who have injected so much life and energy into transforming the social context and disturbing artistic production and vision that allows such art to flourish. Lily has a depropriative attitude to her finished painting, and she imagines it may even be hung in an attic, traditionally the servant's quarters (*TTL* 170). This possibility in part speaks of Lily's uncertainty about the value of her art being recognised, but also suggests a new, working-class audience for such art which, more open to interpretation and emerging from the flux and change of a society in transition, may have a different appeal and meaning for a greater diversity of viewers.

At the end of *To the Lighthouse*, the reader has a sense of stepping out into a void, but also of being poised on a threshold moment of possibility. In terms of the gift economy, this is the effect of the bestowal of a gift. As Hyde points out, 'Bestowal creates that empty place into which new energy may flow' (146), energy that fuels creativity and sustains vitality. The parallels between Lily and Woolf, as they both complete their visions simultaneously and offer their work to the world with some trepidation about how this vision-gift will be received,[30] invite a consideration of the effect of the lacuna created at end of the novel for Woolf herself. Indeed, after the completion of her novel, Woolf records in her diary feeling 'virgin, passive, blank of ideas' (*D3* 131). Yet once she is 'struck' by the idea of writing 'a Defoe narrative for fun', she is flooded with inspiration, conceiving 'a whole fantasy to be called "The Jessamy Brides"' and an original plan 'Suddenly between twelve & one'

108 *Gifts, Markets and Economies of Desire*

(*D3* 131). This inspiration, 'the odd hurried unexpected way in which these things suddenly create themselves', recalls for her the similar experiences of inventing *Jacob's Room* and *To the Lighthouse* (*D3* 131–2). By October 1926 the force of this inspiration leaves her 'in short in the thick of the greatest rapture known to [her]' (*D3* 161), and feeling 'happier than [she had] for months . . . [as she] abandon(s) herself to the pure delight of this farce' (*D3* 162).[31] Although Woolf's ideas for her 'new book', which develops into *Orlando*, come several months later,[32] her annoyance at this earlier point of inspiration about not hearing from Vita, who, like the ladies she imagines with 'Constantinople in view', is far away in the East, may suggest that Vita is at the heart of Woolf's 'escapade' even at this initial stage (*D3* 131, 130). Indeed, Vita's absence is another lacuna in Woolf's life, a gap filled by the receipt on the day after this diary entry of two letters from her, 'full as nuts; delicious; milky, meaty, satisfying every desire of my soul, except darling, for a complete lack of endearments' (*L3* 346).

Many critics have written in detail about the importance of Woolf's relationship with Vita Sackville-West and of the mutual benefit both experienced in personal, erotic and professional ways. Of course, this relationship has a special significance in the creation of *Orlando*, famously summed up by Nigel Nicholson as the 'longest and most charming love-letter in literature' (186), and crucially for an exploration of ideas of about gifts and gift-economies. Possibly more than in any of Woolf's relationships, the exchange of gifts between her and Sackville-West is of crucial importance in both initiating and sustaining their intimacy and connection, and indeed, in their development as writers and their productivity in the literary marketplace.[33] As ever with Woolf, however, this relationship, the gift economy that operates so centrally in it, and the market economy are in some ways interconnected: the Hogarth Press published fourteen of Sackville-West's books between 1924 and 1938[34] but ceased to publish her books after 1938 when John Lehman bought Virginia Woolf's share of the business (Lee, 1996, 705).[35] The first of Sackville-West's books that the Hogarth Press published was *Seducers in Ecuador* (1924), a book dedicated to Woolf in what Sproles has termed a 'message of seduction' (64).[36]

Initially knowing each other through their published work, their ongoing admiration, criticism and support for each other's writing and the professional relationship between them ensured that creative gifts, writing and gifts of books were crucial to their relationship. In particular, Sackville-West's first gift to Woolf (though at Woolf's request) of her biography of her family and their estate, *Knole and the Sackvilles* (1922), her long poem *The Land*, and her semi-autobiographical novel *Challenge* relating her affair with Violet Trefusis (which Woolf she tells Vita she is reading in June 1927 [*L3* 391]), all play their part in the inspiration of and the creative production of *Orlando*.[37] The books given as gifts between them can be seen to have had a mutually sustaining effect on both writers, inspiring their creativity and keeping their

A Gift of Vision 109

literal and artistic gifts in motion.[38] As she writes to Vita, in response to a letter from her in Teheran when working on *To the Lighthouse*, 'I make every fragment you tell me bloom and blossom in my mind' (*L3* 232). Her longing and sense of missing Vita here, combined with her imaginary powers, suggest that her creativity is inspired by her desire.

Woolf's creative gift in writing *Orlando* and the literal gift of the manuscript of the novel given to Sackville-West can be seen as return gifts;[39] however, this also epitomises some of the complexities, ambiguities and power play that gifts can entail. *Orlando* has been seen simultaneously as a sign of Woolf's love and desire for Sackville-West and as a punishment for her infidelity with Mary Campbell (as Suzanne Raitt [1993] and Anna Snaith [2000a] have argued).[40] Sherron E. Knopp sees it otherwise, as 'a way to heighten intimacy – not a substitute for physical lovemaking but an extension of it' (27), and Sproles sees it as 'a multiple creation as it recoups Knole for Sackville-West and Sackville-West for Woolf' (72). Sackville-West's 'thank you' letter suggests both her gratitude and a sense of entrapment. She tells Woolf that she feels like 'one of the those wax figures in a shop window, on which you have hung a robe stitched with jewels',[41] but that she also experiences the richness of *Orlando* as a sensual, overwhelming pleasure, like 'being alone in a dark room with a treasure chest full of rubies and nuggets and brocades' (Sackville-West, 1992, 305).

Orlando is also possibly Woolf's most ambiguous gift because it also became her most lucrative novel and ensured her commercial success.[42] Woolf enjoyed the financial freedoms this 'gift' brought, as she notes in her diary, 'For the first time since I married 1912–1928 – 16 years – I have been spending money' (*D3* 212). Although her 'spending muscle does not work naturally yet', spending money freely 'lubricates' her soul and stimulates her creativity (*D3* 212). Ironically, her gift to her Sapphic lover, which itself grows out of the gift economy established between Woolf and Sackville-West, generates more profit than any of her other texts, bringing Woolf more consumer pleasure than she has experienced throughout her marriage. Woolf's anxiety about the commercial success of her work, especially after her first experience of such success with *To the Lighthouse*, leads her to draw a distinction between making money in the marketplace and her own profits, which she metaphorically and literally turns into gifts.[43] She is also keen to emphasise the importance of the process of creativity itself rather than the results in the literary marketplace. In her diary she notes the way that the profits from *Orlando* also enable her to 'keep [her] brain on the boil', 'to spend freely, & then write' (*D3* 212); that what remains 'the only exciting life is the imaginary one' (*D3* 181); and, as she reflects on *Orlando*, that 'it's the writing, not the being read that excites [her]' (*D3* 200).

During this period, Woolf was also involved with various schemes designed as a kind of modernist patronage to support writers, and especially poets.[44] Dorothy Wellesley began to act as sponsor and editor of the Hogarth

110   *Gifts, Markets and Economies of Desire*

Living Poets, set up 'to edit a series of unsaleable poetry' (*D3* 157) and the Eliot Fellowship Fund was being dissolved (though it was not finally wound up until early in 1928). What these schemes acknowledge is that modernist writing, and poetry in particular, is not sufficiently financially viable to support those without inheritance or investments; but also that the unsaleable nature of the poetry is a sign of its value, originality and innovation. It is too esoteric for the easy consumption required by the market and thus is in need of protection. As Hyde notes, a patron enters the market, makes wealth and 'turns that wealth into a gift to feed the gifted' (275).

It is little wonder in this context, in which Woolf's contradictory concerns about money, gifts, fame, and the vicissitudes of the market are so mixed, that *Orlando* is so overtly concerned with literature's relationship to monetary economies, the literary market, patronage and other gift economies. Like *A Room of One's Own* that was shortly to follow, it foregrounds issues to do with the position of art in relation to money and to financial and literary inheritance. It also seems crucially concerned with the wider question of how an artist's engagement with the market has an impact on both their identity and on the creative process. Woolf's own success with *To the Lighthouse* aroused a sense of danger about becoming 'almost an established figure' and of being taken for granted 'as a writer' (*D3* 137). She takes great pleasure in the unpredictable 'wildness' of *Orlando* and presumably in defying her readers' and critics' expectations in many ways. However, she was also cognisant of the need to include her readers in the 'joke' of her novel and to protect her sales.[45] The novel's ironic preface seeks to disarm objections to and criticisms of *Orlando* and Orlando, and creates a sense of the kind of reader who will be able not only to buy the book, but also to appreciate the subtleties of Woolf's experiment.[46] She thanks her literary ancestors, friends and family (who are largely the secure 'coterie' readership of Bloomsbury), who are sure to appreciate it (if critically), for the advice and help they have given her, though this return gift of thanks is threaded through with the language of the market – of debt, profit and value. She also thanks a nameless 'gentleman in America' for 'generously and gratuitously' correcting the inaccuracies in her other works, thus making clear one of the problems with such gifts, especially unwanted acts of generosity when the motivation is far from disinterested.

Among the many other debates the novel stages in relation to gender, sexuality, creativity and literary production, the complex interaction of monetary and gift economies is significant in the historical transition from art funded by patronage to the development of the literary marketplace that is the backdrop to Orlando's experiences as a male and female writer. Nick Greene is the subversive satirist of the novel's Elizabethan period and, scathing of Orlando's poetry, he reneges on his role as beneficiary by insulting his patron. By the mid-nineteenth century, Nick Greene has been knighted and, as a professor and the most influential critic of the Victorian age, he is the powerful voice of the establishment (though still a recipient of

A Gift of Vision 111

Orlando's patronage [*O* 174]). However, making the same complaint as three hundred years previously, that 'all our young writers are in the pay of the booksellers' (*O* 55, 174), he snaps up Orlando's poem for the literary market, seeing it as simply traditional.[47] Orlando remarks on the greyness of his clothes and that his 'restless, uneasy vivacity had gone' (*O* 175); he is 'so neat, so portly, so prosperous', 'grown plump' and 'grown sleek' (*O* 173, 175). She is confused by the machinery and strategies of the literary marketplace (the idea of publication and promotion of her poems, 'a little puff of her own poems' [*O* 176], and by the royalties she would earn), but realises that the literary authors who are now promoted by powerful figures like Nick Greene are respectable and by conventional with all the energy and risky creativity of their art extinguished by the market power of reviewers.[48]

Orlando's idealised expectations of art and creativity as vivid, forceful and untamed, as 'something as wild as the wind, hot as fire, swift as lightening; something errant, incalculable, abrupt' (*O* 175), are profoundly disappointed. Her own poem does have this energy and vitality and she feels it is almost a separate being, like a child nurtured and secured next to Orlando's heart: 'The manuscript which reposed above her heart began shuffling and beating as if it were a living thing' (*O* 170).[49] At the point of Orlando's profound disappointment with Nick Greene and the state of the literary world, her poem breaks free, seemingly to counter '(t)he violence of her disillusionment' (*O* 175). However, oblivious to the subversiveness of Orlando's poem (for instance, the homoerotic 'contraband' of the 'Egyptian girls' that Orlando riskily smuggles in past the censorship of the Victorian spirit of the age),[50] Nick Greene folds and flattens her 'blood-stained' manuscript so that it fits neatly into his pocket and does not interfere with the line of his coat; nor, this suggests, does it disturb the conventionality of his reputation as a professional literary figure (*O* 166, 176). With this action, Orlando's poem is already on the way to becoming the commodity from which she later feels so distanced.

Orlando's instinct to not entirely 'trust [Nick Greene's] good nature' proves accurate. The implication is that he will sanitise and conventionalise Orlando's poem; that he will make it conform through the process of marketing, promotion and reviewing is confirmed as Orlando ventures once again into commodity-filled London (*O* 176). Feeling bereft of her manuscript, and having telegraphed Shelmardine, she turns 'to beguile herself' in the first bookshop she has ever seen (*O* 177). The sight of 'innumerable little volumes, bright, identical, ephemeral, for they seemed bound in cardboard and printed on tissue paper' confirms what her unique poem, created over three hundred years, and with a life of its own, will become (*O* 177). As she reads Nick Greene's criticisms and reviews, she weeps at their pervasive message of an obliteration of individuality and autonomous expression, and concludes that 'one must never, never say what one thought . . . one must

112 *Gifts, Markets and Economies of Desire*

always, always write like somebody else' (*O* 178–9). This is accompanied by the knowledge, gleaned from reading half a dozen of the hundreds of books she has ordered, that the age of patronage is dead and that it is 'monstrously difficult' for realist fiction to make life into literature (*O* 178). However, before Orlando's conclusion drawn from her reading can be revealed, she too conforms to social expectations as she fulfils the procreative role, and the narrative leaps to the Edwardian period and then to 'the present moment' (*O* 185, 186).

Unanchored from the process of creating 'The Oak Tree', Orlando experiences a sense of fragmentation and dislocation which begins significantly in a department store – a space of fantasy and self-creation where capitalist consumerism promises that desires of all kinds (even those, Felski argues, 'in defiance of traditional patriarchal prohibitions', 90) can be realised and satisfied by the purchase of commodities. It is a space that 'offered a new and intoxicating public space beyond the walls of the familial home' (Felski 90), and especially 'opened up for women a range of new opportunities and pleasures – for independence, fantasy, unsupervised social encounters, even transgressions' (Nava 53). However, Orlando is not seduced by the array of commodities, and her desires are not even especially stirred by a chance glimpse of Sasha, Orlando's first love. Orlando experiences again a youthful longing for her, yet, with Sasha grown fat and lethargic, she is simultaneously repulsed by her. Although time is money in a capitalist mode of production, Orlando's perception and consciousness is seemingly unaffected by this all-pervasive ethos. Even in a department store, emotion, memory and Orlando's experiences as an artist slip beyond such dictums and calculations as past and present emotions and desires merge and diverge. Far more powerful for Orlando than the possibilities that capitalist commodity culture has to offer is the 'contact with any of the arts', which can collapse the certainties of time and place with such immense effects (*O* 191). Orlando's 'love of poetry' makes the capitalist spectacle pale into insignificance, causing her to lose her shopping list and to leave the shop, most of her purchases unmade.

As she speeds through the city, the process of the fragmentation of her identity accelerates: 'body and mind were like scraps of torn paper tumbling from a sack' and she becomes 'a person entirely dissembled' (*O* 192). This is the effect of the 'magic' of modern technology, but it also speaks of the artist's disorientating experience on the modern market. It would seem that the scraps of paper and the multiple selves that compose Orlando (and us all) are not problematic until market forces attempt to shape and control such diversity and complexity. The scraps of paper that Orlando is likened to are the scraps of paper on which her poem has been composed over the centuries; her flux of desires and vacillations of identity have all played their part in the creation of her poem. She reflects lyrically and profoundly on her experience of the joy of creativity, which is for her an experience of generous exchange: 'Was not writing poetry a secret transaction, a voice answering a voice', her (suggestively homoerotic) interaction with the nature that inspires her imagination being 'like the intercourse of lovers' (*O* 203). However, her poem has been turned into a commodity, 'a little square book bound in red cloth', from which she is distanced, as the description of the 'copy of the first edition, signed by author and artist' reveals (202); fame and success on the literary market have reinvented her as an author she does not recognise as herself. She had planned to bury this copy of her poems in the roots of the oak tree as a return gift and symbol of her thanks to the main source of her inspiration, nature itself. However, she realises that this would be a ridiculous gesture, distanced as she is from this commodity and the emptiness of the fame and praise it has attracted. These issues of the artist's experience are specifically gendered: Orlando is dismissive of her prize, 'A porpoise in a fishmonger's shop attracted far more attention than a lady who had won a prize'; Orlando's biographer is annoyed at the undermining of what should have been the peak of her achievement (as it would be for a male subject) and the glorious point of closure to his narrative (*O* 195); and her male literary ancestors are only impressed by the monetary value of her prize (*O* 197).

However, in keeping with the acceptance of the multiplicity, instability and ambiguity of identity that this novel assumes (that 'Nothing is any longer one thing', *O* 190), Orlando's gender identity and her identity as a woman artist are profoundly problematic: 'when we write of a woman everything is out of place' (*O* 195). Whereas the market seeks to 'package' the artist as a knowable entity, to promote and publicise in accordance with commodity trends and gender norms, and, being end-orientated in its desires, in the completion of a sale transaction to increase profit and cultural property, what *Orlando* makes clear is the limitation and aridity of such an approach to art and creativity. The artist, although framed and constituted as an object in the literary market, remains a complex being and part of several interrelated economies (of desire and creativity) and functions in a liminal space between the market and the gift economy, a space of flux and uncertainty which is inimical to the calculation and equilibrium of capitalist exchange.

As Orlando's fragmented selves itemise the various facets of her character, her being 'Generous' is claimed not to 'count' (*O* 194). Yet what remains most central and consistent throughout the novel is the connection between gifts, desire and creativity. Although Orlando as a man is generous as a patron, he is frustrated and limited by his relationship to the literary tradition (and by his heterosexuality). As Lawrence also argues, it is his 'meditation on the vexed relation between sexuality and poetry' that leads to his decision to leave England (Lawrence 264). He seeks to express his love for Sasha but, much as the English language and its conventional figurations are inadequate to the task, so too are the cultural imperatives to acquire and possess, imperatives that are also gendered so that Orlando as a European man perceives Sasha as a foreign other to tame, and as 'his jewel' to possess (*O* 30–1). It is once Orlando is dispossessed (temporarily at least) of property

114 *Gifts, Markets and Economies of Desire*

and of a privileged (male) relationship to the literary tradition that her creativity is revitalised.[51] Her poem grows in diversity and excess when, as a woman, Orlando participates in a more mutual gift economy and in a more fluid economy of desire, premised on multiplicity and flux. Refusing to be limited by the gender codes and conventions that would constrain her as a woman and artist, Orlando 'adopts and discards at will' the various costumes (and the roles and expectations they encode) placed on her, 'exploiting society as a means to the multiplication of desire instead of seeing society as a block to desire' (Olin-Hitt 488).

Adopting the clothing of a young gallant, for instance, Orlando pursues her desire for women and the company of women (bored as she is with the egotistical and misogynistic company of great eighteenth-century 'wits') and picks up a prostitute in Leicester Square. Briefly 'capitalising' on the capitalist exchange expected in this situation (as Woolf's euphemistic description makes clear, Nell is 'of the tribe which nightly burnishes their wares and sets them in order on the common counter to wait the highest bidder', *O* 135), Orlando plays her role and is aware, from her own experience as a woman, of the ways in which Nell flatters her customer's assumed masculinity. Immediately that Orlando reveals herself to be a woman, such gendered artifices are abandoned and more a more open and mutual exchange of conversation begins, as Nell, Kitty and Rose welcome her into the 'society of their own' and tell their own autobiographical tales (of their illegitimacy) and adventures. Although she derived some pleasure in the exchange of banknotes and wine for dedications and instruction from the male writers for whom she is patron, their lack of kindness, generosity and charity, along with the dangers of offending their massive egos, lead Orlando to seek an alternative sphere for her generosity. Continuing to act as 'patron of the arts,' as she 'furnish(es) generously' the punchbowl for the prostitutes (*O* 136), Orlando creates a 'gift-sphere' (Hyde 275) in which women, herself included, can tell many 'fine tales' and 'amusing observations' (*O* 136, 137). These may be subversive stories at the expense of the men who, like the customer who is quickly served and dismissed, consider women to exist only in relation to men and to have no desires (or interests) of their own. These misogynistic and heterosexist views, here clearly linked to the control men assume over money and (women's) desires, and over notions of taste and hierarchies of value, are ridiculed but also subtly undermined. Another male authority suggests that women only 'scratch' when men are not present, yet Orlando had indeed 'scratched out twenty-six volumes' by the late seventeenth century (*O* 109) and, inspired by her love and homoerotic attraction for women, continues to write such love and eroticism into her poem.

However, it is as a woman artist, an identity that for her is not bound by any reductive essentialism, that Orlando has had the most meaningful experiences; her eroticism and creativity are closely aligned. Realising that women write 'not with the fingers, but with the whole person', Orlando acknowledges

A Gift of Vision 115

both the multiple sites of women's erotic pleasures and creative impulses, and suggests the non-linear, plural and expansive forms of expression this might take – the writing of excess, *jouissance* and generosity ('writing the body') that we see throughout *Orlando* itself. The playful, teasing, exuberant and subversive qualities of Woolf's writing in this novel, its 'shimmer of reality', seductiveness, ambiguity and humour, are richly suggestive and offer up a multiplicity of potential meanings. Woolf's ideal reader, a 'fellow worker and accomplice', will need to respond with generosity and openness to get 'the fullest value' from reading this text (*CD* 60). Conceived in part as a gift, however ambivalent and complexly motivated, it proved successful as both gift and commodity, winning Sackville-West's praise and gratitude, as well as earning Woolf the most money she had earned from a single work to date.[52] However, *Orlando* itself foregrounds the dangers of commodification (of both books and their authors). Part of its complex subversion of dominant social and sexual institutions, its parody of norms of gender and sexuality, and its critique of the power dynamics of the literary tradition is a privileging of the gift economy and homoerotic desires as the source of inspiration, creativity and generosity of spirit.

By the time Woolf came to write *Between the Acts* (between 1938 and 1941) the social, political, economic and literary landscape had shifted radically, and her novel records the period of time in which the effects of the rise of fascism in Europe and the potential future danger of war were beginning to be registered in Britain. Although in the early 1930s Woolf sought a position of immunity, by the mid- to late 1930s she had realised that this position was impossible to sustain, a realisation brought to a head when the pacifist position held by some members of the Labour Party was 'brutally overridden' at the 1935 party conference over the issue of pacifism (Lee, 1996, 635, 688). Zwerdling notes, 'the contemplative neutrality of the observer-artist came to be seen as a luxury of another era, no longer honourable in a world on the brink of disaster' (267). The pacifist position she assumed put her at odds with most of her friends and family, who felt that it was necessary to re-arm and to fight Hitler, and that pacifism was irresponsible (Lee, 1996, 690). Woolf battled to keep depression at bay as she simultaneously dealt with the onset of war, and she felt an increasing sense of isolation in her liberal pacifist views. As a writer in an increasingly politicised literary context, she wrote also against the 'new esthetic-political style – activist, partisan, and aggressive' (Zwerdling 268) that emerged in the mid-1930s. Her sense of isolation was also intensified by the personal criticism she received, for example from the Leavises, Roy Campbell and Wyndham Lewis (Lee, 1996, 692, 622). Despite the phenomenal bestseller success of *The Years*, by 1940 she records in her diary that she has 'no public to echo back' (*D5* 304), and the deaths of close friends and family were a significant contribution to this feeling.[53]

Leaska discusses Woolf's anxiety about her loss of audience, suggesting that Bart Oliver's comment in *Between the Acts* that the most important role

116   *Gifts, Markets and Economies of Desire*

is to be the audience 'carries far greater poignancy that we may realize, for one of the most terrifying effects of World War II on V.W. was that she felt she no longer had an audience', and this was what 'she increasingly needed when self-doubt and some means of self-justification began to preoccupy her' (1983, 209). In her essays, Woolf expresses her concerns about the response of her readers and about art being discarded in wartime (see Chapter 1 for a discussion of 'Why Art Today Follows Politics' as an example of this). For her, writing and its reception constituted her identity. As she remarks in her diary in 1933, 'I thought . . . something very profound about the synthesis of my being: how only writing composes it: how nothing makes a whole unless I am writing' (*D*4 161). As always, Woolf's earnings were an indication to her of her success. As her income from her books decreased between 1937 and 1939, the 'disproportionate significance' she gave to earning money corresponded to her need to confirm her identity as a writer (Leaska 461). Woolf's doubts about her own creative gifts in this politically and personally fraught period seem to underpin the questions and anxieties that *Between the Acts* (literally) stages about the purpose and efficacy of art for a society on the brink of war.

Several critics have noted that in this novel Woolf is most 'responsive to contemporary events' (Zwerdling 302). Julie Abraham notes that the novel 'very much reflects the present danger of its own historical moment, when the problem seemed so obviously to have more than literary dimensions and consequences, and to require more than literary solutions' (Abraham 161). Woolf includes real facts from the time in which the novel is set: notably, reference to a newspaper report of the rape of a young girl by a group of guardsmen, mention of the French prime minister, Edouard Daladier's economic decisions, and the gossip about royalty circulating at the time. These facts serve to draw attention to the dominant institutions, values and preoccupations that lead to war.[54] Gillian Beer also suggests that in including these details, 'the novel invokes the larger ordinary community of which [Woolf's contemporary] reader is a part and makes of that stuff the will to survive' (Beer, 1992, xiii). These facts also make a powerful connection between the fictional lives Woolf represents and the real lived experience of her readers; the themes played out in her novel have a direct link to experience and aim to ensure that the role of fiction, and more generally art and the artist, is perceived as important at this time of crisis. At a personal and a political level, Woolf saw it as imperative that bonds and connections be sustained and that a range of interpretations are kept in play as a counter to the tyrannical forces driving Europe to war.

This eclectic, diverse, playful, richly allusive and at times elusive novel also evokes the sense of a shared culture and invites its readers (and its internal audience) to participate in what Mauss calls 'the common store of wealth', by which he means material wealth and cultural richness, a wealth to be shared equally as a basis for happiness and peace (83). A long-term goal for Woolf was to enable everyone, regardless of their class or gender, to access the literary tradition and to experience reading and interpretation as an active, participatory and creative process. The critical work ('Reading at Random' or 'Turning the Page') that she began gathering materials for and writing as she wrote *Between the Acts* was also engaged with the opening up of the history of English literature in a similar way to the *Common Readers* (Silver 357). In her novel, Woolf incorporates a wide-ranging reference to the English literary tradition and so 'unskeining' it and 'set(ting) it unhierarchically among all the goings on of human behaviour' (Beer, 1992, xx). In fact, she sets it loose to interact with the fragments of Ancient Greek drama, popular culture, music hall tunes, nursery rhymes, fictional guidebooks and geological history, and even with the sounds of nature she includes to create a wildly hybrid form, the various elements of which interact productively and resonate across a wide range of experience. The novel facilitates the sharing in the common store of literary wealth, aiming to enable as many readers as possible to engage with and to be part of the diverse community of readers of and in this text. In the novel, the words of this rich cultural heritage become a social tool, helping to create a sense of community and social bonds as characters quote, misquote and ask for help in remembering fragments of poetry, drama, fiction. Kime Scott suggests that *Between the Acts* is characterised by '(a) restless shifting of positions and a sifting through cultural fragments' (1995, 53). As echoes of Eliot's *The Waste Land* throughout the novel may imply, these are indeed the fragments shored up against our ruin in war and the madness of modern life. Cut loose from history and hierarchy, and frequently from their authors, these fragments are also the creative materials out of which new ideas and connections can be made, resisting authoritative interpretations and limited meanings, and giving access to the 'creative feelings' Woolf felt to be so vital to counter war.

The women artists in this novel, Isa and Miss La Trobe, in different ways suggest the regenerative potential of art in the fostering of a sense of community and connection in the face of social fragmentation, political crisis and the threat of war as they act as focal points for this tradition. As Kime Scott notes, Isa 'is assigned the preponderance of the "PH Poetry" [the poetry Woolf wrote and gathered in preparation for this novel] so important in the consistency of the novel' (62). However, although Miss La Trobe draws on this rich tradition in the creation of her pageant to share with her audience, Isa's poetry is only shared with the external reader because she keeps her poems, and the illicit desires they encode, secret. Her creativity is bound, as she is herself, by the economic structures of heterosexual marriage: she records her poems in a book bound like an account book, just as she is also bound to 'her husband, the stockbroker', a description that is repeated throughout the novel (*BTA* 6).

Woolf's essay 'Thoughts on Peace in an Air Raid' (1940) is one that has significant resonance with some of the concerns about the role and power of art

118 *Gifts, Markets and Economies of Desire*

and the artist in the period of crisis explored in *Between the Acts*. In this essay, Woolf proactively seeks a way to counter the education and upbringing of young men which encourages aggression and a desire (felt as an instinct) to be heroic. Woolf's representation of Giles reveals how deeply ingrained and constantly reinforced is the version of masculinity that is militant, repressive and which fuels prejudice and intolerance – all of which constitute the 'subconscious Hitlerism' that predispose men to go to war.[55] It also results in Giles's intense fears about being unmanly – expressed in his fierce denial of being a coward, and in his rejection of what he perceives as effeminate or trivial (as seen in his response to the 'artistic' and effeminate William Dodge and the pageant itself, which he rejects as 'Tosh' [*BTA* 104]). These fears give rise to violent outbursts but also a bitter denial of his desires (for Isa and the land, *BTA* 30–1, 68), forced, as he feels he is, to comply with the economic expectations placed on him as a man to earn money. His job as a stockbroker in the City serves to highlight the connections between the repressive militaristic masculine identity he adheres to and the power of the capitalist economy.

In 'Thoughts on Peace in an Air Raid', Woolf asserts that 'we can fight(ing) for freedom . . . with the mind', with women's 'idea-making' and 'thinking against the current' countering the 'sterile, unfertile' 'emotion of fear and hate' produced in and by war with 'access to creative feelings' (*CD* 168). Woolf's novel as a whole, and in particular her focus on Miss La Trobe, reveals the extent of the struggle faced by those who seek to provide weapons of the mind to replace the gun, and the risk women take, 'perhaps . . . abuse, perhaps . . . contempt' (*CD* 169), to speak out against their own and men's enslavement in dominant values and beliefs, in order to strengthen the will to peace. However, although the novel sheds a stark and critical light on this complex, tense and volatile period of history, Woolf's sense of art as a regenerative gift leads her to write a novel that also sparkles with comedy and playfulness, engaging the reader imaginatively and creatively in the pleasure of her text. The enjoyment of language is conveyed here in the sometimes excessive play on and with words (in the use of imagery, metaphor, cliché, incongruity, puns and repetitions) and with the auditory qualities of language (rhyme, alliteration, assonance and onomatopoeia).[56] In the face of increasingly limited ways of making sense of the world, Woolf insists on generosity and excess; she uses language not as a closed system of meaning, but as an ambiguous, fertile, protean, life affirming key to social connection and harmony.

That the regenerative powers of art can act as a way of fighting for peace in this context is highly ambivalent, however, and this ambivalence coalesces around the specific giving of a creative gift – the pageant that occupies the central space in this novel and encapsulates the potential for the building of bonds and fostering of creative feelings. It aims to create connection and to facilitate an open interpretation; Miss La Trobe's pageant aims to 'enlist' the audience but not through propaganda and not into war. Rather,

A Gift of Vision 119

her pageant invites a collective action of creativity that includes and tolerates difference. As Cuddy-Keane suggests, 'a social group' but one which 'is separated from the concept of homogeneity', is created (1990, 279). This pageant-gift seems to enact the process of fighting war with the mind, with the imagination and with words. The pastiche and parody of the historical and the literary tradition that Miss La Trobe's pageant consists of makes it a gift that undoes hierarchies, defies conventions, rejects authoritative views, privileges indeterminacy and ambiguity, embraces difference, yet offers a collective voice and creates a sense of unity. However, this is not the kind of unity that Freud's theories of group dynamics in Western societies postulated in the works Woolf read as she wrote *Between the Acts*, a unity based on sameness, such that readily coalesces around (patriotic) symbols like Empire Day, the army, and the 'Grand Ensemble, round the union jack to end with' (*BTA* 94).[57] Rather, it is one in which differences can be tolerated, and this coincides with Woolf's aims for the novel as a whole. In the diary entry in which she notes the germ of her idea for *Between the Acts*, Woolf asserts that in her 'random and tentative' creation there will be an absence of a central authority, ' "I" rejected: "We" substituted . . . "We" [. . .] composed of many different things [. . .] we all life, all art, all waifs & strays – a rambling capricious but somehow unified whole' implying her vision of a decentred, plural narration, inclusive and composite in that there will be a 'unified whole' but not a uniform whole (*D5* 135).

The uncertainty, ambivalence, ambiguity, yet the necessary risk of gift-giving seen throughout Woolf's work, and in particular the importance of creative gifts, is given priority in this novel. The way Miss La Trobe chooses to give her gift is itself a significant risk as she stages her pageant in the open air and chances the success of the only performance of the pageant to good weather, accommodating wildlife and minimal technical hitches. The major risk in how the gift will be received and how the recipients will interpret and inscribe it with meaning is emphasised here by the amount of attention given to the responses to the pageant, and by Miss La Trobe's anxieties about the need to sustain an emotional response and connection. The element of risk is especially high given the contradictions this gift entails. Miss La Trobe offers her pageant as a specific gift to her community, but this is complicated by the fact that she is perceived as an outsider and treated as an outcast – she a lesbian who is 'foreign' to the village and possibly to England itself (*BTA* 37). Her village pageant is part of a pagan folk tradition that helps to sustain community bonds. Yet this one in particular is part of a broader act of charity to raise funds for the illumination of the village church, a cornerstone of Christian village life.[58] However, there is a certain futility in this act of fundraising given that the blackout was only six weeks away from the setting of this novel.

The pageant's composition is also highly ambiguous and doubly focused. Its historical scenes and dramatic playlets chart the rise of the British Empire

120 *Gifts, Markets and Economies of Desire*

and cumulatively reiterate the powerful dominant ideologies of class, gender, race and sexuality on which British national identity is based. Simultaneously, Miss La Trobe's pageant works to parody and satirise these ideologies and the sexual, social and monetary economies on which the Empire is built. In doing so, her pageant exposes the violence, repression, prejudice, greed and corruption with which these ideological beliefs are inextricably and historically connected. Miss La Trobe is not afraid to speak out (and like Woolf, who risked and caused a furore with her essay 'Reviewing') –her gift is challenging, provocative and risks 'abuse' and 'contempt' (*CD* 169). The blackbird nursery rhyme that recurs as a motif throughout and which enforces connections between men and money, women and consumption, heterosexuality and authority, demonstrates the powerful transmission of dominant ideologies in the process of cultural socialisation, as it simultaneously deems them facile. In the final part of the pageant, this rhyme and the forces of patriarchy, capitalism, heterosexuality and war that it represents are implicitly the source of unceasing human suffering.

The criticisms the pageant includes are delivered largely through a comic mode that invites laughter. This works to undermine such powerful and authoritative forces,[59] but does not limit the possibilities for interpretation (as the diverse responses of the audience suggest). Instead, the pageant's diversity and parodic excess, its ambivalence and laughter-provoking comedy, like the novel as a whole, ensure that there are multiple ways in which it can be interpreted. It is a sharing in and of a cultural past but not from a single, central perspective. This makes the pageant a highly subversive gift. For instance, there are large gaps in the chronology, which break up the linearity of official history, leaving it up to the audience to remember or imaginatively fill the gaps between the selected periods. Indeed, at one point, there is a gap within a playlet and the audience is instructed to 'imagine' what goes on in this narrative gap. This in one way makes clear the predictability of the heterosexual romance the playlet depicts, but it also decentres any sense of narrative authority. This reaches a crescendo in the 'present time' section, which is thrown open to the many voices and faces of the audience as they are reflected in the mirrors held up to them. This marks a radical break with conventions and hierarchies and, as Leaksa notes, when the actors appear at the end the words given in the text are not from the pageant, but have been spoken, murmured or thought by the various characters in the audience during the novel itself (Leaska 451; *BTA* 109–10). Further, the scenes and playlets within the scenes themselves comically disrupt the power hierarchies that allow only one official version of history, and one reading of the literary tradition, insisting on an ongoing dialogue between the past and the present.

The performance of the pageant itself also extends the sense of dialogue democratically as not only does Miss La Trobe offer a marginal perspective on official history and the literary tradition, but any sense of authority due to her as the writer and director of the pageant is also undermined. She

A Gift of Vision 121

writes the script and orchestrates the performance (indeed, she is likened to a 'commander' and nicknamed 'Bossy' by the actors), but the working-class performers make the pageant their own as they bring their individuality and personality to their roles in a way that repeatedly breaks the illusion of the performance. This dynamic engagement with the script and the context (in which the gramophone is highly unreliable, the wind obscures the sounds of the words, and animal sounds spontaneously fill the gaps) seems to far exceed the effect anticipated or expected when Miss La Trobe wrote her script. What they bring as performers not only brings the pageant to life, but adds something unscripted and unpredictable – a vitality and comedy that gives rise to the laughter of the audience and proliferates its meanings.

The actors are readily identifiable by the audience, and their identity is overlaid onto, and often takes priority over, the characters they play in a comically subversive way. This creates 'the double focus of the stage', a comic duality that Ames argues is part of the carnivalesque quality of what he calls 'Woolf's most explicitly carnivalesque novel' (395, 394). One instance that Ames identifies of this 'comic double vision' is in the playing of Queen Elizabeth by 'the humble Eliza Clark' (395). The audience are drawn in by the successful creation of the illusion of Queen Elizabeth (the symbolic ruff, pearls and silver cape made from scouring pads), even as they simultaneously recognise her namesake, Eliza (*BTA* 52). It is not only that, in typical carnivalesque fashion, high and low are inverted in this scene, but the fusion of their names creates a subversive slippage of reference so that 'Eliza Clark, licensed to sell tobacco' is also the 'great Eliza' whose colonising agents first brought smoking tobacco back to England, making this a lucrative commodity and contributing to the greatness and power of Eliza/beth herself. Here and in other of the dramatic scenes Woolf forcefully brings to the fore the exploitation that underpins of economic power and Empire over time. Not only are distinctions between the shop keeper and the first Queen of Empire blurred, but there is also a sense in which Eliza is 'great' in her own way and brings her own force to the role in a way that both further enhances the illusion of Elizabeth, but which clearly locates her power in her working-class identity. Eliza is large in stature and physically powerful ('She could reach a flitch of bacon or haul a tub of oil with one sweep of her arm in the shop'). This translates into the appropriate authority she projects as Queen Elizabeth, 'For a moment she stood there, eminent, dominant' (*BTA* 52). However, her 'swarthy, muscular arm', symbolic of her working-class identity, comically deflates the illusion of the virgin queen (whose white skin was a symbol of her superiority) especially as she stretches it to imitate an 'ashen haired babe' (*BTA* 53). At this point Eliza's performance begins to unravel – the wind unbalances her already 'top heavy' head dress, her 'ruff had become unpinned and great Eliza had forgotten her lines' at which point the audience bursts into laughter (*BTA* 53).[60] However, the precariousness of this Eliza's power (sustained, as it was for the real queen, by the

122 Gifts, Markets and Economies of Desire

use of carefully controlled spectacle) and Miss La Trobe's authority over her creation have already been suggested by the fact that Eliza 'bawled' her lines, and 'a cow mooed. A bird twittered' in response to the line, 'For me Shakespeare sang' (*BTA* 52). This first dramatic scene and the playlet that follows set up an unpinning of any official or single interpretation of the past, as is evident in the varied responses of the audience.

Perhaps unsurprisingly, the most biting attack is levelled at the Victorian era. Miss La Trobe's playlet representing this targets the brutality and prejudice embedded in its rigidly hierarchical, patriarchal and imperialist social order. The attack is focused largely through its spokesperson, a policeman but also a composite Victorian authority figure whose assertion of his moral duty and authority resonates with menace, violence and self-righteousness. His obedience to Queen and Empire is unquestioning and unquestioned, but equally he claims power and authority for himself as a White man of the British Empire, and he exerts his authority and control (symbolised by his truncheon) over every aspect of life.[61] Taking racist exploitation, class oppression and the suffering of the poor for granted, as 'the price of empire' (*BTA* 97), he impresses the audience as 'A very fine figure of a man', his portrayal convincing as he stands 'eminent, dominant, glaring from his pedestal', leaving no space for disruptive laughter, or for incongruities to undermine his authority (*BTA* 98).

Before this scene, two members of the audience, Lynn Jones and Etty Springett, reminisce fondly over their Victorian childhood and upbringing, discussing the shared past that feeds into their present bond, and they agree that village festivities bring people together. However, although both are affronted and insulted by the representation of the Victorian past, they do concur, for different reasons, with the criticisms implied, to the extent that Lynn Jones feels that the impurity of the Victorian family led to it perishing (*BTA* 103). The attack seems to be most severe on this period, then, in order to expose the tyranny, hypocrisy, cruelty and greed embedded in the dominant institutions that survive into the novel's present moment. It aims to stir up a more personal response and to confront the tensions bubbling beneath the social surface, to acknowledge and so disperse the potential aggression that such differences can engender at this volatile moment in history. Giles, for instance, is the most obvious product of the legacy of Victorian values. The scene stirs vengeful feelings against his aunt Lucy who, Budge/Hammond implies by singling her out from the audience, is irresponsible and disrespectful of authority (*BTA* 96–7). This indictment of Victorian values and structures of authority tries to undermine the influences that frame and constrain interpretation; Miss La Trobe's pageant, like the novel itself, works to resist Victorian certainties and the neat moral conclusions, as well as the bellicosity, of this period.[62]

The final dramatic scene of the pageant, 'The present time. Ourselves', compounds the audience's experience of discomfort ('All their nerves were

A Gift of Vision 123

on edge. They sat exposed') and brings their hostility fully to the surface (*BTA* 106). For instance, the village children who emerge holding the mirrors are referred to derisively as 'the riff-raff' by the disgruntled and disorientated middle- and upper-class audience (*BTA* 109). The first part of this scene comprises ten minutes of the audience unwittingly experiencing 'present-time reality' (*BTA* 107) during which Giles, Isa and William ruminate silently on their unhappiness. Others become increasingly impatient as they wait for the next scene to entertain them, and Bart Oliver complains about the fund-raising aspect of the performance (*BTA* 105). After a shower of rain, one of many organic interventions enhancing the performance and reinforcing the communal nature of this experience (it is a 'sudden and universal' shower *BTA* 107), the performers hold mirrors up to the audience, reversing their gaze on the performers and forcing them to realise their own role and complicity in the present moment of history. This is a culmination of the challenges that Miss La Trobe's creative gift has raised, emphasising that the gift is not always welcome or happily received.

The participation of the audience has been a fundamental aspect of this pageant from the beginning: it is only when they are participating and have recognised that the pageant has begun that it can be said to have begun (*BTA* 49). Miss La Trobe may have written the first words, and 'England' spoken them, but it is only when the audience is receptive ('Muscles loosened; ice cracked') that '(t)he play had begun' (*BTA* 49). However, this overt participation of the audience, and the breaking of the boundaries between audience and performers/performance, is disturbing on several levels, not least, as Bart Oliver's complaint has made clear, in relation to the economic exchange that he feels has taken place. His uncharitable attitude here, revealed in his belief that 'Nothing's done for nothing in England' (105), is in line with his assertion before the pageant begins that his role is to be the audience. Given this, he refuses to contribute anything else, even refusing help with the refreshments, which are so important to the gift economy and to building social bonds (*BTA* 37). However, Miss La Trobe's 'present time' troubles the audience's 'safe' and supposedly unambiguous role (as 'customers' receiving services for which they have paid), which they assume has been guaranteed by their contribution to the fundraising. Their class and economic superiority they feel is challenged and scrutinised by 'the inquisitive insulting eye' of the mirrors and mirror bearers (*BTA* 111). The clear-cut and impersonal experience of capitalist exchange is profoundly undermined by Miss La Trobe's creative gift, as not only are boundaries between audience and performer, customer and market blurred, but human – animal barriers seem also to have dissolved as animals join in the uncontrolled 'uproar' (*BTA* 110).

Even before this cacophonous finale, however, Miss La Trobe's pageant-gift has already offered a scathingly critical representation of 'civilization' – depicted as a wall being rebuilt to the tune of the nursery rhyme which has resonated throughout the novel (especially in relation to Giles and Mrs Manresa),

124   *Gifts, Markets and Economies of Desire*

and which dictates the rigid gender and economic roles of the king and queen, counting money and eating honey. The rain shower that precedes this has a cathartic effect, and is emblematic of the tears 'wept for human pain unending' (*BTA* 107), a sorrow that is also synonymous with this nursery rhyme, 'And the voice that wept for human pain unending said:

> *The King is in his counting house,*
> *Counting out his money,*
> *The Queen is in her parlour . . .*

(*BTA* 107–8)

As the audience applaud the flimsy and '(c)rude' representation of civilization, (the wall was 'a cloth roughly painted'), and the peace and prosperity that it seems to promise, the tune changes and finally there seems to be an attempt to rein in the excesses of Miss La Trobe's provocative and subversive artistic gift: 'O the trees, how gravely and sedately like senators in council, or the spaced pillars of some cathedral church. . . . Yes, they barred the music, and massed and hoarded; and prevented what was fluid from overflowing' (*BTA* 108). However, the rapid and dislocated changes in music that follow suggest that neither the patriarchal powers of local government nor the Church can match the fertile and regenerative powers of this artistic gift, as the inadequacy of both institutions in this novel demonstrates. The 'senators in council' represent the council, which had promised but failed to bring water to the village; and cathedral pillars can be seen to represent the pillar of the local church, Reverend Streatfield, whose trite summing up of the message of the pageant is an attempt to translate the creative excesses of the pageant-gift into a simplified sentiment about common human experience, and so to make it equate to the funds he wants to raise. Despite the interruption of planes zooming overhead, 'collecting boxes were in operation' immediately he gave the signal (*BTA* 115). Miss La Trobe, 'the gifted lady', refuses to come forward to accept the perfunctory 'vote of thanks' for her gift, leaving the singing of the national anthem to end the festivities (*BTA* 115). She may, as Woolf says of Anon, have given her gift in the service of the church, but she maintains her freedom as an outsider to speak her mind (and say what others feel but are unable to say) through her creativity, yet she refuses to delimit the meanings it can have by offering her author/itative interpretation (Woolf [Silver] 'Anon' 384, 380).

For a moment after everyone has gone, Miss La Trobe experiences a euphoric feeling of 'Glory', that the world has 'taken [her] gift', the 'triumph' of her gift being not in what is given but in the process of it being given and received, of social connections being reinforced (*BTA* 124). This is immediately followed by a sense of failure to create unity and connections. She speculates, as others in the audience have done, that having more money to invest in her pageant would have made it 'a better gift' (*BTA* 124). However, the starlings, which begin to attack the tree behind which she had hidden, seem to be also attacking her pessimism and her resorting to monetary economies to ameliorate her sense of failure.[63] With great energy and 'without measure, without stop', the starlings actions and voices reiterate the vital and excessive force of Miss La Trobe's creative gift, 'birds syllabling discordantly life, life, life', (*BTA* 124). They are interrupted by Mrs Chalmers, going to visit her husband's grave with her gift of flowers, who 'cut(s)' Miss La Trobe to indicate her outcast status and the failure of her pageant to build bonds with the villagers (*BTA* 125). However, not the sense of failure, the economic constraints, or the slights of conventional heterosexual women (who must be 'chal(r)mers' to survive sexually and economically, as Woolf says of the heterosexual economy in *Three Guineas*) can suppress the *zoë*-life of her creative gift, and the glimmer of inspiration she had at the beginning of her pageant returns – 'Then something rose to the surface' (*BTA* 124).

Miss La Trobe's creative gift has also had a positive and life-affirming effect on other characters. To Lucy Swithin, Miss La Trobe is 'a lady of wonderful energy' whose gift is in part to bring out the gifts and talents of others (*BTA* 38). She goes to congratulate Miss La Trobe in one of the intervals and, although she struggles to articulate the impact of Miss La Trobe's gift on her, she does convey the emotional and inspirational effect of the pageant in that she feels she 'could have played . . . Cleopatra' (*BTA* 92). Miss La Trobe understands that Lucy's 'unacted part' had been brought to life by her pageant, and the effect of her creative gift has been to bring hidden qualities, desires and creative urges to the surface. Even in the less sensitive and responsive members of her audience, creative states and emotional responses are activated, from Mrs Mayhew who 'sketched what she would have done had it been her pageant', to Mrs Manresa shedding tears that 'for an instant . . . ravaged her powder' (*BTA* 106, 112).

The pageant also succeeds in making the audience question not only what it meant, but also how they see the world and their roles in it. Some of the audience also go away with the idea that 'we all act all parts' (*BTA* 117). Indeed, this is the case, as not only has Miss La Trobe's pageant necessitated the participation of the audience in the 'present time' section, but as Cuddy-Keane has argued, all the characters play their parts like the communal chorus in an Ancient Greek drama 'between the acts': 'for when the curtain rises at the end of the novel, all the previous narrative falls between the acts, and every voice becomes part of the chorus' (1990, 275). Other critics have also pointed out the significance of the references to Ancient Greek drama and the influence of Jane Harrison's feminist interpretations of ancient myth, art and ritual for this novel.[64] In making central the experience of ritual, in which everyone participates, this novel recovers a sense of the communal which heroic dramas supplanted (Harrison 159, 164). It also counters the worship of the hero central to such forms of art, along with its prioritising

126 *Gifts, Markets and Economies of Desire*

of individual achievement and war. Miss La Trobe's pageant, simultaneously a scathing critique of the power hierarchies of English culture and a celebration of this rich cultural store, is also a fertility ritual in itself (with its dancing, singing, and vitality) which functions to expel the forces of death and masculine heroism in war. And, as Harrison argues of ritual, it also attempts to 'make(s) . . . a bridge between real life and art' (Harrison 135).

A positive reading of the ending of the novel might suggest that, in the communication of Giles and Isa, what Isa calls the third ply of life, 'peace', may be achieved. This scene comes shortly after Isa has called for a 'new plot' and for Miss La Trobe to 'c(o)me out from the bushes' (*BTA* 128). As others have noted, the setting of this final interaction resembles the scene that Miss La Trobe imagines for the beginning of her next play: 'There was high ground at midnight; there the rock and two scarcely perceptible figures. Suddenly the tree was pelted with starlings. . . . She heard the first words' (*BTA* 125–6). This makes her alone privy to the words Isa and Giles 'spoke' because she imagines them (*BTA* 130), and including her earlier experience of the starlings reinforces the drive towards 'life, life, life' and further inspiration the birds represent. As Cuddy-Keane suggests, their cries 'lead(s) to new life in her imaginative world by stimulating her next play' and 'the activity of the starlings brings the play to its birth' (1990, 279).

The creative process leading to this point also resonates with the positive associations of community and connection. Miss La Trobe has a glimmer of inspiration as the performers prepare themselves for the beginning of her pageant and her vision comes to fruition (*BTA* 40). However, her ideas are more developed and fertilised in the public house as, increasingly inebriated, she hears the words of the working-class people around her and transforms them into her vision: 'Words of one syllable sank down into the mud. She drowsed; she nodded. The mud became fertile. Words rose above the intolerably laden dumb oxen plodding through the mud. Words without meaning – wonderful words' (*BTA* 125). As suggested above, Tratner argues that in Woolf's writing the working classes do not bring a vision of their own but act as unconscious marginal figures to release the creativity of the artist, and this would seem to be the case here (1995, 58). However, Miss La Trobe's own outcast status as a lesbian, and possibly a foreigner, locates her on the social margins. Her role, and indeed the role of her art, would seem to be that of a bridge 'between' the classes (she brings their words into the 'medley' of her pageant), generations and between a precarious state of peace and the outbreak of war. The final word of the novel, 'spoke', offers hope for connection and the positive regeneration of a world torn apart by fascism through the power of creativity, the imagination and the 'creative feelings' art generates. Unlike the speeches of fascist dictators, however, which are closed and fixed in meaning, the last words of the novel are not disclosed, leaving the reader to speculate and imagine. Importantly, this speaking together also happens in the knowledge of differences between the interlocutors. It is Miss La Trobe's

A Gift of Vision 127

position on the margins of this society that seems to be the key to her perception of, and ability to imagine, the tolerance necessary to sustain communication in this situation of increasing tension and imminent crisis. Miss La Trobe's association with the troubadors,[65] the wandering poets of the Middle Ages, and with Anon, who led 'a roaming life' (Woolf [Silver] 'Anon', 382), suggests that, although much of the novel urges towards hope, continuity and connection, the pleasures her creative gifts can bring to a diverse and divided community, and the resistance they can offer to the darkness and violence of war, can only be temporary.

As a counter to the rise of fascism and the pathway to war, Miss La Trobe's eclectic and excessive pageant serves to open up the differences of view and opinion within this community, so enabling different perspectives on the past to be voiced so as to resist the herd mentality and closed interpretation on which the success of patriotism and propaganda relies. Her pageant opens up multiple ways of interpreting, undermines the notion of a single authority and source of meaning and, by insisting on a democratic production, aims to build a collective feeling that is tolerant of difference. Although there is scope for reading Miss La Trobe's pageant as a failure in this respect,[66] there is also a positive endorsement of its success given the effect on her audience: 'Like quicksilver sliding, filings magnetized, the distracted united. . . . On different levels they diverged. On different levels ourselves went forward; . . . but all comprehending; all enlisted' within a harmonious if diverse community (BTA 112). At the end of The Gift, Mauss argues that gift-exchange practices enable groups 'to oppose and to give to one another without sacrificing themselves to one another', practices it is crucial for the 'so-called civilized world' to learn (82–3). It is such gift practices that Woolf's novel engenders. Between the Acts, like To the Lighthouse, is framed by the idea of giving a gift. However, unlike Orlando's poem or Lily's painting, Miss La Trobe's creative gift does not produce a material object that can be recuperated into a commodity exchange. Rather, her pageant is performed just once. It is this transitory quality that ensures it unquestionably and uncompromisingly retains its integrity as a gift of the creative imagination and of collective participation which cannot be absorbed or contained. When there is an attempt to reduce the pageant to a simple monetary transaction (as in Bart Oliver's complaint that '"All our village pageants . . . end with a demand for money"' BTA 105), this is met by opposition, not only from the characters within the novel, but by the experience and the effects of the pageant itself. Whereas usually Woolf's reader is invited to be a conspirator and an accomplice, to participate in the textual generosity and excess of her writing, Between the Acts includes its own audience as participants as it aims to democratise still further the processes of creating and interpreting. Woolf saw this goal as crucial in the resistance of fascism and in the hope for future peace.

4
Moments of Giving: Generosity and Desire in Woolf's Short Fictions

Until fairly recently, Woolf's short fiction has received relatively little critical attention. However, new studies focusing on her shorter works[1] are building on the sparse critical work that has gone before (notably the work of Dean Baldwin and Avrom Fleishman), and reassessing this aspect of Woolf's *oeuvre* in the light of both modernist literary concerns with form, and the interconnected growth of the short story genre around the turn of the century. The mid- to late nineteenth century saw the blossoming of the short story as the expansion of commercial magazine publication created new opportunities for authors to sell and publish their stories and the readership to read them. Like other art forms affected by the climate of social and political instability and radical cultural transition, by the turn of the century the short story was undergoing a transformation, with 'a wave of experimentalism in British short fiction' (Benzel and Hoberman 3). In particular, Russian literary influences on the form affected its evolution from the mid-nineteenth century norm of a short, contained and unified fiction to a more indeterminate, ambiguous, open-ended, unstable and hybrid form. By the time Woolf began writing and publishing her short fictions and reviewing translations of Chekov in the late teens and early 1920s,[2] the genre had become broader, giving Woolf's experimentation a forum for development.[3] This was also the period in which Woolf's relationship with Katherine Mansfield, a modernist writing exclusively in the short fiction genre, was most intimate and intense. As others have noted, Mansfield, herself very much influenced by Russian writers, was a source of encouragement and inspiration for Woolf.[4] Woolf's *Diaries* reveal the significance she attributed to Mansfield at this time: she valued the 'priceless talk' she and Mansfield shared, seeing Mansfield as 'the only woman . . . with gift enough to make talk of writing interesting' (*D2* 45).[5] The suggestion here of a bond between women, however complex, that is without measure in the monetary economy and that is sealed by the recognition of a gift of some kind is a key idea which can be explored in Woolf's short stories.

The transformation of the short story form paralleled and fed into the development of modernist literary forms more generally. Indeed, for many

Moments of Giving 129

critics the modernist short story epitomises and exemplifies the techniques, structures and political and cultural subversiveness of modernist writing.[6] The short story also epitomises modernism's often contradictory, and potentially subversive, relationship with the market and consumer culture. Woolf's stories engage with market economies in a variety of ways, subverting, as is typical of both short stories generally and much modernist writing, hegemonic gender and sexual norms encapsulated in capitalist and commercial practices.[7] This subversiveness operates at the level of content, form and the relationship with the reader. Hanson suggests that short fiction can act as 'a vehicle for different *kinds* of knowledge, knowledge which may be in some ways at odds with the "story" of dominant culture' (1989, 6). In making central a gift economy and the idea of generosity, Woolf's short fictions enable different affective, libidinal and hermeneutic economies to operate which undermine dominant hierarchies of value and relationship and assumptions about meaning(s). As in Woolf's longer fictions, expressions of generosity and the literal giving of gifts give rise to an alternative economy that runs parallel with capitalist and commercial systems.

Despite the critical assessments of the short story as the quintessential modernist form, and despite the fact that Woolf wrote and reviewed short fiction throughout her life, her short fictions have received relatively little critical attention. Until more recently, critical work on this part of her *oeuvre* has tended to consider these works as a 'testing ground' for ideas and forms developed in her longer fictions, an approach that has been criticised for merely seeking 'quarry for the longer works' (Dick *CSF* 3; Fleishman 44). Even more recent work, such as Julia Briggs' readings of Woolf's later short stories, still frame their readings of this work in relation to the longer works, viewing them as 'a kind of tuning up for *The Waves*' and as 'a playground or exercise yard, or else a sketchbook in which she renewed her search for "the essential thing"' (Briggs 2004, 175, and 2006, 172). One reason for this lies with Woolf's own apparently dismissive comments, whereby '(s)he often emphasizes her stories' provisional, dashed-off feel by referring to them as sketches, little stories, scenes' and commenting on the 'ease and speed' with which she writes them (Daugherty 102), later looking back on her initial success in publishing short stories as 'treats' (*L4* 231, cited in Daugherty 112).[8] As others have noted, Woolf's flippant comments about these works are belied by her rigorous attention to the revision and preparation of her short fictions for publication[9] and her preoccupation in her *Letters* and *Diaries* with both the process of writing and the success (or not) of publication.

Woolf's short fiction is also subject to the major difficulty in criticising short fictions in general, however, which lies with the problem of trying to theorise and define a genre which has such 'protean variety' (Reid 3) and which, like other literary forms, evolves over time with changing conventions.[10] This process is also further hampered, by the marginalisation of the genre owing to a critical prejudice in favour of '(c)omplexity and breadth'

130 Gifts, Markets and Economies of Desire

(Reid 2), and by value judgements which take the novel as the norm (Head 3–5). For Reid, however, it is also the form's popularity in magazine publication that presents difficulties: he points out that the term 'short story' to mean a distinct 'literary product' only appeared in the OED Supplement in 1933, and emphasises the short story's status as a commodity further by suggesting that the genre's 'slightness and slickness . . . do often infect the short story when it is adapting to market requirements' (1). Although not every short story or short-story writer is 'tempted towards the reductive formulae of merchandise' (Reid 3), critics have more recently begun to explore the close connection between modernist writing, and particularly the modernist short story, and the marketplace. Short stories in general exist in a different relation to the market and the monetary economy than other forms of writing, and this seems to be the case for the modernist short story in particular.

For Lawrence Rainey, modernist publication in forums such as 'little' magazines[11] and reviews, and by small presses in deluxe editions, created a new space and value system within, yet separate from, the institutions of mass culture and publication: a niche market in which art becomes elevated as 'a special kind of commodity', not merely an object of simple and immediate mass consumption, but rather 'a rarity capable of sustaining investment value', so that consumption is 'defer(red) . . . into the future' (1999, 43). Tim Armstrong, on the other hand, argues that the publication of modernist short stories in commercially produced American magazines renders them, despite their 'epiphanic, ambiguous, formally perfect' qualities, still only 'a basic unit of magazine publication', 'the "quality" filler in a sandwich comprised of aspirational copy aimed at the middle classes and matched advertising' (2005, 52). He goes on to argue that the little magazines, though intent on distinguishing themselves from mass consumerism, were also inevitably enmeshed in the market economy, concerned with self-publicity as distinctive cultural forms, advertising and identifying audiences (53). Because a short story is more likely than other literary forms to be published in either commercial or little magazines, commissioned by editors and paid for in a single transaction, this genre exists in a more transparent and direct relation with the market. Because of this, it exposes the economic exigencies of modernist publication and the relation of the genre to the literary marketplace in general. As Armstrong attests '(t)he position of the short story can be taken as emblematic of modernism as a whole: "quality" cannot be dissociated from a consumer culture in which it identifies a particular audience' (53).

Although Woolf's co-ownership of the Hogarth Press in many ways freed her from some of these exigencies, her involvement with it brought her face-to-face with issues of marketing and profits in relation to her own work and that of others; she also wrote for publication in commercial magazines and received payment for these stories. However, as with her attitude to her longer works, Woolf's attitude to commercial success as a writer and publisher of short stories was complicated from the outset. On the one hand, the publication of short stories was vital to the initial success of the Hogarth Press, with the first publication (*Two Stories* – consisting of Leonard Woolf's 'Three Jews' and Virginia Woolf's 'The Mark on the Wall') bringing them success. Importantly, this also helped to strengthen Woolf's reputation and led to other commissions for her – 'An Unwritten Novel', published in the *London Mercury* July 1920, and 'Solid Objects' in the *Athenaeum* in October 1920 (Dick, 2004, xvi). As Staveley argues, the writing and production of 'Kew Gardens' brought further success, both in terms of personal pleasure and artistic freedom (the 'tremendous fun' of printing), and, after the review of the story by Harold Child in the *TLS* (1919), in terms of commercial success (*L2* 169, cited in Staveley, 2004, 41).[12] This publication broadened the audience for her work to a 'more mercantilist audience' beyond the 'coterie list of subscribers to the Hogarth Press' (Staveley, 2003, 1). Woolf's decision to reprint this story in 1927 in a limited edition format was, according to Staveley, motivated by the temptation of capitalising on her growing status as a major European writer and maintaining some control over her work (with 'Kew Gardens' being the first to appear in translation in the French periodical *Les Nouvelles Litteraires*), and making a profit (this edition was carefully produced to look expensive and carefully marketed as a collectible) (Staveley, 2003, 1–2, 4–6).

However, Woolf's participation in the market was also accompanied by an antithetical attitude to the values and tastes of it. Although she did sometimes write stories explicitly to make money, for example when she felt her finances were running low she revised 'Lappin and Lapinova' for publication (Briggs, 2004, 175), she found this to be boring (Dick, 2004, xix, cites). It is also obvious that the value of her short fiction was never simply monetary, as her annoyance when her story 'Gypsy, the Mongrel', 'demand(ed)' by *Harper's Bazaar* and tailored for this market (presumably being less 'sophisticated' than her previous submission that was rejected), was paid for but not published; 'The Legacy' was also rejected (*D5* 241; Dick, 2004, xix). However, her annoyance, attributable to the affront to her reputation, but also possibly to the fact that her stories were not in circulation, is offset by other triumphs over the publishing industry. For instance, with £60 payment for her 'little Sapphist story' ('Moments of Being: "Slater's Pins Have no Points"'), Woolf gleefully relays to Sackville-West the fact that the 'Editor has not seen the point, though he's been looking for it in the Adirondacks' (*L3* 431; Dick also cites this letter, 2004, xviii). Her thrill seems to be about the misunderstanding of the transaction that had taken place: the editor assumes that he has bought a commodity on which he can capitalise and which his readers can readily consume, but Woolf knows he is blind to the sexual and economic contraband she has smuggled into her writing. This story is about the awakening to new sexual self-knowledge, and to the inevitable economic implications of being at odds with and resistant to the dominant script of heterosexuality. This moment, then, demonstrates her knowing negotiation

132   Gifts, Markets and Economies of Desire

of the market as she simultaneously subverts its capitalist and heteropatriarchal values from within.

Daugherty reads Woolf's public declarations about the relative insignificance of her short stories as a kind of screen, masking 'a radical freedom' which, along with 'not publishing', allows Woolf to continue 'playing' and 'inventing without pressure',[13] and so 'protect(s) Woolf's freedom to challenge genre norms' (103).[14] The non-publication of her stories is one obvious way in which Woolf locates them outside the literary marketplace, seeing their value as pleasure and enjoyment, a value beyond the monetary economy associated with publication. However, her generic experiments with form, privileging ambiguity, openness and lack of closure, and creating a rich suggestiveness and multiplicity of potential meanings, with the intensity of the relationship between text and reader this writing demands, can also be seen to operate an economy fundamentally at odds with capitalism.[15] Discussing the relation of Woolf's stories to the marketplace, Benzel and Hoberman argue that '(t)he short story, whether it is self-published or sold to a magazine, brings writer and reader into a particularly intense relationship, one in which the act of reading is itself an act of consumption' (10). However, as is the case with all of Woolf's writing, this is not a ready consumption for the reader because the reader must also read with generosity, participating in the ongoing process of generating meaning and assessing value. Although this reading process can be conceptualised usefully as an investment – an emotional and intellectual investment as well as an investment of time[16] – the 'profits' are often not in the form of a clearly demarcated 'return' and may even resemble a loss in capitalist terms. As Nena Skrbic's reading of Chekov's 'Happiness' suggests, the inconclusiveness of the story indicates that meaning lies beyond the ending and notions of economically regulated returns on investment: 'the story's conclusion is a treasure that readers have to find for themselves' (2004a, 29).

Woolf's first highly experimental story, 'The Mark on the Wall', derails the possibility of the reader's easy consumption of this narrative as a commodity. Rather, foregrounding digressions, tangents, associations, and the losses of material objects, it counters, as Woolf's stories repeatedly do, the ethos of the market with the exhilaration of 'the rapidity of life, the perpetual waste and repair', and the complicated pleasures of hermeneutic ambiguity and uncertainty (CSF 84). The plots, subject matter and form of her short fictions foreground a sense of generosity and gifts as they open up rich possibilities for meaning, as they simultaneously question and undermine capitalist values of property and profit, revealing such acquisitive values and such simple exchanges to be of limited worth.

In 'Solid Objects' (1920), John's growing obsession with the 'waste' produced by commodity culture in many ways disrupts capitalist hierarchies of value, and privileges an a-commodity aesthetic, especially at first when he experiences his 'finds' as gifts of nature's bounty and re-values ('repair(s)') as unique what capitalist mass production rejects. As in the process of gift-giving itself, it is the form and the context of finding (and so being 'given') and displaying that imbues these objects with meaning. For example, with a different setting (or context) a piece of beach glass (its function as a manufactured commodity eroded) could become 'a precious stone' and the fragment of china retrieved from the marginal space of the 'wasteland' is revivified (like the furniture and collected objects in 'The Lady in the Looking-Glass') and 'seemed to be pirouetting through space, winking light like a fitful star' (*CSF* 103, 105). As Ruth Hoberman, drawing on Walter Benjamin, argues, John perceives the auratic qualities of these found objects, and, like a traditional modernist artist anxious about the dangers of mass production, attempts to fix their meaning in reaction to the arbitrary and changing values attributed to objects in the marketplace (85–6).

However, his mounting passion for and possessiveness of the objects he collects leaves John increasingly isolated and he hoards his treasures to himself, cut off from communication with others. His obsession becomes violent and invasive, as he 'ransacked all the deposits of earth' in his ambitious drive to lay claim to ever rarer objects (*CSF* 106). Finally, his bounty becomes the spoils of his exploitative actions; he imagines that his first piece of glass could be from the treasure chest of some sunken Elizabethan ship, and his acquisitiveness echoes the greed of the colonial enterprise implied. Despite the promise of the waste of mass production being recycled into something with meaning in excess of that attributed to it by the marketplace, John's attitude to his found objects imitates the acquisitiveness of capitalism itself. In a parallel movement, John's hoarding of objects literally removes them from circulation and closes off the proliferation of their meanings, as it simultaneously removes him from social interaction. What had potential to be a generative, life-enhancing process in tune with the generosity of a gift economy has simply become a deadened and socially deadening collection.

'Kew Gardens' (1918), among other things, also highlights the dangers of capitalist modes of thought and their detrimental effects on relationships and on the fulfilment of desires. All four of the dialogues in this story reveal how desires are thwarted. However, it is the final dialogue of the young couple on the cusp of marriage that is most revealing of the damaging effect of prevalent capitalist values as they channel and stifle desires and possibilities and commodify women. As others have pointed out, for Woolf the exchange of commodities in a capitalist economy and the exchange of women in a patriarchal sexual economy are interrelated (Brigid Elliot and Jo-Ann Wallace, 73). We see this interrelation very clearly in this story. Finding it '(l)ucky' that admission to the gardens is not the sixpence charged on Fridays, the young man reveals a set of values that differ from those of his fiancée, who herself questions whether 'it' would be worth the sixpence admission (*CSF* 94). Taking a feminist narratological approach, Staveley argues that it is 'the conversations in Woolf's gardens [that] speak the story's feminist modernist critique', and that this particular one is a key to understanding the preceding

134 *Gifts, Markets and Economies of Desire*

three (2004, 43, 49). Woolf's sense of the dangers for women of being complicit in social and economic systems that threaten to disempower, objectify and even commodify them is evident here. Staveley persuasively argues that the ambiguity of 'it encodes a critique of the economies of sexual exchange that underpin prevailing assumptions about patterns of courtship, romance and marriage', with the woman 'includ(ing) herself in the afternoon's enterprise' and the admission price (2004, 49). Staveley notes how this couple 'both enact and soon become entrapped by intersecting orthodoxies: romantic, sexual, and economic' (2004, 52). The man, fingering the coins in his pocket with which he will pay for their tea, does so to reassure himself of the reality of his specific and conventional sexual and economic role. The woman, Trissie, on the other hand, acquiesces to her economically dependent and sexually submissive role, the price of which is the curtailing of her unspoken desires to stray from the path to the tea-room, metaphorically to deviate from the conformity to dominant norms that the very English ritual of tea-taking represents. She longs to explore other avenues, to see 'orchids and cranes among wild flowers, a Chinese pagoda and a crimson-crested bird' but such sensual adventures and subversive pleasures are denied her, 'foreign' as they are in this English, heteropatriarchal scene (*CSF* 95; Staveley also cites this part of the story, 2004).

Three stories written and published in the early- to mid-1920s, 'In the Orchard' (1923), 'A Woman's College from Outside' (1926) and 'Moments of Being: "Slater's Pins have no Points"' (1928), in different ways also address and expand on the central issues of 'Kew Gardens'. In particular, they examine the limitations placed on women who are trained for a particular social, sexual and economic role. Capturing the threshold moment of young women on the verge of sexual and emotional maturity, all three stories explore the desires of the young women to transgress the constraints of dominant norms. The various exercises of force (material and ideological) with which these desires are contained indicate the powerful threat that such deviance poses to heteropatriarchal power hierarchies and the capitalist economy in which these hierarchies are enmeshed (the two systems support one another). Both material and ideological, economic force becomes the significant channel for the reinforcement of normative roles and behaviour. Indeed, all these stories have an economic lesson at their heart: what is made apparent to the young women is the economic risk of social and sexual deviance, the consequences of refusing to conform to heterosexual imperatives in a heteropatriarchal and capitalist society in which women are seen as objects of exchange in transactions between men. Talking explicitly about the economic risk of women pursuing their desires for women, Patricia Juliana Smith argues,

> what is at stake for a woman under such conditions is nothing less than economic survival, as the object of exchange is inevitably dependent

Moments of Giving 135

on the exchanger for her continued perceived worth; . . . for a 'commodity' . . . to lack exchange value is tantamount to meaninglessness.

(1997, 6)

However, although for many characters (and authors) this gives rise to what Smith calls 'lesbian panic',[17] this is not the outcome in Woolf's stories (1997, 2). The emphasis on economic issues in these stories is perhaps not surprising because they were written and published as European societies struggled to recover, socially, politically, emotionally and economically from the First World War, and when debate about ways of managing the economy and criticism of existing economic systems came to the fore (notably, in Britain, where issues of economic adjustment were 'perhaps more prominent than most', Aldcroft, 1983, 2). The radical economic ideas of Maynard Keynes, advocate of deficit spending and credit for the consumer to boost the economy, seem to have informed Woolf's experience of and ideas about economic issues,[18] as did her involvement with the women's co-operative guild and Leonard Woolf's work with the League of Nations and the Labour Party.

'In the Orchard' (1923) critically exposes the ways in which dominant social, sexual and monetary economies interconnect and severely limit the potential of Miranda, the story's young middle-class protagonist. In this space of horticultural control, we see the operation of a capitalist economy, defined by Rubin as a system in which 'elements of the natural world are transformed into objects of human consumption' (Rubin 537). The orchard is a space that alludes to the Christian myth of the Garden of Eden, with the apples acting as a reminder of women's potential for transgression of patriarchal law and the terrible consequences of disobedience. Beyond the orchard walls, the school-children are seemingly being primed for a specific class-based role in a hierarchical and capitalist society, and the potential disobedience of the working-class and poor men, women and children is kept in check by physical and social punishments. The violence of this world beyond the walls threatens always to intrude into the seemingly idyllic peace and tranquillity of the orchard, as the harsh sounds of 'the school-children saying the multiplication table in unison, stopped by the teacher, scolded, and beginning to say the multiplication table over again' creates 'a shrill clamour', a brutal noise which assumes a tangible quality as it strikes the truant school-boy picking blackberries and causes him to 'tear his thumb on the thorns' (*CSF* 149). This perhaps suggests that his own harvesting of nature's bounty is somehow a crime against the authority of commercial enterprise. The gender implications of such a social and economic system are made clear with the six poor women being churched.[19] And as the story develops, it becomes clear that the violence that fiercely maintains the social and sexual order outside the orchard also underlies the smooth surface of Miranda's middle-class life. The capitalist economic force of this is evident when, by the

136   *Gifts, Markets and Economies of Desire*

end of the story, we see the extent of its effects as Miranda herself is, like the orchard fruits, perceived as merely a commodity for consumption.

Structured in three similar sections, the first represents a romanticised version of leisured femininity, with Miranda dozing as she reads in her French novel (*Ramuntcho*)[20] about the laughter of girls in the Basque country from her position in the apparent safety of the orchard. Miranda is conventionally identified with nature (her dress is likened to a flower on a stem, and her opal rings flush rosily as the sunlight passes through them). However, even here nature is mediated through the fruit crop, with the sun 'oozing through the apple trees' (*CSF* 149). In this section Miranda is oblivious to the outside world, and the noises from beyond the walls (of rote learning, punishments and women being churched) pass above her head. It is only the squeak of the weather vane that wakes her and reminds her of her duty at the tea table. In the second section, however, Miranda's potentially subversive dreams are revealed, seemingly impacted upon both by the novel she is reading and the noises, especially those of the women being churched. Not only does she sleep and dream with the laughter of girls on her mind, but her lips move as she reads of the laughter of girls resounding, suggesting a heightened physical engagement with this text. The point in *Ramuntcho* at which this spontaneous laughter erupts is one of anticipation and nascent erotic excitement as the village girls wait to see the pelota players, the village 'heroes', practice for an important game; the spontaneous laughter is an expression of their unspoken pleasure and desires. Cixous suggests that women's laughter is subversive in that it can disturb property rights and 'shatter the framework of institutions . . . blow up the law' (1981a, 258). It is when the laughter of the girls enters Miranda's dreams that she feels most in harmony with nature, not claiming it as property or making it a commodity; here pleasure and possibility are seemingly at one with nature's powerful sensuality and with 'life itself' (*CSF* 150).

At first it may seem that Miranda's daydreams (revealing her desire to be somehow at one with the earth, the air and the sea, to be the powerful centre of the natural environment, a 'queen' carried on the back of the world) are to be achieved at the expense of the children and drunken man beyond the orchard walls. The sounds of school-children being scolded and punished and the drunken man's shouts become transformed into the powerful and erotic experience in Miranda's dream and 'she drew breath with an extraordinary ecstasy' (*CSF* 150). However, Miranda is not immune from the exercise of social, sexual and economic power beyond the orchard walls, but, like the poor women being churched, is in an equally vulnerable social and economic position. The sound of the bells ringing following the women being churched cuts into her dreams in a significant way, redirecting her fantasy of escape and her own disruptive desires towards heterosexual romance and the prospect of '(n)aturally' getting married (*CSF* 150). At this point Miranda's potentially transgressive urges and sensual pleasures, triggered by her reading

Moments of Giving   137

about girls' laughter, are reined in, contained via the legitimating discourse of courtship and marriage. Her expansive, sensual and exploratory day-dream (marked by a centripetal movement) is exchanged for a romantic cliché which glosses over the reality of women's economic vulnerability in a heterosexual and capitalist economy, a closing in and down of possibilities as the centrifugal movement (with everything 'moving . . . towards her in a pattern') suggests (*CSF* 150). Although she seems to dictate the scene around her 'by the beat of her own heart', the squeak of the weather-vane recalls her to the reality of her situation and to the anxious necessity of playing by the patriarchal rules (*CSF* 150). That the women being churched are poor is also part of the threat, emphasising their economic vulnerability and dependence on patriarchal institutions, even as such institutions perceive women's (re)productive capacities (and by extension women's sexuality) to be unclean. This point about the economic vulnerability of all women is brutally reinforced in the final section in which Miranda as an individual is effaced, her active desires obliterated and her future revealed to be as bru-tally constrained as that of the working class and poor women.

In this final section, Miranda is displaced from the centre of the narrative; there is no mention of the novel she reads nor of the noises that influence her dreams; even her words are now in parenthesis and she is more fully, and disturbingly, appropriated as a commodity. Here the apple trees assume a more prominent role and are now more evidently a crop: there is a specific number placed (presumably in a regular pattern) so that each has 'sufficient space' but no more, and even the sky seems to be made to fit this pattern (*CSF* 150). Indeed, there is a more overt sense of a masculine and capitalist economy at work here with the emphasis on measurement and calculation, and with the use geometric terms.[21] Further, the cash crop itself seems to be in tune with a masculine libidinal economy as well as with a male-dominated capitalist one: the growth of the straight and phallic tree-trunks seems to have an almost ejaculatory effect: they grow 'with a rush up the trunk which spread wide into branches and formed into round red or yel-low drops' (*CSF* 151), suggesting that it is this virile capitalist energy that brings the fruits into being. Accompanied by an intensified sense of restric-tion and control (the orchard walls have 'compacted' everything inside and the earth itself is 'clamped together'), there is a sense that all of nature's bounty (including Miranda) is appropriated in this commercial enterprise. Miranda's dress is merely a 'purple streak' which forms a 'slit' in the blue green of one corner of the orchard (*CSF* 151). The disturbing image of the purple streak/slit indicates that it is her virginity and/or her reproductive capacity that will accord her any value in the violent social and sexual sys-tem represented here: like the trees, she must fit into an allocated amount of space and is seemingly also a fruit ripe for the picking.

However, this story resists the notion of the marketplace as the ultimate arbiter of value. Woolf's story is not simply a commodity for instantaneous

138   *Gifts, Markets and Economies of Desire*

consumption. Rather, its highly experimental form invites the reader to participate with generosity in the creation of various meanings. Woolf's engagement with literary modernism's ambivalent relationship to the market is a constant preoccupation for her, a preoccupation seemingly given a particular focus in the early 1920s by her involvement with the attempts to raise a fund to support T.S. Eliot. Woolf's response to Ka Cox's dislike of 'In the Orchard' prompts her to consider her own relationship to the market, and importantly to distinguish her own writing from the purely commercial in a way that resonates with the issues 'In the Orchard' raises (*D2* 247–9). At this point, Woolf, still anxiously comparing herself to Katherine Mansfield whose commercial success she both envied and despised, is in the midst of writing 'The Hours' (*Mrs Dalloway*). In her diary, she exalts in the full creative flow of her modernist style, so 'queer' and 'masterful', against her distrust of the 'cheapness' of reality and realism (*D2* 248). She also feels refreshed to be free of 'the motive of praise', a relief expressed as if she had 'slipped off all [her] ball dresses and stood naked . . . a very pleasant thing to do' (*D2* 248). Diane Gillespie discusses this image of divestiture as 'a positive metaphor for immunity from public scrutiny and judgement', and argues that Woolf 'here associates feminine costumes with public approval, and nakedness with writing for its own sake' (2006, 10). Discussing this diary entry in relation to Lady Godiva, she makes the broader point that such nakedness represents a freedom from conventions enabling Woolf to 'speak her mind' (11).

In relation to the 'slit' of Miranda's dress in 'In the Orchard', this image involving the shedding of dresses also signals a rejection of the sartorial signifiers of the objectification and of a brutal exposure of the commodification of women's bodies and sexualities. That this is linked for Woolf with the growing 'body' of her own writing is evident as the diary entry goes on to shift the discussion to Woolf's new found fame and fortune, brought about by the commercial success of her writing rather than from her novels. Significantly, she 'turn(s) now to the body – which is money and America and Mr Crowninshield' (then editor of *Vanity Fair*, *D2* 249). There seem to be two bodies discussed here: the metaphorical naked body of her creative integrity, and the writer's literal body that makes money, which perhaps suggests some anxiety about 'selling out', about prostituting her creativity for the making of material wealth. However, in the face of the vagaries of popularity and success, Woolf insists on her integrity as a modernist writer, asserting this as 'the old feeling of nakedness' that is 'the backbone' of her existence (*D2* 249). She claims not to have 'that "reality" gift' but rather that she 'insubstantise(s), wilfully to some extent' in her creation of modernist forms that can convey reality more truly and with a 'richness' in the implied contrast to the 'cheapness' of realism (*D2* 248). The insubstantial qualities and indeterminacy of 'In the Orchard' demonstrate this modernist richness, and defy any sense of this story as simply a commodity the value and meaning of which derives only from the marketplace.

Moments of Giving 139

Although the story does not engage obviously with the giving of gifts, its highly experimental form, dominated by what would seem 'unprofitable' repetitions and near repetitions, creates a textual generosity that counters the capitalist economic principles of property and profit, principles that short-change women and the working classes by default and transform nature's bounty into a commodity. With an excess of possibilities it resists the commodifying impulse of capitalism, promoting a destabilisation of hierarchies, and a disturbance of property rights. The three sections of the story explore similar external events but offer three different perspectives on these events and on Miranda herself. As in 'Kew Gardens', a woman's barely articulated desires to escape the ideological traps of conventional sexual and economic structures are reined in by the social ritual of taking tea, the service required of women in this ritual reinforcing the idea that, whatever a woman's class, 'all women . . . are . . . in complex ways, bound in service to the consequences of patriarchal ideology' (Staveley, 2004, 57). However, although Miranda's duty at the tea-table punctuates the ending of each section of the story, demonstrating the rigorous, and increasingly ominous, enforcement of this social imperative, Woolf's own experience of the tyranny of the tea-table (described in 'A Sketch of the Past') enables her to develop an oblique approach which, when transferred to her writing, means that she can 'slip in' things that would otherwise be ignored or invisible (*MOB* 164). It is this stylistic sleight of hand that is the foundation of the generosity of this story. This takes the form of literary allusions and formal innovations, which enrich and complicate the story, creating a fluid and indeterminate literary form that Cixous argues can be categorised as a feminine gift economy.[22] The allusion to the French novel *Ramuntcho*,[23] for instance, offers rich potential for other meanings, especially with the impossibility of an exact equivalence between two languages.[24] What is selected from Loti's text refers to girls' (erotic) pleasure and, given the uncertainty of what may be missed in translation, adds further to the potentially subversive qualities of Miranda's dreams, indefinitely increasing the possible meanings of this story and resisting a fixed calculation of value. Although the final section of the story does indicate how Miranda is positioned and perceived as a commodity on display, this story does not endorse this through narrative closure. Rather, the story's circularity and multiple narrative beginnings mean that the reader is sent back to the beginning, looping back to begin again the pattern of a story of three parts that repeatedly refuses to unravel. What is emphasised, in fact, is that Woolf's formal innovations, her 'wilful insubstantising', emphasise the indeterminate qualities of Miranda, a technique that generates different versions of Miranda, rendering her value as a marketable commodity or investment hard to ascertain. She is not a single unified subject, but is multiple, fragmented and incoherent, and as such is a highly problematic commodity to 'price'. Miranda's lack of a fixed and specific value undermines the law of exchange, and without such a quantifiable value an exchange cannot take place.[25]

140 *Gifts, Markets and Economies of Desire*

This is in stark contrast to the Miranda of Shakespeare's *The Tempest*, to which Woolf's story also seems to allude. Shakespeare's Miranda exemplifies the dangers of a gift economy when it is women *themselves* that are given as gifts, 'gifts', that is, that function in accordance with a capitalist exchange. Miranda is given in marriage by her father, Prospero, as a 'rich gift' to the Prince of Naples (*Tempest*, 93), but this is in return for Prospero's own gain in wealth and status. She is knowingly complicit with her status as an object exchanged between men and with the political corruption of those with power. She recognises that men play her 'false' but is content with what she will gain from being a pawn in a patriarchal power game that revolves around making maximum profit in terms of social prestige, political power and material possessions.[26] However, in Woolf's story, there is no narrative closure to 'resolve' the tensions and implicit critiques her writing raises. In contrast to the apparently more knowing Miranda of Shakespeare's play, we see how Woolf's Miranda is unwittingly played false in what Rubin calls 'one of the greatest rip-offs of all time' (Rubin, 550).[27] Woolf's story challenges the objectification of women as either commodity or gift, and demonstrates the limitations of the capitalist exchange. The many interruptions and divergent narrative threads in the three sections send the readers' imaginations off in all directions, refer back to other sections, and invite a reading against the grain of the seemingly inevitable pattern of Woolf's Miranda's future.

At the time of the composition and publication of 'In the Orchard' Woolf was not only re-reading Shakespeare and other Elizabethan writers, but *The Tempest* seems to have been not far from her thoughts in several ways, not least as connected with creativity, publication, sexuality and monetary and gift economies. At this point Woolf was highly involved in what was ultimately a failed attempt on the part of T.S. Eliot's friends and colleagues to raise sufficient funds to enable him to leave his position at Lloyds Bank so that he could devote more time to writing. Ezra Pound began the *Bel Esprit* project in 1922 and Ottoline Morrel set up the Eliot Fellowship Fund to complement this (Ackroyd 122; Lee 446). Given the impression that Eliot's *The Waste Land* made on Woolf (as Lee notes, 443, 453), with its reference to Ariel's song possibly triggering ideas for 'In the Orchard', it would seem that Woolf's attempts to help set in motion a gift economy for Eliot's benefit (and the failure of this) and Shakespeare's play are entwined with her own story about markets and commodities.[28]

This scheme raises interesting issues about modernism's relation to the market. Lawrence Rainey sees it as a 'modernist' form of patronage, updated for the modern world as a form of investment. Ezra Pound 'sold' the scheme to potential patron-investors with promises of the chance of 'infinite profit' to reward their 'great deal of risk' (in a letter to John Quinn, cited in Rainey 1999, 61). The difficulty, as Rainey points out, is that the literary text remains the property of the author and investors do not get a return on their investments

Moments of Giving 141

in terms of increased personal wealth. This is why, he argues, 'the deluxe or limited edition acquired such prominence: it transformed literary property into a unique and fungible object' that could increase in value, suggesting that these changes indicate 'a profound change in the relations among authors, publishers, critics and readers', especially in the sense that collecting and owning become more important in this kind of economy than reading (1999, 62, 55). The schemes to raise money for Eliot do indicate a mismatch between modernist literary value and market values: the Eliot Fellowship Fund appeal claimed as a justification for such a scheme the fact that Eliot's 'literary work is of too high and original a quality to afford by itself a means of livelihood' (quoted in *L2* 590). What is clear is that literary modernism is not sufficiently viable to support those without inheritance or investments; giving to Eliot is a means of countering the pressures of the market, and is necessary to enable original creativity to be sustained. This scheme makes clear the recognition that modernist literature is above this market, a highbrow cultural object and not the popular commodity that 'middlebrow' writers might produce. Its value lies in its artistic integrity and originality, in terms of its technical innovation and its niche-market appeal, not in its moneymaking potential as a bestseller.

Despite Woolf's persistence (and the promise of a copy of all of Eliot's works as published to subscribers) she found 'so few people[,] willing to give at all' because 'most people are as badly off as Tom' (*L2* 542, 548). Eliot's own reticence and anxiety about relying on gifts for his financial security compounded the difficulties of this scheme, and Ezra Pound's part in the scheme further confused the issues.[29] By October 1922 Woolf complains that this 'most ticklish business' has impacted on her whole summer, but that she is the only one on whom the scheme 'reflects credit' (*L2* 565, 572).[30] Despite her own anxieties about money in the summer and autumn of 1922 (as they surface in her concerns about the commercial success of *Jacob's Room* and the future of the Hogarth Press, *L2* 579–80, 583), when a correction to the contribution forms was needed, she also offered to print it at the Hogarth Press (*L2* 575). Woolf's efforts in this scheme raise many issues about gift-giving and about the duty to give in a predominantly capitalist culture. Her own motivations are genuine concern and pity for Eliot's situation,[31] and a sense of responsibility for not making the scheme a success. However, she seems also aware of how to strike a bargain that involves 'gifts' as well as some return profit, as is evident in the negotiations around the editorship of *The Nation*. Maynard Keynes tries to negotiate the literary editorship for Eliot and, to try to ensure the success of this, Woolf appeals to Lytton Strachey for him to offer to contribute to *The Nation* if Eliot were to be editor. She reminds Strachey that 'this is cheaper than contributing the £100 which is your due' and that, as well as more lofty motives (the easing of his conscience and the fostering of English literature), she adds the financial incentive that 'Maynard is going to pay his contributors highly' (*L3* 14–15).

142   *Gifts, Markets and Economies of Desire*

Lee suggests that 'the fund stirred up the competitive issue of how much money they all had' (1996, 446) and that this context reveals much about Woolf's attitude to money and the operation of economies. She is relieved that, unlike Eliot, she is not inhibited about money ('why twist and anguish and almost suffocate with humiliation at the mere mention of money?' as Eliot does [letter to Roger Fry, *L2* 572]) and says that she 'doesn't much like human nature . . . in money matters' (letter to Ottoline Morrel, *L2* 548). However, she is also in a privileged position, when her earlier financial anxieties were resolved by her receipt of an unexpected 'windfall', in the form of money from investments.[32] She has faith that 'always some wind brings down an apple at the critical moment' (*D2* 161). However, although an apple here is metaphorically a store of money,[33] she does not want to hoard this store or exploit it to increase her profits more than she needs. She does participate in a capitalist system, 'to make myself a certain amount of money regularly' as she says, but this is not money for hoarding but is 'pocket money' for immediate spending (*D2* 225), earning to live rather than earning to buy and hoard. Arguably, it is Woolf's relative financial security and class privilege that makes this attitude to money possible, but it also accords with her 'democratic highbrow' attitudes, as Cuddy-Keane discusses (2003, 13). Woolf's charitable giving suggests that she was committed to sustaining the circulations of gifts, wealth and, importantly, books (as Snaith's research, discussed in Chapter 1, demonstrates).

In 1926 Woolf confirmed her commitment to the gift economy and her support for women's higher education when she made a gift of her story, 'A Woman's College from Outside', to the Edinburgh University Women's Union,[34] a story that Susan Dick has noted is connected to 'In the Orchard'.[35] In both stories, fruit plays a key role. However, fruit as a commodity in 'In the Orchard' is transformed into a homoerotic gift in 'A Woman's College'. This was also the period in which Woolf's relationship with Vita Sackville-West was most intense, beginning in December 1922, and marked by the quick and repeated exchange of gifts: the 'new apparition Vita' gives Woolf 'a book every other day' (*D2* 225). Among the early gifts were books in which in which fruit plays a significant role literally and metaphorically. These include Sackville-West's family history, *Knole and the Sackvilles* (1922), a gift that grew to fruition for Woolf in *Orlando*, but which also, as Karyn Z. Sproles discusses, focuses on fruit as a gift of love. In this history, Sackville-West relates how her grandfather would leave a plate of fruit in a drawer of his writing table as a gift for the young Vita to discover. Sproles suggests that this gift of fruit was what Sackville-West shared with Woolf, both metaphorically in the sharing of her personal history and writing, and literally in the basket of peaches she sent with her acceptance to take tea with Woolf: 'with her gift of fruit she handed Woolf a promise of intimacy as sweet and juicy as a peach' (Sproles 62). Sackville-West also gave Woolf a copy of her collection of poems, *Orchard and Vineyard* (1921). In these poems, Sackville-West

Moments of Giving 143

represents the Kent landscape as the epitome of Englishness, romanticised and rich with nature's bounty; here orchards welcome her speakers home and apple trees are weighted down with blossom promising plentiful fruit. In a love poem, 'To Eve', Eve is freed from the garden walls to a palace on the hill with chiming bells (perhaps an influence on Woolf's less romanticised view of English horticulture in 'In the Orchard'). In Woolf's story, 'A Woman's College', the gift of the metaphorical golden fruit does create an idealised, even utopian, moment, but the story also remains firmly connected to the real world and to the economic and ideological constraints on women's aspirations and homoerotic desires.

As Dick notes, 'A Woman's College From Outside' was first planned and drafted as part of *Jacob's Room* (*CSF* 305). In this context, it would have offered a contrast to the masculine world of Jacob's university life and Jacob's situation. As a story in its own right, it explores the aspirations, fantasies and desires of a young woman on the threshold of maturity; a counterpart to Miranda in several ways, Angela is not a commodity-gift to be exchanged, nor is she to be played 'false'. Rather, as a student of 'the science of economics', with a clear understanding of how her parents' earnings make possible her education, and her future 'earning her living', she is very clearly aware of the operation of the monetary economy.[36] This knowledge is not the same as acquiescence in this system, however. It is Angela's awakening to her homoerotic desires, a revelation experienced, as for other of Woolf's female characters, as the bestowing of a gift, that is at the heart of this story's challenge to the social and sexual norms for middle class women and the limitations these norms impose. Angela's homoerotic desires, experienced as synonymous with her participation in a gift economy, intensify the threat that independent, soon to be professional, women already represent as they undermine not only patriarchal structures and masculine values (particularly in their trespass into 'male' areas of knowledge, emphasised here by reference to the *science* of *economics*) but also the interconnected heterosexual libidinal economy and capitalist economy. It is a story, as Hanson indicates, that acts as 'a vehicle for different *kinds* of knowledge', and what Angela learns is indeed 'at odds with the "story" of dominant culture' with its social and sexual norms (1989, 6).

The narrative perspective is, at first, from outside the women's college, moving from the moonlit gardens to a view of Angela reflected in her mirror as if through her window, and finally moving into the women's dormitories. Initially, Angela is described in conservative and highly conventional terms. She is represented gazing at herself in the mirror, apparently caught up, Narcissus-like, in self-admiration, viewing herself as a kind of goddess figure, an idealised eternal icon of femininity – pure, beautiful, angelic and emanating light: a 'lily floating flawless upon Time's pool' (*CSF* 145). However, this image of feminine perfection is immediately shattered when Angela vanishes from the mirror: the fixed view of her in the mirror from a

144 *Gifts, Markets and Economies of Desire*

single perspective seems to be 'visible proof of the rightness of things', but this idea of her can only be sustained while she is immobile and statue-like. The values this image signifies are 'betrayed' by Angela when she springs into life, moves about the room and, significantly, reads her economics book. The attempt here to dispel the relatively new challenge to social and economic structures that women university students represent is indicated by this objectifying gaze on Angela and by the narrator's doubts that she *can* have 'a firm grasp of the science of economics' (*CSF* 145). Women students' trespass into the traditional male domain of higher education (and their anticipated intrusion into male-dominated professions and the market economy itself) is made safe by emphasising what these women lack. They have 'blank, featureless' faces and 'ringless' hands. Their trespass is also made safe by comparing the college to places traditionally associated with women – 'a dairy or nunnery . . . place(s) of seclusion or discipline', – suggesting an implicit equation of women's education and traditional women's roles. Angela's particular intrusion into the male sphere of economics is thus dismissed as ineffectual, and her intelligence assumed to be inferior. However, this perspective on Angela and the other women students is an external one and cannot be sustained: Angela's self-satisfaction and self-admiration are only apparent, as the '*as if* she were glad to be Angela' suggests (145, my emphasis). And the view from inside the college, bodies and minds of the women radically undermines this narrative perspective and the assumption of women's lack of ability to understand economics. On the contrary, these women students are fully aware of the socio-economic status traditionally allocated to them, and they counter the heteropatriarchal economies of desire and capitalist systems of value that are the basis of this status. Indeed, this Angel[a] has a Will[iams] of her own.

The story immediately challenges some of the formalities of male-dominated higher education, and in doing so begins to undermine the masculine economy of value these represent. The name on the dormitory door confers a specific kind of patriarchal power and authority in a masculine economy of meaning. However, here even the first names remain somehow impersonal when they are inscribed on the cards: they are '(a)ll names, nothing but names' and the values signified with the authority of a name, and the compulsion *to* name, are simply not important (*CSF* 146). Indeed, the 'cool white light' of the feminine moon does not emphasise the femininity, delicacy and purity of these students but, rather, with a power to match a masculine sun 'wither(s) . . . and starch(es)' the name cards on the doors (*CSF* 146). Angela's name, 'A. Williams', has the effect of enhancing impersonality because her initial is the indefinite article (*CSF* 145). However, this impression is quickly undermined as the story moves to the woman-centred space behind the dormitory door, a transition marked by the sound of 'soft laughter' and a discussion about women's sexual desires (*CSF* 146). If there is a temptation to see the effects of the moonlight as endorsing a virginal

Moments of Giving 145

and emotionally icy sense of these women students, this is countered here by Helena's assertion that women students are 'not eunuchs', a statement that both refutes a sense of women students as resembling castrated and inferior men, and asserts that they are women with desires of their own (*CSF* 146). The hint of sexual scandal in the college provokes further laughter and excitement, and their conversation suggests a growing awareness of their own sexual and sensual potential.

This laughter is powerfully subversive, bonding together a community of women who partake in the secrets and sensuality of the night and whose values and relations are very different to those imagined, presumed or hoped for from the outside. Even more so than in 'In the Orchard', women's laughter has a disruptive effect, not directly exploding patriarchal law (as Cixous argues, 1981a, 258). Rather, it 'snow(s) under', smothers and silences the central values and (economic and social) investments of this patriarchal institution. It 'gently waft(s) away the hour, rules, discipline', undermining the kinds of 'heroic', martial and intellectual activities here deemed fundamental to the institution of masculinity: the ability 'to extinguish a fire, suppress an insurrection, or pass an examination' (*CSF* 146). Women's laughter not only diffuses the masculine power, authority and values of this institution but, engaging 'mind and body', is 'immensely fertilising', and its 'bubbling' energy spreads like a mist, its influence extending beyond the garden as it moves out into the world, beyond the college spaces conceded to the women, much as their energy and influence will spread when they leave this limited space.

As it infiltrates Bertha's semi-dream state, this 'irresponsible laughter . . . chaotic, trailing and straying' is formless and excessive, creating a utopian sense of limitless possibility, and of carnivalesque pleasure and *jouissance*. It signals a feminine disruption of hierarchies and property rights. This laughter undermines any expectation of compliance with patriarchal rules and assumptions. Instead, these are 'softly' but surely 'uprooted', breaking up, as Cixous suggests, 'the old property crust, carrier of masculine investments' (*CSF* 146; Cixous, 1981a, 258). As we see in *Mrs Dalloway*, women's subversive interactions work in a different timeframe. Clocks that determine 'proper' or appropriate activities for day and night are 'disregarded' by the women: they resist the male-identified 'commands' of the clock striking the early hours of the morning, and rebel against the 'prim-voiced' sound and the respectability it tries to enforce (*CSF* 146).

The richly sensual description of the night, and by extension women's sexuality, further emphasises a sense of generosity, overflow and plenitude, a stark contrast to the regulation and calculation of a rational (daytime) economy of value. The language used to describe the night and the women's experience of this shared and secret time generates a sense of bountiful freedom and unfettered possibility: 'since night is free pasturage, a limitless field, since night is unmoulded richness, one must tunnel into its darkness.

146   *Gifts, Markets and Economies of Desire*

One must hang it with jewels' (*CSF* 146). The value of these night-time experiences and interactions is of a different order to those of the daytime. In this sensual and illicit context the young women play cards, their 'hands were dabbled in the cards', implying a gamble at odds with the regulation and rationality of a capitalist economy of calculation, profit and loss. Although gambling also involves these factors, it is the risk-taking and daring to go beyond what is certain that is privileged. Here there is also a potential slippage between the name cards and the playing cards, suggesting the sense that the women's identities and indeed their destinies are part of the gamble. In this intimate context of shared secrets and the sensuality and pleasure of the night, it is suggested that the empty signifiers of names on doors may become richly invested with immense possibility for the women's future selves.

While the others dream or play cards, Angela and Alice engage in a risky and potentially life-changing gamble of their own, as they engage in romantic talk of the colour of the beach in the evening and arranging to meet in the summer. In this woman-centred, sensual, nurturing and subversive context, Alice's touch on Angela's head creates an explosive effect for Angela, unleashing overwhelming excitement, emotions and energy: Angela feels 'like one possessed of a wild wind-lashed sea in her heart' as she moves restlessly 'up and down the room' (*CSF* 147). Not sure whether Alice has kissed her or simply touched her head, Angela experiences this moment as a precious gift, a golden fruit 'dropped into her arms', the bounty of 'the miraculous tree' of Alice. Like Sally's diamond gift of a kiss in *Mrs Dalloway*, Angela is intoxicated by the radiance of this kiss/touch and feels; like Clarissa, that this gift is not to be in any way recuperated into the everyday world of sensation, thought or language: 'a thing not to be touched, thought of, or spoken about' (*CSF* 147). Although this can be read as a self-censoring of women's homoerotic desires, wanting to keep separate this moment of experience indicates Angela's sense that this gift of Alice's kiss/touch is something rare, precious, hard to attain and almost impossible to hope for. As such it cannot be given an exchange value in any system of experience. For Angela, as for Clarissa, this giving of a gift between women marks a radical shift and enables her to see the world and her future in a very different light, 'after the dark churning of myriad ages here was light at the end of the tunnel; life; the world' (*CSF* 147). The effect of this gift is positive, inspiring in her feelings of confidence and optimism that her future will be 'all good; all loveable' and hers for the taking. Her 'discovery' of 'this good world, this new world', however, creates a conflict with the heteropatriarchal and capitalist world she knows exists beyond this woman-centred space. There is a contradictory impulse in Angela as she longs to get closer to this newly envisioned future in which desire between women is possible, yet also wants to forestall her transition to the world of adulthood, with all of its responsibilities – not least the economic pressures on women who do not marry. It is a moment of

Moments of Giving   147

rebirth, as the image of Angela sucking her thumb suggests, an exciting yet also fearful moment. Drawn to the open window, at the permeable boundary between the inside and outside, college life and adult independence, Angela makes a sound 'as if in pain' as she becomes aware of 'something murmuring in the distance, the world, of course, and the morning coming' (*CSF* 148). This may also be a recognition, like that of Clarissa in *Mrs Dalloway*, of the danger of the violence of the 'granite wall' of homophobia and threat of social and financial impoverishment that her full acceptance of this homoerotic gift would entail (*MD* 40–1).

The story ends with Angela poised literally and metaphorically at a threshold. The ecstasy of her awakening desires and potential future happiness hangs in the balance as she faces what seems the inevitability of this vision being shattered in the male-dominated world beyond the college and in the cool light of day, a world in which she will need to use her knowledge of economics to support herself in a capitalist economy. Alice's kiss/touch creates a utopian moment apparently as equally impossible to sustain as the ideal of femininity with which Angela was introduced in this story: her own sensual play, kissing her reflection in the mirror, is displaced by the more powerful desire for intimacy with Alice, but this brings with it its own risks, dangers and costs. These issues of homoerotic awakening, and the negotiation of economic pressures and constraints consequent on being at odds with the heteropatriarchal capitalist world, are also explored in 'Moments of Being: "Slater's Pins Have No Points"'. Here, what becomes apparent is that Woolf's writing does not present a simple opposition of market and gift economies whereby the gift represents a kind of utopia beyond the market. Expressions of generosity and the literal giving of gifts do work to undermine capitalism's acquisitive ethos and attempts at attributing a fixed value, but equally they take place within a capitalist society. The gift is absorbed in the dominant paradigm of capitalist exchange. However, its profound ambiguity (in terms of motivation, its effect on the relationship between the participants and its value in every sense[37]) has a disruptive effect, suggestively sidestepping the calculation of market exchange. Further, in an increasingly impersonal and rigid economy (especially in the 1920s with the British Government stalwartly adhering to a policy of fiscal and monetary retrenchment in an attempt to return to the stability of the gold standard [Aldcroft, 1986, 6]), the need to counter the impersonality of a commodity society through the exchange of personal gifts becomes more urgent (as Carrier argues, 11).

As in 'A Woman's College from Outside', the giving of gifts in 'Moments of Being: "Slater's Pins Have no Points"' helps to create a sense of intimacy and to realise a different economy of desire between women. However, rather than keeping 'the world' at bay, this story explores the interconnections of market and gift economies, indicating an awareness of the ways that commodity culture can stimulate new desires for objects and experiences as it also creates spaces and opportunities for potentially subversive libidinal

148 *Gifts, Markets and Economies of Desire*

desires to surface. These desires can endanger the hierarchies and heteropatriarchal social order capitalism seems to keep in place because they cannot necessarily be channelled into or satisfied by the purchase of commodities. In this story, shopping and commodities create opportunities to pursue homoerotic desires and facilitate an increased intimacy between the two female characters. However, it is the operation of the gift economy that offers an outlet for such desires, needs and appetites, and signals the release of libidinal longings in excess of the rigid structures of capitalist exchange and heterosexual norms. Displacing the emphasis from the possession of commodities to the pleasures of the gift economy, this story works to generate homoerotic possibility and, potentially, to facilitate the satisfaction of women's more subversive desires. In particular, like in 'A Woman's College from Outside', 'Moments of Being: "Slater's Pins Have no Points"' privileges the giving of non-material gifts, such as the gift of music played to 'reward' and to charm, the giving of compliments, the sharing of a moment of ecstasy, and a kiss. The importance of gifts of stories, and the pleasures and dangers of interacting imaginatively with others by creating stories about them, is foregrounded in 'Moments of Being: "Slater's Pins Have no Points"'. This is seen both in Fanny's invention of stories about her teacher, and in the textual generosity of Woolf's story itself which, with its suggestive indeterminacy, offers an excess of 'points' to explore.

Resonating strongly with Mauss's ideas of the gift, the gifts exchanged in this story are not simply material, but inherently spiritual, even magical, imbued as they are by givers and receivers with the identity or the soul of the donor. It this aspect of the gift that has such significance here. In his reading of the story, Baldwin claims that Fanny is 'too young and inexperienced to grasp the full meaning of what she says about her teacher' and that 'it is not clear that Miss Wilmot understands fully the implications of the kiss' (54). Clearly, the open-endedness of this story helps to create this uncertainty. However, Baldwin's suggestion that 'what the story dramatizes is the unknown forces that may shape character without our being aware' (54) points also to the dominant, familiar and naturalised social, sexual and economic forces that are brought to the reader's and Fanny's awareness by the attention given to the operation of the market economy and the gift economy which both co-exists with and subverts it.

The beginning of the story foregrounds commodities and their acquisition. It also attests to an apparent disappointment with mass-produced objects. The faulty pin that causes Fanny's flower to fall interrupts Julia's playing of a Bach fugue (a 'reward' to her favourite pupil) and so intrudes on both the rarefied atmosphere created by high art, and on the intimacy of a moment of gift exchange between Julia and Fanny. Here it is evident that Woolf's writing does not set up a simple opposition of market and gift economies whereby the gift represents a kind of utopia beyond the market, but that gift exchange takes place within a capitalist society and works to

Moments of Giving 149

undermine capitalism's acquisitive ethos and the fixing of value from within. The title of the story makes clear that there is an intimate connection between the moment of being of homoerotic realisation and the impersonal, transferable commodity of a pin. It is the functional failure of the pin that literally and metaphorically 'unpins' and opens up the subversive potential of this otherwise conventional and acceptable teacher–pupil situation. As in 'A Woman's College', there is a different kind of knowledge conveyed in this story. Beginning with the shock that Julia participates in commercial transactions, Fanny's perception of her music teacher and her own desires undergoes a radical shift as she experiences an emotional and sexual awakening at odds with the dominant script of heterosexuality. This is a story about the awakening to new sexual self-knowledge, but also to the inevitable economic implications of being at odds with and resistant to the dominant script of heterosexuality. The context in which Julia Craye and her pupil Fanny Wilmot come to know one another is created by the business arrangement of buying and selling music lessons, but it is also a scene of 'homoerotically imbued mentoring relations' (Winston 61). Although this relationship is ostensibly premised on a monetary exchange, the interaction of Julia and Fanny exceeds the circuit of this exchange with generosity on both sides, and the lessons about desire and sexual choices that Fanny learns are inextricably bound up with both market and gift economies.

In particular, what is made explicit to Fanny is the economic risk of pursuing her homoerotic desires and the consequences of refusing to conform to heterosexual imperatives in a heteropatriarchal and capitalist society, a risk that also seems to contribute to Angela's sense of trepidation and her denial of the coming day in 'A Woman's College from Outside'. However, Fanny's teacher/mentor, Julia, is a role model for how to be happy to take the risk and live a frugal life, 'counting the cost and measuring out of her tight shut purse the sum needed for this journey, or for that old mirror' (*CSF* 220). Although her 'tight shut purse' seems to refer to both the economic constraint she experiences (Julia has been 'left badly off' after her brother's death, *CSF* 215), and her sexually constrained and closeted position, it is immediately made clear that such frugality also ironically signals her resistance to self-denial: she preserves the right to do what she likes and is obstinate in 'choosing her pleasures for herself', and indeed in sharing them with other women (*CSF* 220). It is also clear that what is valuable to Julia is not material possessions, but rather experiences and memories: she strings her 'memorable days' like precious gems on a necklace, recalling their uniqueness with sensuous (even sexual) satisfaction, 'finger(ing), . . . feel(ing), . . . savour(ing), sighing' over their 'quality(ies)' – not counting their value with avaricious calculation (*CSF* 219).[38] Julia's insistence on her freedom and her own assessment of what is of value seems to be also a reaction to the constraints of her previous living arrangement with her brother and indeed a counter to his acquisitiveness as a collector of rare objects. Like John in

150 *Gifts, Markets and Economies of Desire*

'Solid Objects', Julius hoards his treasures to himself, and the preciousness with which he keeps them encased, even embalmed, in a closed, sterile, and lifeless space, causes both Julia and Julius to be cut off from communication with others so that Julia is also metaphorically fixed in and by his display cases. In contrast to these valuable artefacts, the shoddy mass-produced pins unfix her, release her homoerotic desires, and act as an 'opening' to new relationships and, simultaneously, a new perspective on the world. Julia's opening gambit, then, can be read as her indication to Fanny that she has stepped beyond the constraints of her brother's collection, and the attitudes, assumptions, and values this represents, by demonstrating her involvement in the everyday commercial world.

However, although as a shopper Julia is an agent of exchange, rather than an object of exchange in a heterosexual economy, commodity culture is far from wholly satisfactory or satisfying. Julia is not duped or 'seduced by the glittering phantasmagoria of an emerging consumer culture' (Felski 62). Far from being the passive female consumer that male-driven marketing strategies assume and create, Julia remains in control of her spending and limits her participation in the masculine monetary economy. She is not drawn into the temptations of commodity culture and so does not capitulate to the desires it stirs, which can also keep women in a state of financial dependency on men, needing more money than they can earn to satisfy such desires, and so needing to charm and allure men.[39] Her desire 'to break the pane of glass' could be not only 'to break the spell that had fallen on the house; to break the pane of glass which separated them [Julia and Julius] from other people' (*CSF* 216), but also to break a shop window whose display of commodities for sale could both fascinate and entrap. Indeed, it can be argued that Julia, like Woolf, uses the market economy to facilitate the articulation of her desires: as Fanny suspects, Julia's opening gambit about Slater's pins seems to be made 'at a venture', as a means of forging a more intimate connection with Fanny through the sense of shared experience (*CSF* 216).[40]

It is this sense of shared intimacy between women that most differentiates the experience of Fanny and Julia from the impersonal world of collecting and of retail marketing associated with men. In contrast to the impersonal experience of retail,[41] the story sets up a space of female intimacy from which men are effectively excluded (Julius is dead and Slater's phallic pins are proven to be pointless) and in which a feminine libidinal economy is privileged. This economy is premised on the generosity and risk taking involved in the giving of a variety of gifts, and the story focuses on the power, centrality and passionate possibility of a homoerotically infused gift economy shared by women. Indeed, at the heart of this 'business' of giving music lessons is the personal connection between Julia and Polly Kingston, the spinster principal of the music school. It is significant that Julia teaches only 'as a special favour' to Polly, 'who had "the greatest admiration for her [Julia] in every way"' (*CSF* 216). Polly seems to wish to ameliorate the economic and

Moments of Giving 151

emotional dangers inherent in the resistance to dominant sexual norms, and to counter what Mauss calls 'the mere skimpy life that is given through the daily wages doled out by employers' (69), with her generosity supplementing the harsh and sterile economic system. Her stories are also imaginative gifts and similarly enrich the impersonal practicalities of economic transactions.

The gifts given in this story suggest the giving of pleasure and suggest a lesbian seduction. In this sense, Julia's role as an agent of gift exchange has a more subversive effect than her role as shopper. It serves to disrupt the market economy and trade because it threatens to undermine the notion of a fixed hierarchy and certain measurement of value, and because it defies the economic regulation of profit and loss. Further, the exchange of gifts between women also scuppers the heterosexual economy in which women are the gifts exchanged between men, not the givers or the receivers. In gift exchange between women, then, women are agents ('exchange partners' and 'sexual subjects', Rubin, 542–3) with the power to negotiate their own pleasures and to give pleasures to other women. Julia plays Bach as a gift to Fanny, and this music fills Fanny's ears and fully engages her senses. For Emerson, such a gift of one's talent is a true 'toke(n) of compliment and love', it is '(t)he only gift . . . a portion of thyself' (25), and this musical gift serves to create an atmosphere of intimacy and to charm Fanny. It also sets the gift economy in motion and Fanny's response is to reciprocate. Indeed, it could be that dropping her pin at Julia's feet acts as a pledge, as Mauss's discussion of the importance of the pledge in Germanic law and gift practices suggests. Mauss explains that a pledge makes the interaction between the two parties possible, because each 'possesses something of the other' (1990, 61), and the thing itself ('generally of little value' but also 'normally . . . personal', 61, 62) 'is a bond by virtue of its own power' (61). Such pledges are also wagers, challenges and dares, which 'hol(d) danger for both parties' (62), and are usually thrown at the recipient's feet. In Mauss's contemporary France, pins are the objects given as such pledges (61–2). Fanny's pin, dropped at Julia's feet, then, may be her promise to reciprocate Julia's gift of playing Bach for her, and the dare that prompts Julia's 'venture' about Slater's pins.

The stories in this story also function as gifts, stimulating the imagination and fuelling desires, and, importantly, exceeding simple commercial exchange. Polly relates tales of her tomboy days as she accepts payment for the music lessons. She gives 'little character sketches', which are not only in excess of the monetary exchange taking place, and which contrast significantly with the practical and direct exchange of 'cheques' for 'receipts', but which engender other stories in Fanny's mind and keep this gift in circulation (*CSF* 215). Importantly, it is from Polly's 'indescribable tone' used in the sketch of Julius Craye that Fanny infers 'something odd, something queer' about him and that fires her speculations about Julia (*CSF* 216). Although this 'something' remains elusive for most of the story, a phrase that appears in the version of the story published in *A Haunted House*, but

152   Gifts, Markets and Economies of Desire

not in the version published in *Forum*, significantly belies Fanny's feeling.[42] The hint of there being 'something odd about Julius Craye' (in both versions) is prefaced with 'it was a seductive thought' in *A Haunted House* (105). Rather than evading acknowledgement of Julia's lesbian sexuality and misrecognising her own lesbian desires (as Clements's reading of this story suggests), Fanny's attempted 'readings' of Julia also, more indirectly, reveal her attraction to her tutor. If the gift economy is energised and fuelled by love and generosity, and by a willingness to imagine and speculate, Fanny's stories of thwarted heterosexual romance, for which she can think of almost endless variations, can also be read as a kind of gift.[43] Fanny reads Julia as 'odd' and 'queer' like her brother, Julius. This seems to be an attraction (*CSF* 216), and she assumes that Julia had many admirers in the past, seemingly because Fanny herself admires her (*CSF* 218). Importantly, her speculation about Julia's suitors also reveals the extent to which Fanny is unconsciously attuned to the economics of heterosexual relationships and to the status of women as objects to be exchanged between men (as Baldwin's reading implies). This is evident in her suggestion that Julia's suitors would either have been her brother's friends or ambitious men who were as much attracted to her possessions as to Julia herself (*CSF* 217–8).

The pins of the title have many possible associations. In the story itself, knowledge of pins is something that Fanny considers pertinent only to married women ('None of the Crayes had ever married. She [Julia] knew nothing about pins – nothing whatever' *CSF* 216), and indeed the idea of 'pin money' would confirm this connection between pins and marriage.[44] The title can be seen to foreground the sexual politics of heteropatriarchal capitalism. And the apparent criticism of the shoddiness of the pins as a massproduced commodity can be read as a criticism both of heterosexual and capitalist systems. Neither Julia nor Fanny can rely on such gifts of money from men (indeed Julia's relatively impoverished state after the death of her brother suggests the vulnerability of women in such a system), so their ability to earn their living is a serious business.

However, although pins seem to be pure commodities – impersonal, massproduced, alienable objects – they can suggest other meanings and can cross over into other economies. Material objects, especially commodities, in Woolf's writing are hardly ever all they literally appear to be. Their meanings can be unfixed as they circulate in a new network of associations and desires. As we have already seen, they can unpin and set into circulation other associations and possibilities, in excess of what is intended. This opening up of possibilities can be seen also in the changeability of Fanny's flower once it is released from the pin. Initially, it is a rose (symbolising heterosexual romance and a heterosexual economy of desire) that falls from Fanny's dress, but this becomes a carnation as the story progresses. The 'flower' that is returned and re-pinned to Fanny's breast at the end of the story remains ambiguously coded in this sense (*CSF* 220). The pointless pins, then, give rise to a literal

Moments of Giving 153

and semiotic release and to a fluidity of signification;[45] they make it possible to articulate, though not to reductively pin down, a sexuality perceived to be in excess of a heterosexual economy.[46]

This change in flower may also signify Mauss's idea that 'to give something is to give a part of oneself . . . one gives away what is in reality a part of one's nature and substance, while to receive something is to receive a part of someone's spiritual essence' (10). However, this spiritual dimension of the gift, its *hau*, also sets up the obligation to reciprocate because '(t)o keep this thing is dangerous, not only because it is illicit to do so, but also because it comes morally, physically and spiritually from a person' (Mauss 10). As Julia gives back the flower that dropped out of Fanny's dress at the start of the story, we are aware that this gift is now imbued with Julia's homoerotic desires and with Fanny's awareness of, and somewhat uncomfortable acceptance of, them. It also suggests Fanny's recognition of these desires as her own. The rose that falls suggests Fanny's state on the threshold of heterosexual awakening, but it seems to be a carnation that is returned to her with a kiss at the end of the story.[47] That this returned flower-gift has been imbued with Julia's homoerotic desire and identity is made explicit in what Fanny seems to perceive as Julia's seductive handling of it:

> And she picked up the carnation which had fallen on the floor, while Fanny searched for the pin. She crushed it, Fanny felt, voluptuously in her smooth veined hands stuck about with water-coloured rings set in pearls. The pressure of her fingers seemed to increase all that was most brilliant in the flower; to set it off; to make it more frilled, fresh, immaculate.
>
> (*CSF* 217)

It seems, then, that the flower (and the female sexuality it can be seen to encode) is intensified, excessive and imbued with the disruptive power of lesbian passion. It is this, with the possibility and risk of future exchanges, that Fanny accepts with such trembling excitement and trepidation. In this exchange, Julia appropriates and transforms a somewhat clichéd heterosexual romantic gesture, and in doing so usurps the male role in such exchanges, signalling a displacement of the phallic heterosexual economy. Here we see that far from being deflowered[48] (with the underlying sense of violation and being laid claim to that this term implies), Fanny, like the carnation, is transformed. The word 'immaculate' also suggests that something sacred is taking place, suggestively Fanny's initiation into a new economy of desire.

At the point at which Julia returns the flower, Fanny is given an intimate insight into Julia's passion and we see the immense risk Julia takes, as she reveals her desires:

> She saw Julia open her arms; saw her blaze; saw her kindle. Out of the night she burnt like a dead white star. Julia kissed her. Julia possessed her.

154   Gifts, Markets and Economies of Desire

'Slater's pins have no points', Miss Craye said, laughing queerly and relaxing her arms, as Fanny Wilmot pinned the flower to her breast with trembling fingers.

(*CSF* 220)

This spell-like moment accords well with the 'magical or religious hold' Mauss claims gifts can have (12), and with Georg Simmel's understanding of the giving of a first gift, described as 'beauty, a spontaneous devotion to the other, an opening up and flowering from the "virgin soil" of the soul' (392–3). As Osteen suggests in relation to Simmel's ideas, the gift 'constitutes perhaps the fullest expression of what it means to be human . . . forges social connections and enacts one's true freedom' (14).

The danger implicit in gift-giving is also apparent here. Fanny interprets Julia's desire as intense and exhilarating, but also as having an edge of violence. When Julia crushes the carnation, releasing its energy and vibrant colour, this signals a danger for Fanny who is also embraced passionately, symbolically 'crushed', by Julia at the end of the story. Fanny also experiences this embrace as possession, the danger of which has been made clear in the representation of Julius's collection as life-denying. However, as we have also seen, Julia, unlike Julius, is anti-acquisitive; her urge to possess Fanny expresses a powerful moment of erotic intensity and release, not a desire to fix, own and take out of circulation. As is generally the case with gift-giving, Julia's seemingly spontaneous gesture is a risk for her; there is no guarantee of how her daring and unconventional gifts will be received, or whether they will be reciprocated. Julia's particular gifts are especially loaded with danger, but also with possibility; she seems to seek to awaken a more passionate experience of life and desire in Fanny, to imbue her with a new intensity (as she does with the carnation). However, the questions that the kiss and embrace raise remain unanswered, and the reader is left to speculate beyond the end of the story about the meaning of this moment of generosity and Fanny's response to it. As for Angela in 'A Woman's College From Outside', part of the sense of apprehension and danger for Fanny as she tremblingly accepts her flower and the kiss could be caused by her awareness of the real dangers that openly lesbian women face in a heteropatriarchal society – social ostracism, homophobia and financial constraint.

Woolf's story explores the interconnections between monetary, libidinal and gift economies, and raises questions about the notion of value, artistic production and interpretation. What we see here is the way that a momentary loss of a material object – marked as a commodity in this story – opens up a range of erotic, economic and creative possibilities. The flux and ambiguity of commodity culture are used to subversive ends. Alongside the operation of a gift economy, they give rise to a sense of intimacy and subversive potential. Finding the pin coincides with the revelation and recognition of another economy of desire, a desire that is in excess of both a heterosexual economy and a market economy. Perhaps in a sense, one point of Slater's pin/'Slater's Pins', then, is to prick the bubble of heterosexual romance and open up a different way of relating, bonding, of gaining a sense of identity. The moment of *jouissance*, overflow and energy at the end of the story exceeds rational calculation and opens onto a different way of being. Woolf's experimental style is ambiguous, tantalising and open. It keeps possibilities in play, refusing to absolutely pin down and fix meanings that could indeed invite censure and censorship. The privileging of the gift economy in Woolf's work (including in relation to the reader) seems key in maintaining this fluidity and ambiguity. Just as Fanny's various readings and co-writing of Julia's past make clear '(o)ne could make that [a snippet of information about Julia's past] yield what one liked' (*CSF* 218), Woolf similarly refuses to limit the meaning of her story, but rather offers it up to her readers as a gift for us to make it yield what we like, to co-write and circulate it as we like. The lack of closure to this story leaves the reader reeling, as we too are made to feel Fanny's radically altered perception of her situation and her world. The openness of the ending, and indeed Fanny's newly opened state, leaves us questioning, invites our participation in the creative process, and relies on our generosity in offering our own version(s) of what happens next.

Woolf's short fictions of the 1930s and 1940 continue to engage with market and gift economies, though in this period Woolf's attention was focused more firmly on the writing of her longer fictions and essays. After the publication of 'The Lady in the Looking-Glass: A Reflection' in 1929, Woolf did not publish another short story until 'The Duchess and the Jeweller' in 1938 (though Dick suggests that this may have been drafted in 1932 and then revised for publication in 1937, as with 'The Shooting Party' *CSF* 314). As Woolf's income from her novels decreased in the late 1930s, her anxieties about money intensified and sharpened her attitude toward writing for commercial outlets. Daugherty draws attention to the fact that, acting on Vanessa Bell's advice, Woolf would only write 'The Duchess and The Jeweller' 'if money is paid beforehand' (Daugherty 102; *L6* 157). She also highlights Woolf's chagrin when 'The Legacy', a story commissioned by *Harper's Bazaar* in October 1940, was not published, partly prompted by the editors' discourtesy but also because it was written specifically for money, a point reinforced in her letters to the editors which stress she 'was not prepared to write a story except it was commissioned' and her demand that they pay for it anyway (*L6* 469).[49] Although there is much to be said about Woolf's stories of the later 1930s in relation to the monetary, gift and libidinal economies in operation, it is 'The Legacy' (the last story that Woolf prepared for publication, completed in 1940 and published posthumously in 1943) that most explicitly foregrounds the gift economy, focusing as it does on the bequeathing of a gift – a gift that, like the pin in the earlier story, marks the sealing of a bond and the opening up of unspoken desires. This is simultaneously an important and ritualised giving of gifts, as well as the marking of an intimate

156   Gifts, Markets and Economies of Desire

relationship. Such bequest gifts perhaps best epitomise the central, most important aspects of the gift: the way a gift can both colour and be coloured by the relationship between donor and recipient and can irrevocably forge a connection between object and person.

'The Legacy' may have been inspired by Woolf's being given gifts after Lady Ottoline Morrell's death (*D5* 329–30, note 6; Dick *CSF* 318). Although the story is positive about such gifts, it would seem that Woolf's own experience was an 'uncomfortable' one (*D5* 140). In her diary she records being 'pressed' to take things by Ottoline's husband, as well as having, paradoxically, 'a vulture feeling' compounded by critical self-awareness about 'doing well out of Ottoline' (*D5* 140).[50] Almost inevitably, reading 'The Legacy' after Woolf's death invites autobiographical considerations, dealing as it does with a woman's suicide and her bequests, one of which was her diaries bequeathed to her husband. Lee suggests that 'the idea of posthumous enlightenment from the wife's diaries suggests something nearer home' than Woolf's experience after Ottoline Morrel's death, and 'the story makes a harsh, ironic, exaggerated version of the dark side of her own marriage' (1996, 748). In this story there is still an interconnection between market and gift economies but, as in Woolf's other writing from the late 1930s and 1940, the criticism of the capitalist ethos is much harsher than in the earlier stories considered in this chapter.

In this story Gilbert, the central character, sums up the meaning of the legacy his wife has left him in a way that appears to offer a definitive closure. The form of the story itself seems also to conspire in this closure being, in Fleishman's formalist reading, an example of Woolf's 'word-closed stories' where 'the title acts as the controlling focus throughout, but is mentioned only at the beginning and end' (59). Although Gilbert seems to feel shortchanged by his legacy, '(t)o him, of course, she had left nothing in particular, unless it were her diary', clearly Angela's bequest of her diaries to her husband Gilbert is central to both the form and content of this story, and indeed to his final realisation of 'the truth' (*CSF* 281, 287). What the story also makes clear is that Gilbert's understanding of the truth is, like his understanding of gift-giving, very narrow and limited; he seeks a rational and literal sense of 'truth' to close down possibilities to one meaning. As such, his understanding is a self-contained transaction. Although Fleishman also notes the 'oversimplification' of the conclusion when Gilbert 'discovers all' (60), this formalist reading does not go beyond this point. However, the reader is clearly invited to read beyond the reductive summing up offered by this egotistical, self-centred character and to resist the sense of completion that the circular form seems to suggest.

A focus on the ongoing circulation of the legacy gifts and on the meaning attributed to the process of gift-giving offers a counter to a form which Fleishman also suggests is one that 'reestablishe(s) an equilibrium' and centres on 'the meaning of the given' rather than exploring or 'pursu(ing) the unknown and possibly unknowable' (as a linear form does) (69). With its exploration of two very different attitudes to gifts and gift-giving, 'The Legacy' quite explicitly challenges social, sexual and economic 'givens' through the important and ritualised giving of legacy gifts, a bequeathing of personal possessions heightened still further by the fact that Angela committed suicide in a pact with her lover. In assuming an active role as gift giver and in choosing simply not to return the gifts her husband had given her, Angela not only defies Gilbert's pre-conceived expectations and estimations of her but, contrary to the masculine economy that determines Gilbert's expectation of a simple reciprocal exchange of gifts, she insists that the gift sphere be spread wide. In this way she resists the patriarchal authority he has assumed throughout their marriage and undermines his capitalist ethos not only by denying him a return on his investments (each of the gifts he is given her also 'had some memory for him' *CSF* 281) but by diffusing this value throughout her circle of friends. Indeed, this circulation of gifts transforms the meaning of Gilbert's gifts to Angela, which seem to be an exchange for her 'charms', one of which is her flattering dependence on him for information, for status and, presumably, for financial security. As Woolf's other writing attests, the social and economic imperative for women to charm men indicates their enslavement in a masculine economy that stifles their potential, creativity and desires. In acting on her socialist beliefs and pursuing her illicit sexual desires, Angela challenges this subordinate position, a challenge made manifest by her conversion of Gilbert's pseudo-gifts and the values they signify into gifts of great personal and symbolic significance (as discussed below). In this respect, her gifts also embody the transformation in Angela herself. That she committed suicide in a pact with her lover whose socialist political views challenge Gilbert's right-wing, authoritarian and patronisingly patriarchal beliefs, further compounds the subversiveness of her actions. Although Angela's suicide may be seen as a triumph of Gilbert's values over hers, Woolf's story (and indeed other of her fictions and her own life story) insists on this as a means of taking control and maintaining a sense of independent identity. That her gifts may also signify homoerotic possibilities compounds further the disruptive and challenging nature of the gift economy at work in this story.

Gilbert takes a very pragmatic, materialist and in many ways capitalist attitude to the giving of gifts, which shores up masculine social, sexual and monetary economies. In one way, his concept of the gift could be what Emerson refers to as a 'common gift', which satisfies the material needs of recipient but still ultimately creates a positive social bond (Emerson 25). However, he also very clearly perceives relationships in terms of profits or debts, so that 'gifts' are given in the spirit of capitalist exchange, calculated to bring a return profit or to thriftily cancel a debt. As Cixous claims, 'Man is strategy, is reckoning . . . "how to win" with the least possible loss, at the lowest possible cost' and this is the basis of 'the whole masculine economy',

158 *Gifts, Markets and Economies of Desire*

as is the avoidance of being in debt, in the vulnerable position of 'submission to the enormous weight of the other's generosity' (1981b, 47, 48). Before he realises his wife has committed suicide, her consideration for all of her friends in leaving them each a gift bemuses him. His inability to see the value of such gifts, now imbued with Angela's genuine affection and care, is revealed by the use of the phrase 'a litter of rings and brooches', by the repetition of 'little' to describe his wife's gifts (*CSF* 281). That these are also the gifts he gave to her in exchange for her devotion and dependence indicates also the capitalist thrift inherent in his attitude to gifts – to give as little as possible so as to get the 'returns' he desires. His attitude to seeing Sissy Miller, his wife's secretary, also confirms the masculine economy of values that resonates so clearly with a capitalist system. Because of the length of time Sissy has worked for them, he feels that he '*owe(s)* her . . . this token of consideration' of a private interview, which is a clear contrast to Angela's 'token of her affection' left for Sissy and all her friends (*CSF* 281, my emphasis). For him the 'token' (the interview) is a nominal sign that makes visible, and cancels, his debt; whereas for Angela the 'token' is a visible, tangible gift that embodies her affection, and which stems from generosity.

Angela's gift to Sissy, a pearl brooch, is what Emerson would call a gift of affection, of 'compliment and love', in representing 'a portion' of the giver and conveying the giver's identity (Emerson 25). However, it is also, importantly, what Hyde calls a 'threshold gift', a gift that marks a passage from one stage to another, offers protection and guidance in the process of change and transformation, and makes visible the loss, experienced invisibly, that such transitions entail (Hyde 43–5). Such gifts 'are not so much compensation for what is lost, but the promise of what lies ahead. They guide us toward new life, assuring our passage away from what is dying' (Hyde 44). It is this powerful promise of ongoing life that 'the fluidity of gift exchange assures' (Hyde 44) and that the gift Angela bequeaths to Sissy, imbued as it is with her love, offers. It is this that Gilbert's masculinist, capitalistic thinking, compounded by his conservative class and gender attitudes, threatens to obliterate.

He can see that Angela's gift to Sissy has some personal meaning but misjudges the relationship it signifies: he realises that Angela was able to form a more personal relationship with Sissy, but sees this as a demonstration of Angela's 'genius for sympathy', a paradoxical phrase which suggests that he sees Angela's ability to relate personally to people as an impersonal and innate skill, rather than as an intentional desire to make connections and bonds with others. He sees this relationship, then, as determined by Angela's ability to uncover 'all sorts of qualities in Sissy', rather than as a mutual and equal relationship significant for them both (*CSF* 282). He attributes Sissy's 'terribly distressed' state to the fact that Angela 'had been a friend' and assumes a knowledge of 'what his wife had meant to her', and even of what 'Sissy Miller was thinking' as her gaze rests on the writing table where she

Moments of Giving   159

and Angela worked so closely (*CSF* 282). As he gives Sissy the brooch, he also codes this exchange with a certain formal and formulaic meaning: he simultaneously gives his pre-prepared speech about knowing that Sissy will value Angela's personal possession, which invites what he assumes is also a 'prepared' response from Sissy about how 'it would always be a treasured possession' (*CSF* 282). However, although he remarks that part of the value of the gift for Sissy is that '(h)is wife had often worn it', his limited understanding of the full range of meanings of this gift is made apparent by his superficial thought about appearance. He considers that Sissy would probably have other clothes to wear 'upon which a pearl brooch would not look quite so incongruous' as the 'little black coat and skirt' which seem to be 'the uniform of her profession' (*CSF* 282). Here Gilbert is both objectifying and judging her by his own conventional sense of taste. Yet he misses the point that this brooch is not simply an ornament to adorn clothes, but that its inherent meaning is beyond such assessments of appearance or taste. Although he then realises that Sissy's black clothes indicate her mourning of her brother, he still remains insensitive to the cumulative meanings of Angela's gift for Sissy. He sees this gift as merely an object with a conventional usage as accessory or ornament. And he misses the way that this gift and the occasion of giving it symbolise and reinforce an intimate bond, carrying as they do the spirit or identity of Angela. (And, as we assume from the later revelations, this gift may convey Angela's feelings for Sissy's brother.) He disparages the brooch as a somewhat unsuitable gift, '[a] rather incongruous gift' for a woman of Sissy's 'kind': 'drab little women in black carrying attaché cases' (*CSF* 282). Unable to appreciate that one important motivation in giving gifts is purely to give pleasure and aesthetic satisfaction with total disregard for any practical or utilitarian function, he considers a more appropriate, because more useful, gift to be 'a sum of money, or even the typewriter' (*CSF* 282). However, the gifts he would have given confirm that he sees Sissy only as an employee; money and a typewriter are both impersonal gifts and merely confirm her role in the monetary economy as a professional woman earning her own living. Indeed, they could be seen as an investment in keeping this economy (and its limited places for women) in motion. His later offer of 'help' and his plan to offer financial assistance by letter confirm that he sees this legacy gift as a *payment* for Sissy's loyalty of service (so discharging the debt he feels he owes her), and an inappropriate one in need of being made more substantial, meaningful and suitable as he sees it. Hyde discusses the significance of 'market exchange . . . on the threshold' (44) as not only inappropriate but also a denial of the 'aegis of the [threshold] gift' under which we can safely undergo a spiritual transformation to the next stage of life. That Gilbert thinks in capitalist terms about Angela's and his own potential gifts indicates that he cannot accept or recognise his loss and that, not allowing the gift to protect him, he will die 'a dead-end death' – 'the death we rightly fear' (Hyde 45).

160   Gifts, Markets and Economies of Desire

Hyde's point that 'ideologies of market exchange have become associated with the death that goes nowhere' (45) is confirmed also by Gilbert's response to the gift bequeathed to him, Angela's diaries, his reading of which leads him nowhere beyond his own ego and self-concern. He is immune to the transformation and passage away from loss that this precious revelation of the private 'portion' of Angela could effect. His reading of the diaries resembles a capitalist approach to acquiring knowledge and making meaning. He seeks only what he sees as profitable to himself in being about himself ('His interests slackened' as 'His own name occurred less frequently' [*CSF* 285]) and discards as waste the details of Angela's private self, her desires, interests and losses – 'the little trifles, insignificant, happy, daily trifles that had made up her life', all written 'in her schoolgirl hand' (*CSF* 284). He had no idea about her grief over not having children, and his estimation that their '(l)ife had been so full, so rich as it was' means that he does not take this desire seriously now (*CSF* 284). Although he comprehends the facts of the life that she had, until now, kept private from him, he makes no attempt to empathise with the intimate revelations to which Angela has given him access. His negligence, self-conceitedness and dismissal of his wife's emotions, intelligence and values in his reading say much about Angela's life with him. He cannot understand her political commitments, nor anything else that contradicts his sense of possession of her as the perfect, submissive wife – an 'angel' woman. Once Angela's relationship with B.M. becomes recorded more prominently, Gilbert finds the diary 'more and more inexplicable' (*CSF* 286). He cannot appreciate the quality and potential of her generosity, just as he cannot appreciate the extent of Sissy's offer to explain anything more beyond the identity of B.M. There is "'Nothing! . . . Nothing!"' that Sissy can tell him beyond this fact, from which he deduces his 'legacy': 'She had stepped off the kerb to join her lover. She had stepped off the kerb to escape from him' (*CSF* 287).

Sissy's offer to explain and support Gilbert is, in fact, the second 'threshold' gift he refuses to accept, Sissy's offer of help being made significantly as she stands in the doorway: 'For a moment, on the threshold, as if a sudden thought had struck her, she stopped' and offers her help with a 'sympathetic yet searching [expression] in her eyes' (*CSF* 283). It is also a continuation of Angela's gift, motivated as it is by Sissy's feeling for Angela – it would be a 'pleasure' to help him for Angela's 'sake' (*CSF* 283). The final words of the story leave many questions unanswered and many possibilities unexplored. That these facts mark the point of closure for Gilbert, of the story and of his relationship with Angela, however, does lead the reader 'nowhere'. In fact, his rejection of further explanation, and the transition and transformation this second threshold gift could bring about, echo the 'nothing in particular' with which he estimated her gift of her diaries towards the beginning of the story, confirming that this really is a dead-end death for Gilbert.

Moments of Giving   161

For Sissy, Angela's gift is genuinely 'a treasured possession', a 'token of affection' and a vehicle for Angela's love, as the thrice repeated '"For Sissy Miller, with my love"' makes clear. Indeed, as Krystyna Colburn in her lesbian reading of this story points out, this is 'the only direct statement of love in the entire story' (2004, 72). Colburn makes clear the centrality of this gift to the lesbian possibilities in this story, asserting that '(i)t is the brooch that is the key to this story' and that it 'means more than a simple remembrance' (2004, 72). As Colburn points out, the fact that it is a pearl brooch is significant as a symbol of intimacy and possibly desire between Angela and Sissy, given the subversive potential of pearls read as clitoral imagery.[51] That this gift object is made of pearls points also to the palimpsestic nature of the relationship between the women to open up the subversive potential of this otherwise conventional and acceptable employer–secretary relationship through the story's erotic subtexts. Colburn excavates the palimpsestic layers of meaning through a close reading of the various drafts and versions of this story. She concludes that Woolf's revisions and rewritings suggest a certain struggle in her representation of 'the nature of the relationship between the women' (2004, 71). Indeed, what Dick considers '(t)he major change VW made as she reworked the story' in identifying 'B.M.' as Sissy's brother[52] may be an attempt to 'make safer' the homoerotic desires in this story and to 'explain' the unusual intimacy between Sissy and Angela, normalised by confirming Angela's illicit *heterosexual* relationship. However, as the effects of the pin in 'Moments of Being": Slater's Pins Have No Points' suggest, this brooch may symbolically pin together emotions and desires that are more complex than would at first appear, holding together a triangle of intimate relationships that threaten to unpin the foundations of heteropatriarchal and capitalist economy. Angela escapes her marriage from Gilbert and the meaning he attributes to her, just as her gifts also unpin themselves from Gilbert's property and circulate in a sexually subversive and socialist-inspired gift economy that threatens to destabilise heterosexual and market economies.

As this small selection indicates, in Woolf's hands the short story is an incredibly economical form, rich in potential meanings far in excess of the lengths of short fiction, and resisting the process of commodification. Her short fictions are not finished commodities with a specific meaning and literary value, but operate an economy of textual generosity, of association and possibility resistant to a simple process of interpretation. Although some of her short fictions may participate in a market economy by being sold and bought commercially, they demonstrate a preoccupation with and preference for the ongoing circulation of ideas, desires and meaning. Indeed, the reader's involvement becomes more of an emotional and intellectual investment in this circulation and in the creation of meanings, building a sense of intimacy collusion. The ambiguity, suggestiveness and indeterminacy of the form of Woolf's stories can also be read as textually generous. They give rise to a wealth of potential meanings, and invite a generosity from the reader

162 Gifts, Markets and Economies of Desire

who may participate, investing time, imagination, emotion and intellect to explore their many possibilities. Such generosity also puts these stories at odds with the dominant processes of commodification because they are not a closed and finished products with a specific meaning and literary value for ready consumption. As usual, Woolf seems to have in mind a reader-accomplice who will generously participate in the creative and ongoing process of making meanings so that ideas and possibilities remain in circulation.

5
Conclusion

There is a tendency in recent thinking and writing about the gift to dismiss it as merely 'disguised self-interest' or 'as a remnant of a golden age of pure generosity' (Osteen 1), and to 'conjure the gift away, refusing its magic or madness in the name of reason, of reducing everything to economic exchange' (Still, 1997, 172). Writing in a period of dramatic social, political and, importantly, economic upheaval, Woolf's privileging of the gift confirms its importance in sustaining social bonds in an increasingly (and dangerously) impersonal world. That gifts are complex, ambiguous and indeterminate, and that the risk in giving them is great, are factors central to Woolf's own sense of her creative gift, to her negotiation of the literary market, and to her own acts of generosity. Concepts of the gift facilitate the exploration of the subversive politics of Woolf's writing, offering a different perspective on the challenges to hegemonic authority and norms and resonating with the generosity of its suggestive forms.

However, although in brief moments the gift does take on utopian qualities, in Woolf's writing gift economies are contiguous with market economies. Instead of the oppositional thinking that leads to the explaining away of the gift, the two economies are interrelated. Expressions of generosity and the literal giving of gifts do work to undermine capitalism's acquisitive ethos and the fixing of value, but they take place within a capitalist society and so subvert this economic system from within. Just as gift-giving is never perfectly altruistic or uncomplicated by conflicting desires and motivations, in Woolf's writing participation in market economies and in economic transactions can be generous and doubly-focused both on what is transacted and how this takes place. The gift is not an impossibility in Woolf's writing, nor is it a 'fiction'; rather, it becomes a central dynamic in all the exchanges that take place – within her texts and between her writing and her readers.

It is easy to perceive Woolf's writing as a gift offered to her readers, its richness, intensity and indeterminacy offering scope for ongoing and endlessly proliferating meanings. However, what is also clear is that the process of reading itself is also a gift, an act of generosity that brings Woolf's writing to

164   *Gifts, Markets and Economies of Desire*

life; as her last novel makes clear, it is only when the audience begin to respond that the work of art is given meaning, its circulation and creative gifts put in motion by the generosity of the reader.

My reading of Woolf is not an attempt to define and limit the complexity and problematic aspects of her work, but to read with generosity and a sense of the contradictions the immense possibilities that the idea of the gift can bring to her writing.

Notes

Introduction

1. Abbott cites Jennifer Wicke's *Advertising Fictions: Literature, Advertisement, and Social Reading* and Jonathan Freedmans's *Professions of Taste: Henry James, British Aestheticism, and Commodity Culture* in this respect. Michael Tratner suggests that Cheryl Herr's *Joyce's Anatomy of Culture*, R. B. Kershner's *Joyce, Bakhtin and Popular Literature* and Franco Moretti's *Signs Taken for Wonders* continued this focus on Joyce and the market.
2. These studies include: Jennifer Wicke's 'Mrs Dalloway Goes to Market: Woolf, Keynes, and Modern Markets', in which she argues that 'modernism contributed profoundly to a sea-change in market consciousness' (5); Paul Delany's *Literature, Money and the Market*; Ian Willison et al.'s *Modernist Writers and the Marketplace*, Jane Garrity's 'Selling Culture to the "Civilized": Bloomsbury, British Vogue, and the Marketing of National Identity' and 'Virginia Woolf, Intellectual Harlotry, and 1920s British *Vogue*', and Leslie Hankins' 'Virginia Woolf and Walter Benjamin Selling Out(siders)'.
3. This was first translated into English in 1954 by anthropologist and French scholar, Ian Cunnison (James 10).
4. Such as in acts of hospitality and festivals, donations to the arts, the co-operative groupings, such as Friendly Societies in Britain, in the movement to provide unemployment benefits in Britain, and state interventions in France, such as social insurance legislation and family assistance funds (Mauss 65–9).
5. Although, Mauss identifies the co-existence of gift and market economies in other non-Western cultures as well, with market exchanges being 'marked by very hard bargaining' which is 'unworthy' of gift exchange for the peoples of the Trobriand Islands, for example (Mauss 22).
6. Malinowski is one of the ethnographers whose work Mauss engages with most fully in *The Gift*.
7. Carrier refers to the way that the gift 'takes on a special meaning for the people involved that is over and above, and may even contradict, its meaning as a commodity-sign or even its utility' (8–9).
8. See Zwerdling (1986) and Whitworth (2005) for discussion of these changes and their impact.
9. She inherited money from her Aunt Caroline Emelia, her father and Thoby, amounting to £9000 (Delany, 1993, 5). This was carefully invested by Leonard to produce 'a strategic reserve, not to be depleted for ordinary living expenses' (ibid., 6).
10. Vanessa Bell remarks in a memoir, 'my father, like most Victorians, was mad on the subject' of money, and was 'never happy unless he had an enormous balance at the bank' (1998, 99). She recalls the terrifying experience of presenting the weekly accounts to her father, a duty she assumed after Stella's death, which 'almost always led to groans, sighs and then explosions of rage' (1998, 72) – something that Woolf remembered. Woolf's concern with money was partly at least to stave off a deeply rooted anxiety instilled by Leslie Stephen, about the disasters consequent

166   *Notes*

on not having enough – bankruptcy and the workhouse (Bell 67). Mitchell Leaska argues that his 'prophesies of starvation and poverty [were] all cruelly invented to use money as his manipulatory weapon of power' and that his use of the threat of financial ruin was a means of exerting his patriarchal power (1983, 459).

11. Woolf published five articles in *Vogue* between 1924 and 1926, as well as two photographs (Garrity, 2000, 191–2, 200, 202).

12. See Garrity's discussion of Woolf's fluctuating attitude to Dororthy Todd, for example (2000).

13. As Michael Tratner argues, 'Woolf . . . sees the demise of capitalism not in the elimination of private experience, but in the elimination of property, of the ownership of private space by a single dominant individual. Joint ownership and multiply generated private experience mark the step beyond capitalism' (2000, 132).

14. As Delany remarks, 'It would hardly be fair to call the Hogarth Press a profitable investment', given the 'years of shrewd judgement and grinding effort' it took to increase its value, the fact that the Woolfs 'took relatively little income out of the business', so that the money the made from the sale of Woolf's portion to John Lehmann 'was really deferred compensation rather than profit' (1993, 6). The Woolfs also resisted an offer from Heinemann which would have given the Press potential for development because they feared a loss of their freedom to publish what they chose to (D2 215).

15. 'Swift's Journal to Stella' was published in the *TLS* September 1925.

16. Armstrong and Trotter discuss the reading practices that modernist writing invites in similar ways. This notion of Woolf's ideal reader as a 'fellow worker and accomplice' is most overtly discussed in her essay, 'How Should One Read a Book?'

1   The Business of Writing

1. From the publication of her first review in 1904, her determination to make money from her writing and to enter this profession by doing so was clear. As she wrote to Violet Dickinson, her first review was sent not with the desire to obtain the 'candid criticism' of an editor, but only 'her cheque!' (to Violet Dickinson, *L1* 154). Some of her initial enthusiasm to make money from her writing was also partly to do with the necessity of affording her medical bills.

2. These are two volumes of *The Common Reader*, *A Room of One's Own* and *Three Guineas*, and those collections published posthumously by Leonard Woolf, *The Death of the Moth, The Moment, The Captain's Deathbed, Granite and Rainbow, Contemporary Writers* and four volumes of *Collected Essays*.

3. Namely, the *Times Literary Supplement*, the *Nation and Athenaeum*, the *Bookman*, the *Criterion*, the *Dial*, the *Manchester Guardian*, and *Scrutiny* (Rosenburg and Dubino, 1–2).

4. They have been 'relegated . . . to the traditional role of "minor" genre' (Gualtieri 4), and considered 'only in the context of her fiction', with only a small selection attracting feminist and Marxist analysis since the 1970s (Rosenberg and Dubino 2; Lee, 2000, 94).

5. Woolf's 1927 essay, 'Street Haunting: A London Adventure', for instance, was published first in the *Yale Review*, but was one of the '"minor works"' that the Woolfs published as 'attractively designed pamphlets or short books', limited editions produced to increase profits from Virginia Woolf's non-fictional writings (Lee, 1996, 558, citing Mepham). It was published by The Westgate Press, San Francisco, in 1930 (ibid.).

Notes 167

6. See also Garrity's discussion of Woolf's ambivalent feelings about her appearances in *Vogue* (2000, 195–6).
7. See Tratner, *Deficits and Desires: Economics and Sexuality in Twentieth Century Literature*, and Wicke, 'Coterie Consumption: Bloomsbury, Keynes, and Modernism as Marketing' and 'Mrs Dalloway Goes to Market: Woolf, Keynes and Modern Markets'.
8. These ideas are also articulated in Woolf's fictional writing. In *Jacob's Room*, for example, Woolf mentions the displays of women's clothing in which 'the parts of a woman were shown separate' (*JR* 105), with the implication that every part requires attention, clothing and things.
9. Again reading across Woolf's essays that focus on the economies of the City, Woolf's description in 'The Docks of London' of the 'sinister dwarf city of workmen's houses' confirms the working-class status of the woman in the boot shop, as well as exposing the 'dismal' squalor of the source of the commodities for sale (*CD* 108). The docks, with their 'dingy, decrepit-looking warehouses' and the ruthless efficiency of the purposeful weighing out and pricing up, expose the cold calculation of the capitalist system that underpins the glitter and gush of Oxford Street. See Pamela Caughie's 'Purpose and Play in Woolf's London Scene Essays' for an illuminating analysis of Woolf's engagement with the commercial, aesthetic and political in the London Scene essays.
10. It may even contain some of the novels written by women that have been distorted by dominant masculine social and literary values, and which 'lie scattered like small pock-marked apples in an orchard, about the second-hand bookshops of London' (*AROO* 71).
11. In *A Room of One's Own*, of course, Woolf expands on the relation between women writers, the marketplace and independent income.
12. As 'Oxford Street Tide' makes clear when it maps the transformation of raw materials into commodities as they move from the Docks to Oxford Street, and the corresponding alteration of 'the human form' – its movements, responses, attitudes and even language itself (*CD* 113).
13. This was the working title for *A Room of One's Own* and is the title of an article published in *Forum* March 1929, a shorter forerunner to *A Room of One's Own*; it is the topic that Woolf's narrator has been invited to address in her lecture recounted in *A Room of One's Own*.
14. Significantly, one of the treasures to which the narrator is denied access is the manuscript of William Thackeray's novel, *Henry Esmond*, a manuscript that actually belonged to Leslie Stephen's first wife, Minny (the youngest daughter of Thackeray) and which was donated to Trinity College by Woolf's father, Leslie Stephen (Rosenbaum, 205, note 8). In her later essay, 'Reviewing', Woolf singles this novel out as one that Thackeray felt had been ruined by the capitalist operation of the literary market.
15. Her income in 1929 was £2936, only to be beaten by a 'surge' in her income when *The Years* became a bestseller in 1938, '£2972, the highest year's income of her life' (1996, 558).
16. This was banned in 1928 and Woolf was involved in its defence.
17. In the manuscript Woolf is far more explicit. It reads:

<I read> *She said* 'Chloe liked Olivia; the shared a—' <the words came at> the bottom of the page; the pages had stuck; while fumbling to open them there flashed into my mind the inevitable policeman; the summons; the order to attend the

168 *Notes*

court; the dreary waiting; the Magistrate coming in with a little bow; the glass of water; the counsel for the prosecution; for the defense; the verdict; the book is *called* obscene; & flames rising, perhaps on Tower Hill, as they consumed <that> mass of *print* paper. Here the pages came apart. Heaven be praised! It was only a laboratory. [IN MARGIN: that was shared]. <Chloe and Olivia> They were engaged mincing liver which is apparently a cure for pernicious anaemia. But the thread by which we took hold to a book is so stretched, so attentive, is so intense a process, that one jar like this breaks it, and away the mind flew, thankful for a rest, on some other theme.

(Rosenbaum, 114; italics indicate words crossed through).

18. Lee attributes her self-censorship to the anxieties she declared in her *Diary* in October 1929 that she would be 'attacked for a feminist and hinted at for a sapphist' (1996, 527, citing Woolf's *Diary* for 23rd October, 1929).
19. This is a fundamental aspect of traditional economics premised on limiting flows of money and controlling consumption, which Keynesian economics, with its emphasis on unrestricted economic flows and deficit spending, challenges.
20. See also Naomi Black for a discussion of Woolf's political involvements with feminist groups and actions.
21. This was established in 1926 as the Women's Service Library, temporarily named the Millicent Fawcett Library during the Fawcett Library Appeal between 1938–41 (Snaith, 2003, 20), renamed as the Fawcett Library in 1953, and again as The Women's Library in 2002.
22. As Snaith notes, Woolf encountered such sexism in relation to being allowed to sit on the committee of the London Library, her father, Leslie Stephen, having declared there would be no women on this committee (Snaith, 2003, 23).
23. *Three Guineas* was published in early June before the Munich Agreements of 30 September 1938, in which Hitler's occupation of Czechoslovakia was agreed in the last attempt to maintain a fragile peace in Europe.
24. See Vara S. Neverow's illuminating essary for further discussion of Woolf's engagement with Freudian ideas in relation to fascism in *A Room of One's Own* and *Three Guineas*.
25. For example, used to distinguish 'margarine . . . pure butter . . . the finest butter' (*TG* 24).
26. In her *Diary*, Woolf notes that the inspiration for *Three Guineas* came in as she lay in the bath thinking about her talk, 'Professions for Women' (*D4* 6). Snaith (2003, 21) and Lee (1996, 599) also refer to this connection.
27. See 'Castration or Decapitation?' and 'The Laugh of the Medusa', for example.
28. One contributor, Viscount Rhondda, donated 'twice what she would have given had she not read *Three Guineas*' (Snaith, 2003, 22–3).

2 Queering the Market

1. Leonard Woolf stood, somewhat reluctantly, as Labour parliamentary candidate. During the short period in which Labour were in office, he served as secretary to the two sections of the Advisory Committee on International and Imperial Questions (Glendinning, 2006, 257–8).
2. Anticipating her meeting with 'the lovely gifted aristocratic Sackville West' (*sic*) in December 1922, and drawn romantically to her long ancestry 'like old yellow wine',

Notes 169

Woolf was also snobbishly disparaging about the 'incurably stupid' Nicolsons, and critical of Vita's showiness (*D2* 216, 236, 239).

3. Abbott similarly suggests that commodities signify more than their materiality for Clarissa in *Mrs Dalloway*: 'Clarissa transforms the commodity before her into part of her past, her own identity, rather than relying on the commodity as a signifier of her lifestyle or as something to transform her lifestyle' (200).

4. For instance, in a review of *Mam Linda* by Will N. Harden, *TLS* 3 October 1907, cited in Kirkpatrick, (292).

5. Which includes her admiration of its form, 'the sentences ending; the characters – how one talked about them as if they were real', and her praise for the mid-Victorian novel's superiority over anything produced by 'the moderns', especially anything modern written 'about death' loss (*CSF* 155).

6. Abbott attributes the lack of purchasing in Woolf's texts to what he calls an 'acommodity aesthetic', defined as 'balanced patterns of shopping without spending and consumption without commodities' (209).

7. Jennifer Wicke, arguing that there is a more fluid sense of the market economy in *Mrs Dalloway*, discusses the overlapping of gift and market economies in a way that also addresses the blurring of distinctions and the collapsing of hierarchies. She argues that 'the generosity of her [Clarissa's] gendered acts of consumption' means that 'consumption is reformulated as the nature of the gift' (1994, 18). As such, Clarissa's consumption has the potential to liquefy distinctions and hierarchies: 'The city of women – Clarissa's London, for instance – is the site not only of all the hierarchies and divisions of the gendered social world, but also their liquefaction in gifts of consumption' (1994, 19).

8. The early and tragic death of Sylvia is sketchily revealed in *Mrs Dalloway*. Peter Walsh reflects on Clarissa's loss of her sister owing to her father's negligence and notes Clarissa's appraisal of Sylvia as 'the most gifted of them' (*MD* 87). If we read this reference to Sylvia in 'Mrs Dalloway in Bond Street' as referring to Clarissa's sister, the brevity of this reference to the female intimacy of Clarissa's past represents, as in *Mrs Dalloway*, the marginalisation and dismissal of exclusive female intimacy, other libidinal possibilities, and the 'gifts' of the feminine in Clarissa's society. See Elizabeth Abel for a more detailed discussion. See also Boone, who discusses this aspect of the novel in his persuasive exploration of the interrelations of Woolf's narrative techniques and form and the libidinal currents at play in *Mrs Dalloway*.

9. Corinne E. Blackmer uncovers a further lesbian encoding in this story when she suggests that the character of Miss Anstruther is a reference to Vernon Lee's long-time companion, C. Anstruther-Thomas. Blackmer comments that '(w)hile Lee was reluctant to acknowledge her lesbianism even to her close friends, her writings on aesthetics, which influenced Woolf, were replete with encoded homosexual references' (86).

10. The style of glove Clarissa desires, however, may also be a highly encoded reference to her more subversive sexual desires. That the gloves are French suggests romance and even a sense of the risqué, and pearls and buttons can be read as an erotic lesbian code in some of Woolf's texts. See Paula Bennett's work and my essay for further discussion. At the point at which she is composing her story, the French language and French culture have a special appeal for Woolf, signifying 'a kind of levity and frivolity and congeniality' and, travelling in France and Spain (March–April 1923), she finds France to be 'much more enjoyable in some queer way . . . than England!' (letter to Jacques Raverat, *L3* 23).

11. Clarissa's willingness to collude in this system and to accept her identity as property exchanged between the men of two families is apparent in her brief recollection of

170　*Notes*

her family history: 'Down Bond Street the Parrys had walked for a hundred years, and might have met the Dalloways (Leighs on the mother's side) going up' (*CSF* 155). As she herself walks down 'the narrow crooked street' she seems happy to locate her identity between these patriarchal family lines.

12. As Woolf herself suggests in *Orlando*, 'Clothes are but a symbol of something hid deep beneath', which may or may not reveal a consistent gender identity or sexuality (*O* 117). It was at the time of working on 'Mrs Dalloway in Bond Street' that Woolf read Katherine Mansfield's collection of stories called *Bliss* (as she notes in her *Diary*, *D2* 192), in which the story called 'The Little Governess' appears. In this story the little governess' awakening desires and sexual fantasies are signalled in part by her removal of her gloves and, given Woolf's intense feelings about Mansfield (and the fact that when she has read some of Mansfield's stories she needs to 'rinse [her] mind', as she notes in the same entry, *D2* 138), it may not be too speculative to suggest that this somewhat uncomfortable erotic moment in Mansfield's story may act as an intertext for the eroticism of gloves in Woolf's story.

13. The shop assistant apologetically explains that '"(g)loves have never been quite so reliable since the war"' (*CSF* 158) and, of course, it was during the war that women occupied traditional male roles, gaining a sense of independence and sexual autonomy. This suggests that in this post-war period the unreliability and inconsistency of gloves is possibly not only the only thing being referred to here.

14. In 'The Hours', this gift-giving is conveyed as even more fluid, with the sense of a more continuous movement. Rather than the discrete phrases that divide the gift of the flower from the kiss, the two are part of the same gesture: 'They were alone together. . . . Sally took her arm.) Then the most exquisite moment of her life arrived simply that Sally picked a flower & as she gave it her. *she* put *her arm round her* <shoulder> & kissed her' (Wussow, 49; italics indicate words crossed through). It is not that this kiss enables Clarissa to see the world differently in 'The Hours', but it is as if she is physically transplanted, '*It seemed as if she had been wafted away* by that kiss' (ibid.; italics indicate words crossed through).

15. As indeed Richard in the present time of the novel tries to dismiss Clarissa's suspicions of their daughter's apparent infatuation with Doris Kilman as 'only a phase . . . such as all girls go through', feelings which will 'pass over if you let them' (*MD* 14, 132). This sense of homoerotic desire between women as a 'passing phase' is highly distressing for Clarissa given that she knows only too well how long such a 'phase' can take to pass.

16. See Boone, Abel, Jensen, Smith (1997) and Brimstone, for instance.

17. The gift for Evelyn, for instance, aims not only to make Clarissa's visit easier for her, but also to ameliorate Evelyn's suffering, to act as a 'cordial', to bring refreshment and revitalise a 'dried up' (menopausal) woman, as well as to break usual (polite and distanced) pattern of relationships in her society and to bring her closer to women (*MD* 12). Although Clarissa seems overly critical and scathing about Evelyn, this may also be her internalisation of dominant values and may be a projection of what she feels about herself as a woman who is, or is soon to be, also menopausal.

18. Critics have read this moment in the novel in a variety of ways. Abbott sees 'something more meaningful to both [Clarissa and Miss Pym] and quite different from the professional façade of shop women' but does not speculate about *how* this could be more meaningful, except to liken it to the more personalised commercial exchanges of the Victorian period (201). Others have commented more explicitly on the homoeroticism of this scene: see Eileen Barrett for instance. Smith comments that Miss Pym, 'presumably independent . . . in her florist's shop, connected

with the "lesbian" image of flowers', is one of 'the minor "queer" characters in the novel, whose own romantic or sexual histories go unrevealed and unremarked' (1997, 194, note 30). She reads the significance of 'this brief idyll' of 'female homosocial/homoerotic pleasure' as a key moment in Clarissa's experience of lesbian bliss, which acts as a parallel scene to that experienced earlier by the urn with Sally (1997, 43).

19. Several critics have explored the significance of flowers in Woolf's work as they operate as symbols of female sexuality and sexual power (see Cramer 1992b, for example, who reads flowers as symbols of lesbian desire). Wicke also argues that flowers function to drive Woolf's language ('(a)lmost every page is rampant with blooms') and to epitomise the 'modernist . . . commodified spectacle' in her work (2001, 393).

20. That these are not the exotic flowers Abbott notes as 'essential for any social event of the 1920s and 1930s' suggests that Clarissa is not a dupe of the 'sophisticated consumer strategy' which creates such 'essentials' (200), but rather that she exploits the consumer experience, like Clarissa of the short story, for other ends.

21. However, as we see later, flowers also have a key role to play in the operation of heteropatriarchal and capitalist economies in this novel, and work in a less obvious way as part of a gift economy which has disruptive potential.

22. Wicke also discusses the way that this image is attenuated, but identifies it as an example of the 'market consciousness' of Woolf's 'modernist aesthetic development', whereby 'consciousness and consumption are conflated, in confluence with each other' (1994, 17).

23. The advertising function of the aeroplane that supplants the crowd's fascination with the car reinforces this link between such forces and capitalism.

24. This contrasts, for instance, with Lucrezia's thought that the car contains 'the Queen going shopping' (*MD* 18). Abbott also points out this difference, but attributes this difference to 'Clarissa's obliviousness to commodity spectacle' (203).

25. There are several interpretations of Clarissa's response to Doris Kilman and the significance she has for her. See Barrett for a useful summary of several key readings of Doris Kilman's importance in the novel (159). Boone argues that Doris 'becomes an emblem of a hidden side of Clarissa's psyche, of repressed contents striving for expression that call into question the exaggerated love of life that animates her desire to serve as a meeting point, a site of connection for others' (194).

26. Indeed, this scene would suggest that Clarissa's interpretation of Elizabeth either being or falling in love with Doris (*MD* 14) is far from accurate because in it Elizabeth clearly perceives Doris's desperate desire for her but is eager to escape.

27. Although the Army and Navy store is a co-operative and so, Tratner argues, is in tune with the Woolfs' ideas for greater economic equality, it is also clearly associated with the hegemonic forces that this novel criticises. See Tratner, 2001, Chapter 4.

28. The sense of distorted mirroring in *Mrs Dalloway* is made stronger by Woolf's alterations to her earlier draft. In 'The Hours', Elizabeth's reflection on the relationship between her mother and Doris comes to light as she emerges from the department store out onto Victoria Street, and the flowers Clarissa gives to Doris are not specifically from Bourton. The relocation of Elizabeth and her thoughts about the relationship between Clarissa and Doris to the interior of the department store and the specific association of Clarissa's gift of flowers with Bourton works to echo more clearly, and to contrast with, Clarissa's remembrance of her youth at Bourton inside Miss Pym's shop.

172 *Notes*

29. As Mica Nava suggests, '(t)he department store was an anonymous yet acceptable public space and it opened up for women a range of new opportunities and pleasures – for independence, fantasy, unsupervised social encounters, even transgression (—as well as, at the same time, for rationality, expertise and financial control)' (53). However, anonymity and desire are experienced more negatively as loneliness and dissatisfaction here.

30. We see this reciprocal ambivalence when, for instance, Doris is overcome by emotion and almost bursts into tears at Clarissa's laughter, which she perceives as an insult (*MD* 142). The idea that this interaction with Clarissa 'revived the fleshly desires' Doris strives to contain, causes her to be self-conscious about her appearance, and makes Doris (for some reason inexplicable to herself) 'wish to resemble her' (*MD* 142) raises questions about the nature of her feeling for Clarissa. Barrett argues that 'on some level Doris . . . perceives Clarissa's lesbian identity' (160). However, I think that it is more complex than that: paradoxically she wants to 'unmask' Clarissa (*MD* 138) and expose her lesbian desires, and yet wants to be more like her and possibly attractive to her.

31. Tratner, for instance, argues that Doris represents 'a certain kind of socialist whom Virginia and Leonard opposed, ones who denigrated consumption as the source of economic problems rather than the solution' and for whom the rejection of private property became 'a form of asceticism' and self-denial that only brings her further suffering and denial (2001, 104).

32. Richard's clichéd romantic gift serves to underscore the fact that he never had a main part in the romance plot of Clarissa's youth; it was Sally and Peter who were the real rivals for Clarissa's love.

33. 'As a person who has dropped some grain of pearl or diamond into the grass and parts the tall blades very carefully, this way and that, and searches here and there vainly, and at last spies it there at the roots, so she went through one thing and another . . . ' (*MD* 133–4).

34. Although it is probably the roses that are moving, the use of 'one' here is slightly ambiguous and could be referring to Richard or Clarissa moving apart from the other.

35. In the context of a network of images and allusions that associate plunging and treasure with homoerotic desires, that Clarissa had 'once thrown a shilling into the Serpentine, never anything more' (*MD* 203) can be read as an acknowledgement of her denial of her lesbian desires and the economic risk that acting on them may entail. This simultaneously attests to her metaphorical death in marriage (see Emily Jensen).

36. As Peter confesses his enduring love and desire for Clarissa, his realisation that '(o)ne could not be in love twice' seems to accord with Sally's feeling, 'what could she say?' (*MD* 212). Her own enduring love and desire for Clarissa is suggested by her 'often' finding refuge in her garden, where 'she got from her flowers a peace of mind which men and women never gave her' (*MD* 212, 213).

3 A Gift of Vision

1. See Zwerdling (1986) and Whitworth (2005) for discussion of these changes and their impact.

2. Levenback discusses these events in detail, pointing out that Woolf kept a careful record of the progress of the strike and noting that the strike created an unsettled

Notes 173

atmosphere of 'class war' that temporarily 'undermined [Woolf's] ability to continue writing the novel', specifically and significantly, putting a halt to the writing of 'Time Passes' for the duration of the General Strike (95, 101, 100, 87–8). See also Kate Flint.

3. These polarisations have been critically explored for the related dichotomies of science and art, heroism and creativity, rationality and intuition, intellect and emotion, war and peace, philosophical (propositions) and the metaphorical.

4. Compare Janet Winston's different reading of this moment (1996, 39).

5. As Winston points out, although Mrs Ramsay is a victim of heteropatriarchal and colonial ideology, she is also 'the seemingly limitless force of empire' as comparisons with Queen Victoria indicate (1996, 50). Mary Lou Emery, in her discussion of class and colonial otherness in the novel, also reads her insistence on marriage for Lily as both a form of conscription into 'the institution of marriage' and an appropriation of Lily's (colonial) otherness: 'Lily's marrying will alleviate the strangeness of her Chinese eyes and her eccentricities' (219–20).

6. Though, as Lynda Nead argues, the role of women's social investigations is a form of colonisation of the working classes and would further compound Mrs Ramsay's power and influence over the lighthouse men. Tratner also discusses the patronising attitude of middle-class philanthropists (1995, 57), and Zwerdling suggests that '(b)y the twentieth century this form of middle-class benevolence had begun to appear both ineffectual and bogus' (1986, 100).

7. James' envy and resistance to being the measuring tool for this stocking is testimony to this giving of herself.

8. See also Emery's persuasive discussion of how this novel resists closure as it 'invites a return to the chaos it recuperates, and it displaces its own center' (232).

9. Joseph L. Blotner, for instance, reads Mrs Ramsay as a conflation of the primordial goddesses Rhea, Demeter and Persephone (172); Clare Hanson argues that Mrs Ramsay 'is linked with the mythical mother Demeter who is at once opposed to and necessarily complicit with patriarchal law' (1994, 77).

10. For example, Patricia Cramer (1992a) in relation to *The Years*, and Melba Cuddy-Keane and Patricia Maika in relation to *Between the Acts*.

11. In his discussion of Ezra Pound's ideas about money, Hyde recalls Pound's labelling of the Bank of England as an 'evil bank' because of its detachment from the natural world and any sense of 'natural increase', an idea compounded by the Bank's 1694 prospectus in which it claimed to have 'benefit of the interest on all moneys which it creates out of nothing' (cited in Hyde, 258), making clear the essence of the capitalist ethos on which it is based.

12. Although Helen had vast numbers of suitors, it was her father who chose Menelaus to be her husband, for the advantages of wealth and power that this son-in-law could bring to him; the ten-year Trojan War was also fought to rescue Helen from her kidnappers, again suggesting that Helen is merely an object of men's rivalry.

13. Other critics have explored Woolf's work in relation to the work of modern ethnographers she may have known through her friendship with Harrison and others with Cambridge connections. Meg Albrinck offers an interesting exploration of Lily's 'ethnographic sensibility' and 'ethnographic methods' (197).

14. Emery argues that Mrs McNab and Mrs Bast are primitive 'wild, savage, inarticulate forces' (231) whose gender 'indeterminacy' is 'directly related to the modernity of Lily Briscoe' (222).

15. That of Septimus in *Mrs Dalloway*, for instance.

174 *Notes*

16. As explored by Ruth Vanita, for example, and as made more explicit in the holograph draft as William Bankes's recalls the comic, but also homoerotic, memory he has of seeing Mr Ramsay naked (*TTL Holograph* 32–3).
17. The connection between the gift economy and homoerotic desire is also suggested in William's response to Cam's refusal to give him a flower. In part this causes him to reflect on his regrets about not having children, but also makes him feel 'dried and shrunk' a feeling commensurate with the loss of the 'pulp' in his relationship with and desire for Mr Ramsay in the past (*TTL* 20). Vanita suggests that Cam's refusal 'triggers in Bankes an awareness of society's condemnation if him' and his '"wrong" loyalty to the buried friendship' and his homoerotic feelings for Mr Ramsay in the past (1997, 172). However, instructed to give a flower, Cam's refusal is actually a refusal to give a false gift, a refusal to obey the imperatives of a patriarchal society in which women are forced to be the sources of generosity and the 'gifts' to be exchanged and consumed like commodities. Her wildness, spontaneity and impulsiveness are more radically in tune with the gift economy's disruptive qualities, and her energetic refusal to obey gender conventions is a source of vitality, new hope and energy, as we see when Lily closes her paint-box (*TTL* 50). In the holograph draft, the effect of Cam's refusal is not so great. It would seem that in the published version Woolf puts more emphasis on how women are trained to give (as part of their 'proper' role as women), on the broader sense of women as gifts, and the centrality of this so-called 'gift' economy to the heteropatriarchal social organisation of relations between the sexes. Key here, of course, is also Cam's girlhood defiance, something that is eroded as she gets older.
18. See Tratner's discussion of Woolf's representation of working-class women as central to social and political transformation, to the development of modernist art and the emergence of the woman artist (1995, Chapter 2). See Emery for a detailed discussion of the contradictions and middle-class feminist limitations of Woolf's representation and use of the working-class female characters in this novel. Other critics also discuss Woolf's class politics in this novel. Tracey Hargreaves notes that 'Woolf's ambivalence towards the working class is well known' but that some of her reactions are more to do with her anger 'towards political officialdom' in its orchestration of the celebrations at the end of the war and the impossibility of completely distancing herself from her fellow war civilians (139). Her representations of working-class characters also act as 'an index of Woolf's concern with a genealogy of writing and the advent of the modern in its various cultural representations' (146).
19. Minta loses her brooch, given to her by her grandmother, at the point at which she agrees to marry Paul Rayley. This heirloom is imbued with her grandmother's identity ('the brooch her grandmother had fastened her cap with till the last day of her life' and was 'the sole ornament she possessed', *TTL* 71). It is a terrible loss, though not only for its value as an object, nor even for its connection to her grandmother and the continuity of their specific kinship it represents, but seemingly for the loss also of a broader 'kinship' and, given the sexual significance of pearls in Woolf's and other women's writing, the loss of homoerotic connection with women. Lily's wish to restore this brooch is in order to restore this connection and to save this feminine yet tomboyish woman (whose potential for homoerotic desire is suggested as she unlocks new desires and fantasies of foreign places and questions in other women) from the heterosexual economy of marriage, which suggests Lily's homoerotic desire. It also serves as a stark contrast with Paul

Notes 175

Rayley, who mistakenly thinks he can replace this inalienable gift with a bought commodity and so be the 'hero'. Osteen describes heirlooms as 'symbols of memory, kinship and continuity' that like 'art works' occupy a different level of meaning and value than other objects and commodities (234). It is little wonder, then, that this loss gives rise to an uncharacteristic display of emotion from Lily as she too expresses her desire to find Minta's brooch and to restore the various woman-centred connections it represents. Later, the failure of the Rayleys' marriage is bound up for Lily with proving Mrs Ramsay wrong though it also indicates that Paul's overriding of the gift economy with the monetary economy has backfired. It is unsurprising that he becomes an economist and, with his marriage to Minta becoming simply a friendship, has as a mistress 'a serious woman' who 'shared Paul's views . . . about taxation of land values and capital levy' (*TTL* 165). It would seem that Minta's independent life may possibly include homoerotic relationships.

20. Zwerdling is describing Woolf's response when she attended a conference of the Co-operative Working Women's Guild, which is in part recorded in her introductory letter in *Life as We Have Known It* (1931).

21. Haule, Levenback and Tratner (1995) comment on the reduction of her stature and importance in the published version.

22. In the holograph draft, this spiritual connection between the two is more pronounced, as Haule describes it: 'Mrs McNab . . . begins as an ageless seer who cooperates with the 'ghostly presences' all about her. In the original conception, she sees the ghost of Mrs Ramsay come to cooperate in the regeneration' (166). However, I disagree that '(by) the final versions, McNab merely thinks of her former employer and "drinks and gossips as before" '.

23. The song of the second birth of Dionysis, the Spirit of Vegetation (Harrison 77, 104, 102) that later Lily will more fully embody in her art.

24. Haule comments on the alterations made between the holograph draft and published versions in terms of the reference to war being altered and reduced, with '(d)irect identification of the war with male destructiveness and sexual brutality has been eliminated altogether' (166). It would seem that a more important focus in the published version is on working-class women's civilian experience, but also on the forces of resurrection and rejuvenation, on life forces rather than death.

25. This is suggested by the apparent return of 'the voice of the beauty of the world . . . murmuring . . . entreating the sleepers' to see the night in all his glory as if through the eyes of a child (*TTL* 135–6) and to see things as unchanged. As Levenback notes of the immediate post-war period 'Increasingly, the war was being presented as a bad dream – and one from which the populace, civilians and ex-servicemen could awake, as if the fact of war had been transformed to a fiction and its reality to an illusion' (30). Augustus Carmichael sees the house in this way; Levenback also notes his lack of awareness of change (109).

26. As William Bankes notices earlier, Lily wears shoes that "allow(ed) the toes their natural expansion" (*TTL* 17).

27. A position that Mrs Ramsay's complicity in seeing women as inferior supported: significantly, she felt herself to be not even good enough to tie his boot strings (*TTL* 30).

28. The choice of 'flare' here recalls Mrs Ramsay's admiration for the difference Lily's creative gift makes to her as a woman, and suggests that Lily's gift to Mr Ramsay has brought about a brief disruption of his traditional, conservative values and outlook.

29. In the holograph draft she also berates herself and Mr Carmichael for their acquiescence in Mrs Ramsay's exhaustion, their passivity significantly expressed in

176   *Notes*

terms of their being mere commodities: 'Are we fish, *are we*[or] (crossed through) or coal – are we things that can be packed in barrels and rattled across the world without protest?' (*TTL Holograph* 303).

30. Woolf's anxiety about the reception of her work and about sales is typical of her response on completion of a novel. However, her sending a dummy copy of blank pages inscribed with the message, 'In my opinion the best novel I have ever written', followed by a letter to Sackville-West in which she was keen to make clear that this was 'A joke, a feeble joke', suggests her concern was intensified due to the possibility of this boast being circulated among Sackville-West's influential literary connections (*L3*, 372).

31. Significantly, she also mulls over *The Waves* and her lecture, which was to become *A Room of One's Own*, and which, like 'Professions for Women', is a text connected to *Orlando* in many ways, not least in its concern with women's creativity, the male-dominated literary tradition and the woman writer's place in it. Issues of the relation of success to money, the impact of gender norms and ideologies, as well ideas about literary innovation and a focus on the lives of unconventional women (Aphra Behn, for instance) also create an overlap between these two texts.

32. In September 1927 she considers writing outlines of her friends with Vita to be 'Orlando, a young nobleman' (*D3* 157). In October, having completed four articles for the *New York Herald Tribune*, she feels 'free again' to create and imagine, and sketches out the plot of *Orlando* to be written 'for a treat' (*D3* 161).

33. One of the most ready sources of mutual admiration and professional criticism is the letters exchanged between these two writers, especially during this and Vita's previous journey to Persia. They reveal both the intensity of the desire between them, and their admiration for (and criticism of) one another, and for their own and each other's writing.

34. See Woolmer, *A Checklist of the Hogarth Press*.

35. Sproles notes this and that 'Sackville-West's relationship with the Hogarth Press was discontinued after Woolf's death' (216, note 9).

36. She adds that this was a 'highly unusual' gesture for Sackville-West, as well as an indication of the 'passionate connection' between them and 'suggest(ing) a fantasy of future intimacy' (64).

37. Woolf includes quotations from *The Land* as Orlando's poem, 'The Oak Tree', draws on the details of *Knole* and on the cross-dressing figure of Julian/ Vita in *Challenge*.

38. For example, Sproles explores the ways in which Woolf and Sackville-West's biographical writings are interrelated and share the same focus on the emergence of women as desiring subjects. She argues that Sackville-West's biographical work on Aphra Behn contributes to the 'revolutionis(ing) [of] biography in a night' (*L3* 429) that Woolf claimed *Orlando* to be. She discusses Sackville-West's memory in *Knole* of the fruit her grandfather would hide for her in the draw in his writing table, known as 'Vita's drawer' (48), and remarks not only on the literal gifts of fruit Sackville-West gives to Woolf (which bring so much pleasure), but extends this as a metaphor for the fruitful uses to which Sackville-West puts her inheritance. Karen Lawrence also explores the ways that Sackville-West's *Passenger to Teheran* (1926) and her letters from Persia both informed Woolf's 'erotic and political projections onto the "East"' and her ideas about the 'mobility of desire', establishing 'the important relationship between travel and female desire, and particularly the orientalizing of this desire' that is powerful in *Orlando* (256). Raitt argues that *To the Lighthouse* and *Orlando* were an influence on *All Passion Spent*, and that motifs from these novels recur in Sackville-West's writings (1993, 107).

Notes   177

39. Sproles suggests that *Orlando* 'is another heaping of ripe fruit from a writing table' (71), but also that *Orlando* is made fruitful by mutual influence: it 'accomplishes the double restoration of Sackville-West and Knole through an indeterminate narrative voice that Woolf and Sackville-West created between them' (72–3).

40. In a letter to Sackville-West, Woolf teases her, but with a serious edge, about her suspected infidelity with Mary Campbell for which Vita has forfeited a 'love letter' from Woolf. Her accusation is couched in terms of a market economy, 'You know for what price – walking the lanes with Campbell, you sold my love letters. Very well' (*L3* 428). The underlying assumption is that this affair will be inferior by being somehow commercial (and with Vita's tendency to turn her life into 'copy' this may literally be true), a distinction that reinforces the idea that Woolf's and Sackville-West's relationship is distinct from this, being premised on a gift economy. However, this letter also conveys Woolf's concern about becoming the subject of one of Lytton Strachey's books – presumably a modernist biography – her betrayal exposed by 'being bound in morocco by Lytton and read by all the tarts of the moment' (*L3* 428). Although the reality of Vita's infidelity would be 'worse', this comment reveals Woolf's concerns with her public image (and that of Vita), which is confirmed as the letter goes on. She tells Vita her plans for *Orlando*, outlining the possible consequences of Vita being identified as Orlando, and asking her permission to be part of this experiment of 'revolutionis(ing) biography' (*L3* 429).

41. Also cited in Raitt 40.

42. As Robin Majumdar and Allen McLaurin remark, with the increase in sales after *Orlando* the Woolfs were 'always well off' (6).

43. As she describes the car she and Leonard buy after the success of *To the Lighthouse*: 'We have a nice little shut up car. . . . The world gave me this for writing The Lighthouse, I reflect, a book which has now sold 3,160 (perhaps) copies' (*D3*, 147), a point she also makes in her essay, 'Professions for Women' (*CD* 104).

44. A fund was set up to enable the indebted MacCarthys to have a holiday. Desmond 'resents his gift of money a little' (*D3* 148), suggesting further evidence of the problem of the gift.

45. For instance, the risk of the mis-shelving of *Orlando* in the biography section was a serious concern before its publication (*D3* 198).

46. Sproles also discusses Woolf's 'creation of the ideal reader' and notes that the gentleman from America would not understand *Orlando* (105–6). Woolf makes self-conscious reference to the fact that *Orlando* is a commodity for sale, but one that is not readily consumable, when her biographer–narrator attempts to forestall a complaint from a reader expecting a more conventional biography (about the 'life', meaning the external actions, of its subject but only getting a recounting of the passing of the seasons because Orlando is simply sitting, thinking and imagining) who could have 'save(d) his pocket whatever sum the Hogarth Press may think proper to charge for this book' (*O* 167).

47. Given that some of 'Orlando's' poem is quoted from Sackville-West's very successful poem *The Land*, this may be a swipe at Sackville-West who, Woolf thinks, 'never breaks fresh ground' (*D3* 146), though it is also possibly 'jealousy' as Woolf admits, given Sackville-West's success which 'verberates and reverberates in the Press' (*D3* 141).

48. The detrimental impact of which Woolf frequently criticises, in her essay 'Reviewing' (1939), for instance (discussed in Chapter 1).

49. In contrast to the birth of Orlando's son, which happens 'outside' the text with Orlando simply being handed her baby by the midwife, her poem is the child of

178 *Notes*

her creation. The bond between Orlando and her writing is intense and intimate, such that she understands its desire 'to be read', for which it needs to enter human society (*O* 170). To achieve its goal of being read, Orlando faces the discomfort of 'modern conveniences' – the rattle and smuts of the train, and the crush and roar of the City (*O* 171–2). Woolf reflects similarly on *Orlando*: it is 'as if it shoved everything aside to come into existence' (D3 168), suggesting that *Orlando* almost has a life of its own.

50. Much as Sackville-West herself had smuggled these lines from her prize-winning poem *The Land* past any censors of her present day.

51. Karen Lawrence similarly argues that Orlando's 'sex change not only occasions her loss of property but drastically alters her relation to poetic inheritance'. She goes on to argue that 'Orlando's repatriation illustrates more than the hostile climate for a woman writer; it represents a revisionary Romanticism', subverting the gender politics of Romanticism by giving the woman artist the imaginative and generative powers traditionally gendered masculine (273–4).

52. Majumdar and McLaurin note that *Orlando* sold more in its first month than *To the Lighthouse* in a year, and was Woolf's first commercial success (5).

53. Many of those who died in the 1930s were the accomplices and readers named in the acknowledgements of *Orlando*. They included some of Woolf's closest friends and family. Lytton Strachey died in 1932, Roger Fry in 1934, Julian Bell, Janet Case and Stephen Tomlin in 1937, Ottoline Morrell in 1938, and Mrs Sidney Woolf in 1939.

54. They also draw attention to the social inequalities embedded in class hierarchies, to the violence and sexism of patriarchal militarist institutions, and to the dangers of the misuse of economic power. As Leaska notes, Leonard Woolf criticised Daladier as someone who refuses to learn from the past and sustains division by not agreeing to collective economic control in *The Barbarians at the Gate* (Leaska 197). Marina Mackay suggests that the significance of this reference to the French prime minister is to highlight 'the economic vulnerability of France that brings British defeat closer' (27).

55. A glimpse of Giles' childhood and upbringing is seen in the 'game' Bart Oliver plays with his grandson, Giles's son George, in which he disguises himself as a monster and scares George, concluding that his grandson is 'a cry-baby' and a coward (*BTA* 10, 14). He then turns to the newspaper report about the economic concerns that are so closely tied to the war, perhaps as a consolation for his disappointment with George's lack of 'manliness'.

56. Music and musical qualities in language are key in the creation of harmony in this novel, and, Ames suggests, 'the musical metaphor for community is unmistakable' (404).

57. Woolf read *Group Psychology and the Analysis of the Ego* and *Civilization and its Discontents* around this time. In Freud's theories of the group found in these texts, a central figure of authority (a primal father) proscribes the group's values and beliefs, and individual differences are erased or repressed; the aggression and tension that result from this repression are projected onto outsiders, a process that further strengthens the identity of the group. As Cuddy-Keane notes, Woolf was profoundly disturbed by '(t)he implications of these theories . . . and by 1939, [Freud's] words had become darkly prophetic of the rise of German nationalism under Hitler' (1990, 274).

58. The pageant's double pagan/Christian focus is one that resonates throughout the novel and is highlighted, for instance, in the comparison implied between the church and the barn: both have been built at the same time, both are made of the same stone, yet the barn, to which the audience go for refreshment in the

Notes 179

interval, has its own natural illumination and symbolises a maternal plenty in keeping with other pagan and mythic resonances found in Woolf's writing. As in Harrison's uncovering of myths of the powerful feminine supplanted by patriarchal, heroic sagas, here the worship of a patriarchal god is overlaid onto, but does not mask or obscure, the earlier pagan roots of communal worship in ritual.

59. As Cuddy-Keane (1990) and Ames discuss.

60. In 'Anon', Woolf discusses the significance of Elizabethan dress, considering that its purpose may have been 'to enforce the individual' and to write fame onto the body in the absence of other forms of visual publicity (Woolf [Silver] 388). The slippage of Eliza's dress perhaps compounds the slippage of individual identity, further enforcing the sense of 'we-substituted' and the communal representation/recreation of the past in this pageant.

61. Leaska notes that the fact that the publican is referred to by two different names, Hammond and Budge, is likely to be an error on Woolf's part, but his exploration of the significance of these names also uncovers a possible reference to Victorian hypocrisy, homophobia and sexual repression. He notes that Charles Hammond was the operator of a male brothel that caused a Victorian scandal involving the royal family through the involvement of the superintendent of Prince Edward's stables (whom he called Podge) after its discovery in 1889 (235–6).

62. Ames also notes that '(t)he most stinging parody is reserved for the Victorian age – precisely because that era is still associated with the parents of the audience and thus with that official seriousness that the carnival spirit lampoons' (399).

63. It is worth noting that the participation of animals, and nature more generally, has repeatedly sustained and reinforced Miss La Trobe's vision for her creative gift and helped to sustain the emotional response so crucial to the successful creation of connection and community; the birds seem to be continuing in this role here.

64. Maika and Ames, for example.

65. See Leaska, 209.

66. As several critics argue. Annette Oxindine claims that 'La Trobe's pageant ultimately does little to displace the behemoth of English hegemony' (1999, 126). Zwerdling argues that 'The audience is unchanged' and 'far from being a powerful force for unity, art has become an evanescent event, at best a momentary stay against confusion' (321), and 'It is inevitable that the pageant's concluding sketch . . . should show the utter fragmentation of life in the modern period' (321, 319). Leaska and Abraham also claim that the pageant is a failure.

4 Moments of Giving

1. For example *Trespassing Boundaries*, edited by Benzel and Hoberman, and *Wild Outbursts of Freedom* by Nena Skrbic.

2. Benzel and Hoberman argue this point (4), and Nena Skrbic demonstrates the importance of Russian writers, especially Chekov, on the development of Woolf's short fictions as she not only reviewed their work but took inspiration from the 'paradigm of aesthetic experience' that she found in them (2004a, 30). The period in which Woolf reviewed and commented on much Russian writing coincided with 'her most fertile short story writing period, 1917 to 1925' (Skrbic, 2004a, 38).

3. Avrom Fleishman cites 1904 as the 'inception' date for the passing on of Russian influence to English and Irish writers (45).

4. See, for instance, Angela Smith, *Katherine Mansfield and Virginia Woolf: A Public of Two*, and Lee, *Virginia Woolf*. Benzel and Hoberman (2004, 3–4) and Alice

180   Notes

Staveley ('Conversations at Kew: Reading Woolf's Feminist Narratology' [2004, 59, 62 note 17]) also refer to this relationship as significant, as does Woolf herself (see *D2* 226–7, 237–8, for example).

5. Woolf's relationship with Mansfield was, however, very complicated: she both envied and admired Mansfield's work. Although at times she disparaged Mansfield's stories and Mansfield herself, the value she placed on her writing is evident in the fact that Mansfield's 'Prelude' (1918) was the second Hogarth Press publication.

6. For Clare Hanson, it 'is the paradigmatic form of early twentieth century literature, best able to express a fragmented sensibility' (1985, 57). For Dominic Head, it 'encapsulates the essence of literary modernism, and has the ability to capture the episodic nature of twentieth century experience'. He continues 'the modernist short story ... exemplifies the strategies of modernist fiction', and discusses the way short stories expose the ideological contexts in which they are written and critique their social, political and cultural norms (1992, 6, 26–31). For Tim Armstrong, from the short stories of Turgenev, Joyce and Mansfield, 'the short story has become definitional to modernism' (2005, 52).

7. Hanson refers to the genre as 'a form of the margins' that is 'favoured by writers who find themselves to be personally opposed to the society in which they live' (Hanson 1989, 2, and 1985, 12). Like several earlier theorists and critics of the short story (notably O'Connor and Reid), Hanson suggests that the short story represents characters who are in some way marginal(ised), focusing especially on 'the ex-centric, alienated vision of women' (1989, 3).

8. Critics have taken up this attitude and have treated her short stories as less important and significant than her longer works, an evaluation compounded by the fact that she published very few of the stories she wrote, publishing only five of the seventeen stories she wrote between 1926 and 1941 (Dick, 2004, xix).

9. As Dick notes (2004, xix). Colburn also discusses the lengthy preparation of stories in order to disguise their lesbian content (2004).

10. Head also discusses the need for diachronic and synchronic considerations (2–3).

11. See also Mark S. Morrison for discussion of 'little' magazines.

12. Staveley argues that this review 'led to the outpouring of public interest in "Kew Gardens", which, in turn, launched the Hogarth Press toward commercial viability and Woolf, with time, onto the sometimes contradictory path of prosperous avant-gardism' (2004, 45). She also makes reference to the 'flurry of orders' for 'Kew Gardens' and Leonard Woolf's own estimation of the importance of this story to the financial success of the Press (2004, 60, note 6).

13. For example, in the wake of the success of *Jacob's Room* and in anticipation of the success of *Mrs Dalloway*, Woolf takes refuge from this new level of fame and financial success, likened to 'a looking glass flashed in her eyes', by 'dig(ing) deep down into [her] new stories' (*D3* 9).

14. Other critics also discuss the ways in which Woolf challenges, revises and adapts the genre norms. One of Head's central arguments is that modernist short stories do not reject 'conventional story forms' but 'provid(e) structure and referential landmarks, even where such conventions are subject to revisionist or ironical treatment' (17), and demonstrates how this is the case in Woolf's short stories. Benzel and Hoberman also suggest that Woolf's stories can be read 'as ambitious and self-conscious attempts to challenge generic boundaries, undercutting traditional distinctions between short fiction and the novel, between experimental and popular fiction, between fiction and non-fiction, and, most of all, between text and reader' (2).

Notes 181

15. Indeed, Daugherty convincingly argues that Woolf's stories and longer fictions are both independent 'products' and part of an interdependent process of creativity and generation of new texts. Drawing on Brenda Silver's suggestion that the 'awareness of [Woolf's] manuscripts and our study of Woolf's revising practices' means that 'the distinction between "final" version and draft' is blurred, she argues that 'Woolf's stories, when written, actually function in . . . multiple ways' (103, 105). This analysis again suggests that neither Woolf's short nor long fiction can be considered fixed and stable products or commodities with specific value and single meaning.

16. Discussing Henry James' story *The Turn of the Screw*, Armstrong argues similarly, that 'modernist texts propose readings constructed in terms of an interchange between text and reader, creating circles of investment and inclusion' (61). David Trotter, discussing ways of decoding and 'processing' modernist literary experiments, also argues for a greater investment of 'our mental and emotional resources' to 'generate richer contextual effects', though he adds that this (economically informed) theory of interpretation 'doesn't always work in practice' (1993, 67–8).

17. Smith argues that lesbian panic is 'the uncertainty of the female protagonist (or antagonist) about *her* own sexual identity' and 'occurs when a character – or, conceivably, an author – is either unable or unwilling to confront or reveal her own lesbianism or lesbian desire' (1997, 3–4, 2, Smith's emphasis). Both of these stem from 'the fear of the loss of identity and value as an object of exchange, often combined with the fear of responsibility for one's own sexuality' (6).

18. See, for instance, Jennifer Wicke's essays 'Coterie Consumption: Bloomsbury, Keynes, and Modernism as Marketing' and 'Mrs Dalloway Goes to Market: Woolf, Keynes, and Modern Markets' as examples of the importance of Keynesian ideas on Woolf's fiction.

19. This refers to a church service concerned with purifying women after childbirth, as David Bradshaw notes (2001, 107).

20. Bradshaw has identified this novel as Pierre Loti's *Ramuntcho* (1897), ibid., 107.

21. Such as 'the line of the boughs' the 'wagtail flew diagonally' and finally 'the apples hung straight across the wall again' – only temporarily disturbed by the wind (*CSF* 151).

22. See 'Castration or Decapitation?' (1981b) and 'The Laugh of the Medusa' (1981a) for example. Another literary allusion here, most obviously in the anxiety about being late for tea, is to Lewis Carroll's *Alice in Wonderland/Through the Looking-Glass* stories. This is another rich site for the exploration of young women's desires (to be queen, for instance), of dreams and identity in a heteropatriarchal and capitalist society, and of the ambiguity and arbitrary nature of language and of the importance of the ongoing circulation of stories or 'love-gift(s)' as the fairytale is referred to in the poem that prefaces *Alice Through the Looking-Glass and What Alice Found There* (141). Like Shakespeare's Miranda, Alice finally becomes queen at the end of the story as a result of playing chess.

23. Miranda's engagement with this novel suggests an escape through imagination and the sensuality of language beyond the walls of this English orchard, language and culture in a way that seems to accord with Woolf's own feelings expressed shortly before the story was published. Travelling in Spain and France in March–April 1923, Woolf's passion to learn French and about French culture is expressed to Jacques Raverat: 'I felt a kind of levity and frivolity and congeniality upon me with the first sight of Dieppe. How much more enjoyable in some queer

182 Notes

way France is than England! But how does one learn the language? I must and will. I want to know how the French think. After the English, they seem so natural, so much akin to all one likes' (*L3* 23).

24. As Woolf's own experience of working with S.S. Koteliansky on the translation of Tolstoy's letters to Valeriya Arsenyeva and a memoir of Tolstoy by Alexander Goldenveisers at this time would have confirmed (both published by the Hogarth Press in 1923).

25. The setting of 'In the Orchard' may also allude to the garden and orchard at Monk's House, with its proximity to St Peter's Church. Woolf also bought a statue that she named Miranda in 1931 (*D4* 3). I thank Elisa Sparks for drawing my attention to this and for suggesting that this naming may be a joking reference back to 'In the Orchard'. If so, it is a joke also at the expense of the commodification of Miranda in her story.

26. There are obviously other similarities between Woolf's story and Shakespeare's play, not least the theme of the control and commodification of nature's bounty and the natural resources of the island referred to as 'Paradise' (*Tempest* 102), as well as violence towards, and punishment of, individuals who challenge the power and capitalist drive of those who assume authority. It is also a play having potential to be read as subversive and post-colonial, or as one that consolidates the Renaissance colonial ideology. Thus it clearly raises issues of the ambiguity of meaning on which Woolf's story effectively capitalises.

27. Rubin draws attention to the way Levi Strauss avoids a denunciation of the sexism inherent in the kinship structures he explores, but rather attributes this 'as the root of romance' (550).

28. In her diary, Woolf records the impact of hearing T.S. Eliot read *The Waste Land* (*D2* 178). In the same entry, she records her anxieties about *Jacob's Room*, as well as her writing of 'a story for Eliot' ('In the Orchard' was published by Eliot in *The Criterion*).

29. Pound wanted to raise £300 per year for Eliot (£10 per annum from 30 people – Rainey, 1999, 61; Ackroyd 122), though Eliot himself considered £500 per annum for life would be what he needed to give him the security to leave the bank (Ackroyd 129; Lee 1996, 446). Ottoline Morrel, without consulting the others involved in the Eliot Fund, sent a circular asking for £300 for five years (Lee, 1996, 446). Eliot also did not want his plans to leave the bank made public, but people were reluctant to subscribe to the fund assuming Eliot would remain in employment (as Woolf's letter to Richard Aldington, suggests, *L3* 9). Eliot also 'disapproved of it' because it 'seemed too much like charity' (Ackroyd 122).

30. The term 'ticklish' is also used by Woolf to describe the fickleness of the creative urge when writing to Eliot about her plans for 'In the Orchard' (*L2* 521) and about her wanting his judgement of her work, in what is perhaps a further unconscious connection between this gift scheme and her story. In this letter, she also asks when she can read *The Waste Land*, so she can offer her view of his work.

31. Both he and his wife, Vivien, had been recurrently ill and depressed, and Vivien was in an institution; at this time the scheme aimed partly to relieve Eliot's depression.

32. This was actually from the disembursement of assets resulting from the failure of a company in which Woolf had invested.

33. As the representation of the apples in 'In the Orchard' makes clear, apples can be a store with capitalist and masculine connotations.

34. Edinburgh University Women's Union printed Woolf's story in their publication, *Atalanta's Garland* in 1926.

Notes 183

35. Woolf's references to Angela as "Miranda" four times in the holograph and once in the typescript suggest a link between the young woman in this story and Miranda in "In the Orchard"' (*CSF* 304).

36. Instead of marking a place in a romanticised coming-of-age novel, as Miranda's finger does, Angela's finger marks her place in a black economics book (*CSF* 145).

37. Carrier refers to the way that the gift 'takes on a special meaning for the people involved that is over and above, and may even contradict, its meaning as a commodity-sign or even its utility' (8–9).

38. This is a similar image that Woolf uses in her *Diary* (20 April 1925) to convey her own contentment and pleasure in writing and 'street sauntering and square haunting', imagining a dress she may get made, and her hopes for her success with her novels: 'Happiness is to have a little string onto which things will attach themselves . . . that is the string, which as if it dipped loosely into a wave of treasure brings up pearls sticking to it. . . . And my days are likely to be strung with them' (*D3* 11).

39. As Woolf argues in *Three Guineas* (see Chapter 1).

40. Heather Levy also considers that Fanny interprets this comment about Slater's pins as a 'seductive device', but explains this comment as being an indication of Fanny's adoration of Julia, a feeling in part stimulated by the social inequalities between them (89).

41. Giving the shop a family name is an attempt to personalise the retail experience. However, because the name 'Slater's' is a near-palindrome for 'retails' with only the letter 'i' (I) missing, this still suggests that shopping ultimately remains an impersonal activity. I thank my colleague Alison Johnson for pointing out this near-palindrome. Further, Woolf's pointed disparagement of pins and their association with men and the commercial world could have a source in her experience recounted in a letter to Vanessa Bell in May 1926. Having spent some time promoting a new book published by the Hogarth Press, Woolf expresses her disgust with the commercial world, with the 'mediocrity' and drabness of Kensington High Street and the women shopping there. However, she is especially disgusted by a man on the tube sitting next to her 'who picked his ears with a large pin – then stuck it in his coat again' (*L3* 265). Because Dick suggests that it was in early September 1926 that Woolf began her story, it seems reasonable to suggest that this experience on the tube may have contributed in some way to the conception of this story.

42. In the 'Editorial Procedures' for *Virginia Woolf: The Complete Shorter Fiction*, Susan Dick explains the discrepancies between the versions as being due to the fact that Leonard Woolf reprinted the story in *A Haunted House* from the typescript rather than from the version published in *Forum* in 1928 (9).

43. It is worth remembering that shortly after Woolf finished this story in July 1927, she began her own imaginative recreation of the history of a woman she very much loved and lusted after (see Woolf's letter to Vita Sackville-West, *L3* 428–9). Her own willingness to speculate and imagine in her fantastical version of Vita Sackville-West's past and present did actually become a gift to her lover in 1928 (see above).

44. Pin money is an allowance traditionally given to a woman by her husband for her personal expenditure, or it is used to refer to women's earnings to indicate their traditionally marginal position in the workplace and to trivialise their earning power.

45. Fleishman also notes the change from a rose to a carnation and points out the further ambiguity of 'whose breast' the flower is returned to at the end; however,

184 *Notes*

for him the ambiguity of this ending is 'disturbing' (62). Clements and Winston also discuss the confusion of pronouns that gives rise to a fluidity in terms of the identity of the characters.

46. At this time Woolf was learning French and in her letters of this period these lessons seem to be associated with homoerotic frisson. In letters to Vita Sackville-West she remarks on looking forward to learning French and on getting closer to Vita (*L3* 438, 469); and to Mary MacCarthy she writes of looking forward to the flirtation of the classroom (*L3* 134). It may be that she also knew the French for 'pin', *épingle*, and its homophone, *épingles* (meaning, according to Judith Still, a certain kind of gift – usually jewellery given to women to enhance a business relationship or to evade tax). Still discusses this connection in her consideration of the importance of pins in eighteenth-century culture, especially in economic texts and treaties (183–5). As we see in Woolf's story, there is a similar sense of slippage between economies, one that suggests a close interconnection between the market, the gift and economies of desire.

47. A carnation is also used to symbolise lesbian desire in Katherine Mansfield's story 'Carnation' (1918), a story that Winston claims as an intertext for Woolf's 'Slater's Pins' (1997, 63–4). 'Carnation' also ends with the gift of a flower from one woman to another, as Eve drops a flower down the front of Katie's dress – what Eve calls a '*souvenir tendre*'. The meaning of the flower gift in Woolf's story is more ambiguous, and there seems to be a resistance to pinning down and labelling the gift in the same way.

48. I am grateful to my friend and colleague, the late Mike Davis, for suggesting this possible word play.

49. See also her letters to the editor of 23 January 1941 (*L6* 463).

50. Woolf's earlier mixed feelings about Ottoline Morrell and her disgust at her wealth, fashionableness and insincerity found an outlet in Woolf's criticism of 'the social system' in *Mrs Dalloway* (*D2* 248). At some level, Woolf's complex and uncomfortable feelings about Ottoline's 'legacy gifts' may also have found their way into her story, recalling her earlier intentions and the original conception of her novel in which Clarissa Dalloway, also the wife of a Conservative member of parliament, was to commit suicide.

51. See Paula Bennett for a discussion of clitoral imagery in writing by women. I discuss this imagery in 'Pearl-diving: Inscriptions of Desire and Creativity in H. D. and Woolf'.

52. 'In neither the holograph nor what appears to be the first typescript draft is he Sissy Miller's brother' (Dick *CSF* 318).

Bibliography

Abbott, Reginald. 'What Miss Kilman's Petticoat Means: Virginia Woolf, Shopping, and Spectacle'. *Modern Fiction Studies* 38.1 (1992). 193–214.

Abel, Elizabeth. *Virginia Woolf and the Fictions of Psychoanalysis*. Chicago and London: University of Chicago Press, 1989.

Abraham, Julie. *Are Girls Necessary? Lesbian Writing and Modern Histories*. New York and London: Routledge, 1996.

Ackroyd, Peter. *T.S. Eliot*. London: Sphere, 1985.

Adburgham, Alison. *Shops and Shopping 1800–1914: Where, and in What Manner the Well-Dressed Englishwoman Bought Her Clothes*. London: Allen, 1964.

Albrinck, Meg. 'Lily the Ethnographer: Discovering Self in *To the Lighthouse*'. *Woolf and the Art of Exploration: Selected Papers from the Fifteenth International Conference on Virginia Woolf*. Ed. Helen Southworth and Elisa Kay Sparks. South Carolina: Clemson University Digital Press, 2006. 196–202.

Aldcroft, Derek H. *The British Economy Between the Wars*. Oxford: Philip Allan Publishers Ltd., 1983.

———. *The British Economy Volume One: The Years of Turmoil, 1920–1951*. Sussex: Wheatsheaf Books Ltd., 1986.

Ames, Christopher. 'Carnivalesque Comedy in *Between the Acts*'. *Twentieth Century Literature* 44.4 (1998). 394–408.

Armstrong, Tim. *Modernism: A Cultural History*. Cambridge and Malden: Polity Press, 2005.

Baldwin, Dean. *Virginia Woolf: A Study of the Short Fiction*. Boston: Twayne Publishers, 1989.

Barrett, Eileen and Patricia Cramer (eds). *Virginia Woolf: Lesbian Readings*. New York and London: New York University Press, 1997.

Barrett, Eileen. 'Unmasking Lesbian Passion: The Inverted World of *Mrs Dalloway*'. *Virginia Woolf: Lesbian Readings*. Ed. Eileen Barrett and Patricia Cramer. London and New York: New York University Press, 1997. 146–64.

Beer, Gillian. Introduction to *Between the Acts*. London: Penguin, 1992.

Bell, Vanessa. *Sketches in Pen and Ink*. Ed. Lia Giachero. London: Pimlico, 1998.

Bennett, Paula. 'Critical Clitoridectomy: Female Sexual Imagery and Feminist Psychoanalytic Theory'. *Signs: Journal of Women in Culture and Society* 18 (1993). 235–59.

Benzel, Kathryn R. and Hoberman, Ruth (eds). *Trespassing Boundaries: Virginia Woolf's Short Fiction*. New York and Basingstoke: Palgrave Macmillan, 2004.

Black, Naomi. *Virginia Woolf as Feminist*. Ithaca and London: Cornell University Press, 2004.

Blackmer, Corinne E. 'Lesbian Modernism in the Shorter Fiction of Virginia Woolf and Gertrude Stein'. Barrett and Cramer, 78–94.

Blotner, Joseph L. 'Mythic Patterns in *To the Lighthouse*'. *Virginia Woolf, To the Lighthouse: A Casebook*. Ed. Morris Beja. London: Macmillan, 1970. 169–88.

Boone, Joseph Allen. *Libidinal Currents: Sexuality and the Shaping of Modernism*. Chicago and London: University of Chicago Press, 1998.

Bourdieu, Pierre. Selections from *The Logic of Practice*. In *The Logic of the Gift: Toward an Ethic of Generosity*. Ed. Alan D. Schrift. London and New York: Routledge, 1997. 190–230.

186 Bibliography

Bowlby, Rachel. *Still Crazy After All These Years: Women, Writing and Psychoanalysis.* London and New York: Routledge, 1992.

Bowlby, Rachel (ed.). *Virginia Woolf. The Crowded Dance of Modern Life: Selected Essays Volume 2.* London: Penguin, 1993.

Bradshaw, David. *Virginia Woolf. The Mark on the Wall and Other Stories.* Oxford: OUP, 2001.

Briggs, Julia. '"Cut deep and scored thick with meaning": Frame and Focus in Woolf's Later Short Stories'. *Trespassing Boundaries: Virginia Woolf's Short Fiction.* New York and Basingstoke: Palgrave Macmillan, 2004. 175–191.

———. *Reading Virginia Woolf.* Edinburgh: Edinburgh University Press, 2006.

Brimstone, Lyndie. 'Towards a New Cartography: Radclyffe Hall, Virginia Woolf and the Working of Common Land'. *What Lesbians Do in Books.* Ed. Elaine Hobby and Chris White. London: The Women's Press, 1991. 86–108.

Brosnan, Leila. *Reading Virginia Woolf's Essays and Journalism.* Edinburgh: Edinburgh University Press, 1997. Rpt 1999.

Carpentier, Martha. C. *Ritual, Myth and the Modernist Text: The Influence of Jane Harrison on Joyce, Eliot and Woolf.* Netherlands: Gordon and Breach Publishers, 1998.

Carrier, James G. *Gifts and Commodities: Exchange and Western Capitalism Since 1700.* London: Routledge, 1995.

Carroll. Lewis. *Alice's Adventures in Wonderland* and *Through the Looking-Glass.* London: Book Club Associates. 1976.

Caughie, Pamela L. Purpose and Play in Woolf's London Scene Essays. *Women's Studies* 16 (1989). 389–408.

———. *Virginia Woolf and Postmodernism: Literature in Quest and Question of Itself.* Urbana and Chicago: University of Illinois Press, 1991.

——— (ed.). *Virginia Woolf in the Age of Mechanical Reproduction.* New York and London: Garland Publishing, 2000.

Cheal, David. *The Gift Economy.* London and New York: Routledge, 1988.

Cixous, Hélène. 'The Laugh of the Medusa'. 1975. Translated by Keith Cohen and Paula Cohen. *New French Feminisms: An Anthology.* Ed. and Introductions by Elaine Marks and Isabelle de Courtivron. Hertfordshire: Harvester Wheatsheaf, 1981a. 245–64.

———. 'Castration or Decapitation?' 1976. Trans. and intro. Annette Kuhn. *Signs: Journal of Women in Culture and Society* 7.1 (1981b). 36–55.

Clements, Susan. 'The Point of "Slater's Pins": Misrecognition and the Narrative Closet'. *Tulsa Studies in Women's Literature* 13 (1994). 15–26.

Colburn, Krystyna. 'The Lesbian Intertext of Woolf's Short Fiction'. *Trespassing Boundaries: Virginia Woolf's Short Fiction.* Ed. Ruth Hoberman and Kathryn N. Benzel. New York and Basingstoke: Palgrave Macmillan, 2004. 63–80.

Cramer, Patricia. '"Loving in the War Years": The War of Images in *The Years'. Virginia Woolf and War: Fiction, Reality and Myth.* Ed. Mark Hussey. New York: Syracuse, 1992a. 203–24.

———. 'Notes From Underground: Lesbian Ritual in the Writings of Virginia Woolf'. *Virginia Woolf Miscellanies: Proceedings from the First Annual Conference on Virginia Woolf.* Ed. Mark Hussey and Vara Neverow-Turk. New York: Pace University Press, 1992b. 177–88.

Cuddy-Keane, Melba. 'The Politics of Comic Modes in Virginia Woolf's *Between the Acts'. PMLA* 105.2 (1990). 273–85.

———. *Virginia Woolf: The Intellectual, And the Public Sphere.* Cambridge and New York: CUP, 2003.

Bibliography 187

Daugherty, Beth Rigel. '"A corridor leading from Mrs. Dalloway to a new book": Transforming Stories, Bending Genres'. *Trespassing Boundaries:Virginia Woolf's Short Fiction*. New York and Basingstoke: Palgrave Macmillan, 2004. 101–24.

Davis, Natalie Zemon. *The Gift in Sixteenth-Century France*. Oxford: OUP, 2000.

Delany, Paul. 'A Little Capital: The Financial Affairs of Leonard and Virginia Woolf'. *The Charlston Magazine*, Summer/Autumn 1993. 5–8.

Delany, Paul. *Literature, Money and the Market: From Trollope to Amis*. Basingstoke: Palgrave Macmillan, 2002.

Derrida, Jacques. *Given Time: I. Counterfeit Money*. Trans. Peggy Kamuf. Chicago and London: University of Chicago Press, 1992.

DeSalvo, Louise and Mitchell A. Leaska (ed.). *The Letters of Vita Sackville-West to Virginia Woolf*. London: Virago, 1992.

Dettmar, Kevin J. H. and Stephen Watt. *Marketing Modernisms: Self Promotion, Canonization and Rereading*. Ann Arbor: University of Michigan Press, 1996.

Dick, Susan. Foreword. *Trespassing Boundaries: Virginia Woolf's Short Fiction*. Ed. Kathryn R. Benzel and Ruth Hoberman. New York and Basingstoke: Palgrave Macmillan, 2004.

Doan, Laura. *Fashioning Sapphism: The Origins of a Modern English Lesbian Culture*. New York and Chichester: Columbia University Chicago Press, 2001.

DuPlessis, Rachel Blau. *Writing Beyond the Ending: Narrative Strategies of Twentieth-Century Women Writers*. Bloomington: Indiana University Press. 1985.

Elliot, Bridget and Jo-Ann Wallace. *Women Artists and Writers: Modernist (Im)positionings*. London and New York: Routledge, 1994.

Emerson, Ralph Waldo. Selection From Essays and Lectures (1844). In *The Logic of the Gift: Toward an Ethic of Generosity*. Ed. Alan D. Schrift. London and New York: Routledge, 1997. 25–7.

Emery, Mary Lou. '"Robbed of Meaning": The Work at the Center of *To The Lightouse'*. *Modern Fiction Studies* 38.1 (1992). 217–34.

Felski, Rita. *The Gender of Modernity*. Massachusetts and London: Harvard University Press, 1995.

Fleishman, Avrom. 'Forms of the Woolfian Short Story'. *Virginia Woolf: Revaluation and Continuity*. Ed. Ralph Freedman. London and California: University of California Press, 1980. 44–70.

Flint, Kate. 'Virginia Woolf and the General Strike'. *Essays in Criticism*. (1986). 319–34.

Freedman, Jonathan. *Professions of Taste: Henry James, British Aestheticism, and Commodity Culture*. Stanford: Stanford University Press, 1990.

Garrity, Jane. 'Selling Culture to the "Civilized": Bloomsbury, British *Vogue*, and the Marketing of National Identity'. *Modernism/Modernity* 6.2 (1999). 29–58.

———. 'Virginia Woolf, Intellectual Harlotry, and 1920s British *Vogue*'. *Virginia Woolf in the Age of Mechanical Reproduction*. Ed. Pamela L. Caughie. London: Garland Publishing, 2000. 185–218.

Gaskell, Elizabeth. *Cranford*. London: Penguin, 1988.

Gasché, Rodolphe. 'Heliocentric Exchange'. In *The Logic of the Gift: Toward an Ethic of Generosity*. Ed. Alan D. Schrift. London and New York: Routledge, 1997. 100–17.

Gillespie, Diane E. 'Godiva Still Rides: Virginia Woolf, Divestiture and *Three Guineas'*. In *Woolf and the Art of Exploration: Selected Papers from the Fifteenth International Conference on Virginia Woolf*. Ed. Helen Southworth and Elisa Kay Sparks. Clemson: Clemson University Digital Press, 2006. 2–27.

Glendinning, Victoria. *Leonard Woolf: A Life*. London: Simon and Schuster, 2006.

188 *Bibliography*

Gualtieri, Elena. *Virginia Woolf's Essays: Sketching the Past*. Basingstoke and London: Macmillan, 2000.

Hankins, Leslie Kathleen. 'Virginia Woolf and Walter Benjamin Selling Out(Siders)'. *Virginia Woolf in the Age of Mechanical Reproduction*. Ed. Pamela L. Caughie. New York and London: Garland Publishing, 2000. 3–35.

Hanson, Clare. *Short Stories and Short Fictions, 1880–1980*. Basingstoke: Macmillan, 1985.

——. *Re-Reading the Short Story*. Basingstoke and London: Macmillan, 1989.

——. *Virginia Woolf*. Basingstoke and London: Macmillan, 1994.

Hargreaves, Tracy. 'The Grotesque and the Great War in *To The Lighthouse*'. *Women's Fiction and the Great War*. Ed. Suzanne Raitt and Trudi Tate. Oxford: Clarendon Press, 1997. 132–49.

Harrison, Jane. *Art and Ritual*. London: Williams and Norgate, 1918.

Haule, James M. '*To the Lighthouse* and the Great War: The Evidence of Virginia Woolf's Revisions of "Time Passes."' *Virginia Woolf and War: Fiction, Reality, and Myth*. Ed. Mark Hussey, New York: Syracuse University Press, 1991. 164–79.

Head, Dominic. *The Modernist Short Story: A Study in Theory and Practice*. Cambridge: CUP, 1992.

Herr, Cheryl. *Joyce's Anatomy of Culture*. University of Illinois Press, 1982.

Herrmann, Anne. *Queering the Moderns: Poses/Portraits/Performances*. Basingstoke: Palgrave Macmillan, 2000.

Hoberman, Ruth. 'Collecting, Shopping and Reading: Virginia Woolf's Stories about Objects'. *Trespassing Boundaries: Virginia Woolf's Short Fiction*. Ed. Ruth Hoberman and Kathryn N. Benzel. New York and Basingstoke: Palgrave, 2004. 104–32.

Hussey, Mark. *The Singing of the Real World: The Philosophy of Virginia Woolf's Fiction*. Columbus: Ohio State University Press, 1986.

——. 'Living in a War Zone: An Introduction to Woolf as a War Novelist'. *Virginia Woolf and War: Fiction, Reality, and Myth*. Ed. Mark Hussey, New York: Syracuse University Press, 1991. 1–13.

Huyssen, Andreas. *After the Great Divide: Modernism, Mass Culture, Postmodernism*. Bloomington and Indianapolis: Indiana University Press, 1986.

Hyde, Lewis. *The Gift: Imagination and the Erotic Life of Property*. London: Vintage, 1999.

Irigaray, Luce. *This Sex Which is not One*. Trans. Catherine Porter and Carolyn Burke. New York: Cornell University Press, 1985.

James, Wendy. '"One of Us" Marcel Mauss and "English" Anthropology'. *Marcel Mauss: A Centenary Tribute*. Ed. Wendy James and N.J. Allen. New York and London: Berghahn Books, 1998. 3–26.

Jensen, Emily. 'Clarissa Dalloway's Respectable Suicide'. *Virginia Woolf: A Feminist Slant*. Ed. Jane Marcus. Lincoln and London: University of Nebraska Press, 1983. 162–79.

Kirkpatrick, B.J. 'Virginia Woolf: Unrecorded *Times Literary Supplement* Reviews'. *Modern Fiction Studies*, 38.1 (1992). 279–83.

Kershner, R.B. *Joyce, Bakhtin and Popular Literature*. Chapel Hill and London: University of North Carolina Press, 1989.

Knopp, Sherron E. '"If I Saw You Would You Kiss Me?": Sapphism and the Subversiveness of Virginia Woolf's *Orlando*'. *PMLA*, 103.1 (1988). 24–34.

Kucich, John. 'Transgression and Sexual Difference in Elizabeth Gaskell's Novels'. *Texas Studies in Literature and Language*, 32.2 (1990). 187–213.

Lakoff, George and Mark Johnson. *Metaphors We Live By*. Chicago and London: Univeristy of Chicago Press, 1980; rpt. with new afterword, 2003.

Lawrence, Karen R. 'Orlando's Voyage Out'. *Modern Fiction Studies* 38.1 (1992). 253–77.

Leaska, Mitchell A. (Ed.) *Pointz Hall: The Earlier and Later Transcripts of Between the Acts*. New York: University Publications, 1983.

Lee, Hermione. *Virginia Woolf*. London: Chatto and Windus, 1996.

———. 'Virginia Woolf's Essays', in *The Cambridge Companion to Virginia Woolf*. Ed. Sue Roe and Susan Sellers. Cambridge: CUP, 2000. 91–108.

Levenback, Karen L. *Virginia Woolf and the Great War*. New York: Syracuse University Press, 1999.

Levy, Heather. '"Julia Kissed Her, Julia Possessed Her": Considering Class and Lesbian Desire in Virginia Woolf's Shorter Fiction'. *Virginia Woolf: Emerging Perspectives. Selected Papers From the Third Annual Conference on Virginia Woolf*. Ed. Mark Hussey and Vara Neverow-Turk. New York: Pace University Press, 1994. 83–90.

Mackay, Marina. *Modernism and World War Two*. Cambridge: CUP, 2007.

Maika, Patricia. *Virginia Woolf's Between the Acts and Jane Harrison's Con/spiracy*. London: UMI Research Press, 1987 [1984].

Majumdar, Robin Allen McLaurin (ed.). *Virginia Woolf: The Critical Heritage*. London: Routledge and Kegan Paul Ltd., 1975.

Mansfield, Katherine. 'Carnation' (1917) and 'The Little Governess' (1920). *Katherine Mansfield: Selected Stories*. Ed. D.M. Davin. Oxford: Oxford University Press, 1981. 184–97.

Mauss, Marcel. (1950) *The Gift: The Form and Reason for Exchange in Archaic Societies*. Trans. W.D. Halls. New York and London: W.W. Norton, 1990.

Laura Marcus. *Virginia Woolf*. Second Edition. Tavistock: Northcote House. 2004. First ed. 1997.

———. 'Virginia Woolf and The Hogarth Press'. Ian Willison et al. *Modernist Writers and the Marketplace*. Basingstoke: Macmillan, 1996. 124–50.

McVicker, Jeanette. '"Six Essays on London Life": A History of Dispersal Part 1'. *Woolf Studies Annual* 9.1 (2003). 143–65.

Meese, Elizabeth. 'Theorizing Lesbian: Writing – A Love Letter'. *Lesbian Texts and Contexts: Radical Revisions*. Ed. Karla Jay and Joanne Glasgow. New York and London: New York University Press, 1990. 70–87.

Moretti, Franco. *Signs Taken for Wonders: Essays in the Sociology of Literary Forms*. Revised Edition. London: Verso, 1988.

Morrison, Mark S. *The Public Face of Modernism: Little Magazines, Audiences, and Reception 1905–1920*. University of Wisconsin Press, 2001.

Nava, Mica. 'Modernity's Disavowal: Women, the City and the Department Store'. *Modern Times: Reflections on a Century of English Modernity*. Ed. Mica Nava and Alan O'Shea. London: Routledge, 1996. 38–76.

Neverow, Vara S. 'Freudian Seduction and the Fallacies of Dictatorship.' *Virginia Woolf and Fascism: Resisting the Dictator's Seduction*. Ed. Merry M. Pawlowski. Basingstoke: Palgrave, 2001. 56–72.

Nicholson, Nigel. *Portrait of a Marriage*. London: Weidenfield and Nicholson, 1990.

Olin-Hitt, Michael R. 'Desire, Death, and Plot: The Subversive Play of *Orlando*'. *Women's Studies* 24 (1995). 483–96.

Osteen, Mark. *The Question of the Gift: Essays Across Disciplines*. London and New York: Routledge, 2002.

Oxindine, Annette. 'Outing the Outsiders: Woolf's Exploration of Homophobia in *Between the Acts*'. *Woolf Studies Annual* 5 (1999). 115–31.

Rainey, Lawrence. *Institutions of Modernism: Literary Elites and Public Culture*. New Haven and London: Yale University Press. 1998.

190   Bibliography

———. 'The Cultural Economy of Modernism'. In *The Cambridge Companion to Modernism*. Ed Michael Levenson. Cambridge: CUP, 1999. 33–69.

Raitt, Suzanne. *Vita and Virginia: The Work and Friendship of V. Sackville-West and Virginia Woolf*. Oxford: Oxford University Press, 1993.

Reed, Christopher. 'Design for Queer Living: Sexual Identity, Performance, and Décor in British *Vogue*, 1922–1926'. *GLQ: A Journal of Lesbian and Gay Studies* 12.3 (2006). 377–403.

Reid, Ian. *The Short Story*. London: Methuen, 1977.

Rosenberg, Beth Carole and Jeanne Dubino (eds). *Virginia Woolf and the Essay*. Basingstoke and London: Macmillan, 1997.

Rosenbaum, S.P. (ed). *Virginia Woolf. Women & Fiction: The Manuscript Versions of A Room of One's Own*. Oxford: Blackwell, 1992.

Rosenfeld, Natania. *Outsiders Together: Virginia and Leonard Woolf*. Princeton: Princeton University Press, 2000.

Rubin, Gayle. 'The Traffic in Women: Notes on the "Political Economy" of Sex'. *Literary Theory: An Anthology*. Ed Julie Rivkin and Michael Ryan. London: Blackwell, 1998. 533–60.

Sackville-West, Vita. *The Letters of Vita Sackville-West to Virginia Woolf*. Ed. Louise De Salvo and Mitchell A. Leaska, London: Virago, 1992.

Sarker, Sonita. 'Three Guineas, The In-corporated Intellectual, and Nostalgia for the Human'. *Virginia Woolf in the Age of Mechanical Reproduction*. Ed. Pamela L. Caughie. New York and London: Garland Publishing, 2000. 37–66.

Schrift, Alan D. (ed.). *The Logic of the Gift: Toward an Ethic of Generosity*. London and New York: Routledge, 1997.

Scott, Bonnie Kime. *Refiguring Modernism: Postmodern Feminist Readings of Woolf, West, and Barnes. Volume 2*. Bloomington: Indiana University Press, 1995.

Simmel, Georg. 'Faithfulness and Gratitude.' *The Sociology of Georg Simmel*. Trans. and Ed. Kurt H. Wolff. Illinois: The Free Press, 1950.

Skrbic, Nena. '"Excursions into the literature of a foreign country": Crossing Cultural Boundaries in the Short Fiction.' *Trespassing Boundaries:Virginia Woolf's Short Fiction*. Ed. Ruth Hoberman and Kathryn N. Benzel. New York and Basingstoke: Palgrave, 2004a. 25–38.

———. *Wild Outbursts of Freedom: Reading Woolf's Short Fiction*. Connecticut and London: Praeger, 2004b.

Shakespeare, William. *The Tempest*. London and New York: Routledge, 1989.

Silber, Ilana. 'Modern Philanthropy' Reassessing the Viability of a Maussian Perspective. In *Marcel Mauss: A Centenary Tribute*. Ed. Wendy James and N.J. Allen. New York and Oxford: Berghahn Books, 1998. 134–50.

Silver, Brenda. '"Anon" and "The Reader": Virginia Woolf's Last Essays.' *Twentieth Century Literature* 25.3/4 (1979). 356–441.

Simmel, Georg. 'Faithfulness and Gratitude.' In *The Gift: An Interdisciplinary Perspective*, Ed. Aafke Komter. Amsterdam: Amsterdam University Press, 1996. Cited in Mark Osteen *The Question of the Gift: Essays Across Disciplines*. London and New York: Routledge, 2002.

Simpson, Kathryn. 'Pearl-diving: Inscriptions of Desire and Creativity in H.D. and Woolf.' *Journal of Modern Literature* 27.4. 37–58.

Smith, Angela. *Katherine Mansfield and Viriginia Woolf: A Public of Two*. Oxford: Clarendon Press, 1999.

Smith, Patricia Juliana. *Lesbian Panic: Homoeroticism in Modern British Women's Fiction*. New York: Columbia University Press, 1997.

Bibliography   191

Snaith, Anna. *Virginia Woolf: Public and Private Negotiations*. Basingstoke and London: Macmillan Press, 2000a.
———. 'The Three Guineas Letters.' *Woolf Studies Annual* vol. 6, NY: Pace University Press. 2000b. 1–168.
———. '"Stray Guineas": Virginia Woolf and the Fawcett Library.' *Literature and History* 12:2 (2003). 16–35.
Sproles, Karyn Z. *Desiring Women: The Partnership of Virginia Woolf and Vita Sackville-West*. Toronto, Buffalo, London: University of Toronto Press, 2006.
Staveley, Alice. 'Woolf's Q factor: "Kew Gardens" 1927'. The Annual Conference on Virginia Woolf, 2003. Unpublished conference paper.
———. 'Conversations at Kew: Reading Woolf's Feminist Narratology.' In Trespassing Boundaries. Ed. Benzel and Hoberman. London: Palgrave Macmillan, 2004. 39–62.
Still, Judith. *Feminine Economies: Thinking Against the Market in the Enlightenment and the Late Twentieth Century*. Manchester and New York: Manchester University Press, 1997.
Tratner, Michael. *Modernism and Mass Politics: Joyce, Woolf, Eliot and Yeats*. Stanford University Press, 1995.
———. 'Why Isn't *Between the Acts* a Movie?' *Virginia Woolf in the Age of Mechanical Reproduction*. Ed. Pamela L. Caughie. New York and London: Garland Publishing, 2000. 115–34.
———. *Deficits and Desires: Economics and Sexuality in Twentieth Century Literature*. Stanford: Stanford University Press, 2001.
Trotter, David. *The English Novel in History 1892–1920*. London and New York: Routledge, 1998 [1993].
Vanita, Ruth. 'Bringing Buried Things to Light: Homoerotic Alliances in *To the Lighthouse*.' *Virginia Woolf: Lesbian Readings*. Ed. Eileen Barratt and Patricia Cramer. New York and London: New York University Press, 1997. 165–79.
Whitworth, Michael H. *Virginia Woolf* (Authors in Context). Oxford: OUP, 2005.
Wicke, Jennifer. *Advertising Fictions: Literature, Advertisement, and Social Reading*. New York: Columbia University Press, 1988.
———. 'Mrs Dalloway goes to Market: Woolf, Keynes, and Modern Markets.' *Novel: A Forum on Fiction* 28.1 (Fall 1994). 5–23.
———. 'Appreciation, Depreciation: Modernism's Speculative Bubble.' *Modernism/Modernity* 8.3 (2001). 389–403.
Willison, Ian, Warwick Gould and Warren Chernaik (eds). *Modernist Writers and the Marketplace*. Basingstoke: Palgrave Macmillan, 1996.
Winston, Janet. '"Something Out of Harmony": To the Lighthouse and the Subject(s) of Empire.' *Woolf Studies Annual* (1996). 39–70.
———. 'Reading Influences: Homoeroticism and Mentoring in Katherine Mansfield's "Carnation" and Virginia Woolf's "Moments of Being: 'Slater's Pins Have No Points.'"' *Virginia Woolf: Lesbian Readings*. Ed. Eileen Barrett and Patricia Cramer. London and New York: New York University Press, 1997. 57–77.
Woolmer J. Howard. *A Checklist of the Hogarth Press 1917–1938*. London: The Hogarth Press, 1976.
Woolf, Leonard. *Barbarians at the Gate*. London: Victor Gollancz Ltd., 1939.
Woolf, Virginia. '"Anon" and "the Reader": Virginia Woolf's Last Essays'. Ed. Brenda R. Silver. *Twentieth Century Literature* 25 (1979). 356–441.
———. *Between the Acts*. London: Penguin, 1992.
———. *The Diary of Virginia Woolf*. 5 vols. Ed. Anne Olivier Bell and Andrew McNeillie. London: Penguin, 1977–85.

192   *Bibliography*

———. 'The Docks of London.' *Virginia Woolf. The Crowded Dance of Modern Life: Selected Essays Volume 2.* Ed. Rachel Bowlby. London: Penguin, 1993. 107–13.

———. 'The Duchess and the Jeweller.' *Virginia Woolf: The Complete Shorter Fiction.* Ed. Susan Dick, London: Triad Grafton Books, 1991. 248–53.

———. 'Gypsy, the Mongrel.' *Virginia Woolf: The Complete Shorter Fiction.* Ed. Susan Dick. London: Triad Grafton Books, 1991. 273–80.

———. 'A Haunted House.' *Virginia Woolf: The Complete Shorter Fiction.* Ed. Susan Dick, London: Triad Grafton Books, 1991. 122–3.

———. 'A Haunted House.' *A Haunted House and Other Stories.* Harmondsworth: Penguin, 1973. 9–11.

———. 'How Should One Read a Book?' *Virginia Woolf. The Crowded Dance of Modern Life: Selected Essays Volume 2.* Ed. Rachel Bowlby. London: Penguin, 1993.

———. 'Gypsy, the Mongrel.' *Virginia Woolf: The Complete Shorter Fiction.* Ed. Susan Dick. London: Triad Grafton Books, 1991. 273–80.

———. *'The Hours': The British Museum Manuscript of Mrs Dalloway.* Ed. Helen M. Wussow. New York: Pace University Press, 1997.

———. 'In the Orchard.' *Virginia Woolf: The Complete Shorter Fiction.* Ed. Susan Dick, London: Triad Grafton Books, 1991. 149–51.

———. *Introductory Letter to Margaret Llewelyn Davies. Life as We Have Known It by Co-operative Working Women.* Ed. Margaret Llewelyn Davies. London: Virago, 1977. xvii–xxxxi

———. *Jacob's Room.* London: Penguin, 1992.

———. 'Kew Gardens.' *Virginia Woolf: The Complete Shorter Fiction.* Ed. Susan Dick, London: Triad Grafton Books, 1991. 90–5.

———. 'The Legacy.' *Virginia Woolf: The Complete Shorter Fiction.* Ed. Susan Dick, London: Triad Grafton Books, 1991. 281–7.

———. *The Letters of Virginia Woolf.* 6 vols. Ed. Nigel Nicolson and Joanne Trautmann. New York: Harcourt, Brace, Jovanovich, 1975–80.

———. 'Modern Fiction.' *Virginia Woolf. The Crowded Dance of Modern Life: Selected Essays Volume 2.* Ed. Rachel Bowlby. London: Penguin, 1993. 5–12.

———. 'Moments of Being: "Slater's Pins Have no Points."' *Virginia Woolf: The Complete Shorter Fiction.* Ed. Susan Dick, London: Triad Grafton Books, 1991. 215–20.

———. 'Mr Bennett and Mrs Brown.' *A Modernist Reader: Modernism in England 1910–1930.* Ed. Peter Faulkner. London: Batsford, 1986. 112–28.

———. *Mrs Dalloway.* Harmondsworth: Penguin, 1974.

———. 'Mrs Dalloway in Bond Street.' *Virginia Woolf: The Complete Shorter Fiction.* Ed. Susan Dick, London: Triad Grafton Books, 1991. 152–9.

———. *Orlando: A Biography.* London: Grafton, 1989.

———. 'Oxford Street Tide.' *The London Scene: Five Essays by Virginia Woolf.* New York: Random House, 1975. 16–22.

———. 'Reviewing.' *Virginia Woolf. The Crowded Dance of Modern Life: Selected Essays Volume 2.* Ed. Rachel Bowlby. London: Penguin, 1993. 152–63.

———. *A Room of One's Own.* London: Grafton, 1989.

———. 'A Sketch of the Past.' *Moments of Being.* Ed. Jeanne Schulkind. London: Grafton. 1990 (second edition).

———. 'Solid Objects.' *Virginia Woolf: The Complete Shorter Fiction.* Ed. Susan Dick, London: Triad Grafton Books, 1991.102–7.

———. 'Street Haunting: A London Adventure.' *Virginia Woolf. The Crowded Dance of Modern Life: Selected Essays Volume 2.* Ed. Rachel Bowlby. London: Penguin, 1993. 70–81.

Bibliography 193

——. 'Thoughts on Peace in an Air Raid.' *Virginia Woolf. The Crowded Dance of Modern Life: Selected Essays Volume 2.* Ed. Rachel Bowlby. London: Penguin, 1993. 168–72.

——. *To the Lighthouse.* London: Vintage, 1992.

——. *To the Lighthouse: The Original Holograph Draft.* Ed. Susan Dick. London: The Hogarth Press, 1983.

——. *Three Guineas.* London: The Hogarth Press, 1991.

——. *Virginia Woolf: The Complete Shorter Fiction.* Ed. Susan Dick, London: Triad Grafton Books, 1991 [1989].

——. 'Why Art Today Follows Politics.' *Virginia Woolf. The Crowded Dance of Modern Life: Selected Essays Volume 2.* Ed. Rachel Bowlby. London: Penguin, 1993. 133–6.

——. 'A Woman's College From Outside.' *Virginia Woolf: The Complete Shorter Fiction.* Ed. Susan Dick, London: Triad Grafton Books, 1991. 145–8.

——. *Women & Fiction: The Manuscript Versions of A Room of One's Own.* Ed. S.P. Rosenbaum. Oxford: Blackwell, 1992.

Wussow, Helen M. (Ed.) Introduction to *'The Hours': The British Museum Manuscript of Mrs Dalloway.* New York: Pace University Press, 1997.

Zwerdling, Alex. *Virginia Woolf and the Real World.* Berkeley, Los Angeles and London: University of California Press, 1986.

Index

Bold indicates main pages

Abbott, Reginald, 1, 52, 58, 70, 75, 169 n. 3, n. 6, 170 n. 18, 171 n. 20, n. 24
Adburgham, 52
Adorno, Theodore (1903–1969), 17, 18
Albrink, Meg, 4, 173 n. 13
Aldcroft, Derek, H., 3, 5, 135, 147
Ames, Christopher, 121, 178 n. 50, 179 n. 59, n. 62, n. 64
Armstrong, Tim, 130, 166 n. 16, 180 n. 6, 181 n. 16
audience, 1, 9, 17, 28, 79, 130, 131, 164; *see also* readers/reading

Baldwin, Dean, 148
Bel Esprit, 140; *see also* Eliot Fellowship Fund
Bell, Vanessa (1879–1961), 155, 165 n. 10, 183 n. 41
Benjamin, Walter (1892–1940), 27
Bennett, Arnold (1867–1931), 21–2
Bennett, Paula, 169 n. 10, 184 n. 51
Benzel, Kathryn R. and Ruth Hoberman, 1, 128, 132, 179 n. 1, n. 2, n. 4, 180 n. 14
Ezra Pound and, 140, 141, 182 n. 29
Virginia Woolf and, 141
Black, Naomi, 39, 168 n. 20
Blackmer, Corrine E, 169 n. 9
Bloomsbury, 4, 16, 110
Boone, Joseph Allen, 6, 64, 66, 67, 69, 73, 74, 80, 81, 169 n. 8, 170 n. 16, 171 n. 25
Bourdieu, Pierre, 3
Bowlby, Rachel, 12
Bradshaw, David, 181 n. 19, n. 20
Briggs, Julia, 129, 131
Brosnan, Leila, 14

capitalism, 2, 3, 4–5, 6, 7, 9, 13, 14, 15, 16, 18, 19, 20, 21, 22–3, 24, 25–6, 27, 28–9, 31, 32, 33, 38, 39–40, 43, 45, 46; *see also* individual works
carnivalesque, 121, 145
Carrier, James G., 43, 147
Caughie, Pamela, 17, 40, 42, 46–7, 167 n. 9
Chekov, Anton (1860–1904), 128, 132, 179 n. 2
Cixous, Hélène, 52, 58–9, 83
'Castration or Decapitation', 53
feminine gift economy, 6, 29, 32, 39, 78, 139
jouissance 6; *see also* individual works
masculine economy, 3, 6, 53, 57, 62, 157–8
the paradox of the gift, 3, 56
women's laughter, 44, 136, 145
class, 7, 24, 39, 47, 48, 51, 86–7, 87, 97, 130, 174 n. 18; *see also individual works*
Colburn, Krystyna, 55, 161, 180 n. 9
commodities/commodity culture, 2, 7–8, 13, 14, 15, 16, 18, 19, 20, 21, 22, 23, 24, 26, 27, 37–8; *see also* 'women as commodities' *and* 'writing as commodity'; *see also* individual works
Cox, Ka, 51
Cuddy-Keane, Melba, 119, 125, 126, 142, 178 n. 57, 179 n. 59

Daughtery, Beth Rigel, 129, 132, 155, 181 n. 15
Delany, Paul, 165 n. 2, n. 9, 166 n. 14
Derrida, Jacques, 3
Dick, Susan, 83, 129, 131, 142, 143, 155, 156, 161, 180 notes 8, 9, 183 notes 41, 42
Dickinson, Violet (1865–1948), 166 n. 1
Doan, Laura, 60
Durkheim, Emile (1858–1917), 4

Index 195

education, 7, 28, 29, 37, 38–9, 43, 44–5,
  47, 118, 142
University of Cambridge, 28, 29
Eliot Fellowship Fund, 110, 140, 141,
  142; *see also* Bel Esprit
Eliot, T. S. (1888–1965), 182
  The Waste Land, 117, 140, 182
  and *The Nation*, 141; *see also* Bel Esprit
    and Eliot Fellowship Fund
Emerson, Ralph Waldo (1803–1882), 2,
  89, 103, 151, 157, 158
Emery, Mary Lou, 173 notes 5, 8 and 14
Empire, 86, 173 n. 5; *see also individual*
  works

fascism, 13, 18, 37, 42, 43, 44, 45, 46, 47
Felski, Rita, 23, 38, 59, 61, 112, 150
feminine economy, 2, 6, 16, 29, 64;
  see also Cixous
feminism, 1, 5, 8, 11, 15, 18, 38, 44, 87,
  90, 95, 133, 168 n. 18, 20
  feminist criticism, 166 n. 4, 174 n. 18,
    179–80 n. 4
fertility myths; *see also* 'goddess figure'
  and To the Lighthouse
Fleishman, Avrom, 156, 179 n. 3, 183–4
  n. 45
flowers, (commodities) 58, 174 n. 17
  and homoerotic/desire; *see also*
    individual works
France, 151, 169 n. 10, 178 n. 54, 181–2
  n. 23
Frazer, James George (1854–1941), 4
French, 58, 116, 136, 139; language, 169
  n. 10, 181–2 n. 23, 184 n. 46
Freud, Sigmund (1856–1939), 9, 42
fruit,
  apples: 135, 136, 137, 142
  and creativity, 92–3, 94
  as gift, 142, 146
  peaches, 142

Garrity, Jane, 8, 166 n. 12, 167 n. 6
Gaskell, Elizabeth (1810–65), 53, 54
  Cranford, 53–4
General Strike (1926), 86–7, 172–3 n. 2
gift,
  artistic/creative, 13, 17, 19, 28, 29,
    30, 52, 85–6; *see also* individual
    works

counter to war, 19, 40, 86; *see also*
  individual works
homoerotic desires, and, 143, 146;
  see also individual works
legacy gifts, 174–5, n. 19; *see also*
  individual works
monetary, 19, 28, 29, 40, 45–6,
  109–10, 177 n. 44
pseudo-gifts, 50, 62; *see also*
  individual works
spirit of the gift, 3, 4, 63, 148, 153,
  157; *see also* individual works
threshold gifts, 53, 63–4; *see also*
  individual works
Woolf's gifts, 7, 10–11, 38–9, 47–8,
  109,142; *see also* individual works
Gillespie, Diane F., 138
Glendinning, Victoria, 168 n. 1
goddess figure; *see* To the Lighthouse and
  'A Woman's College From Outside'
Gualtieri, Elena, 1, 12, 13, 14, 17, 36

Hall, Radclyffe Marguerite (1880–1943)
  The Well of Loneliness, 20
Hankins, Leslie, 8, 21, 22, 27, 165 n. 2
Hanson, Clare, 64, 94, 100, 128, 129,
  143, 180 n. 6, n. 7, 173 n. 9
Harper's Bazaar, 131, 155
Harrison, Jane Ellen (1850–1928), 4, 90,
  111, 125, 126, 173 n. 13, 175
  n. 23, 179 n. 58
Haule, James M., 175 n. 22, n. 24
Head, Dominic, 130, 180 n. 6, n. 10, n. 14
Helen of Troy, 91, 173 n. 12
Herrmann, Anne, 50
heteropatriarchy, *see patriarchy*
highbrow, 8–9, 14, 25
Hoberman, Ruth, 25–6, 52, 133; *see also*
  Benzel, Kathryn R. and Ruth
  Hoberman
Hogarth Press, 9–10, 108, 130–1, 141,
  166 n. 14, 180 n. 12
homoerotic desire, 2, 6, 11, 30, 31, 51,
  52, 86, 184 n. 46; *see also*
  individual works
Huyssen, Andreas, 1
Hyde, Lewis, 6–7, 63, 96, 98, 160,
  101–2, 106, 110, 114, 159
  artistic gift, 9, 10, 51, **85**, 86; *see also*
    individual works

196 Index

Hyde, Lewis (cont.)
money, 173 n. 11
threshold gift, 107; see also individual
works

identity, 8, 19, 20, 23, 26, 32, 50, 52,
59, 66, 70, 92, 103, 110, 112,
113, 114, 116, 118, 120, 121,
153, 155, 157, 169 n. 3, n. 11,
170 n. 12, 172 n. 30, 178 n. 57,
179 n. 60, 181 n. 17; see also
'subjectivity'
Irigaray, Luce, 6

Jensen, Emily, 78, 170 n. 16, 172 n. 35
jouissance; see Cixous and individual works

Keynes, John Maynard (1883–1946), 7,
135, 141, 20
A Tract on Monetary Reform, 51
deficit spending, 3, 16, 168 n. 19
influence on Woolf, 51, 16
Kucich, John, 54

Labour Party, 7, 51, 82, 95
Lakoff, George and Mark Johnson, 65, 66
Lawrence, Karen, 113, 178 n. 50
League of Nations, 48
Leaska, Mitchell A., 115–6, 120, 166 n. 10,
178 n. 54, 179 n. 61, n. 65, n. 66
Lee, Hermione, 8, 10, 12–3, 15, 16, 17,
18, 28, 29, 31, 34, 36, 38, 39, 42,
108, 115, 142, 156, 166 n. 5, 168
n. 18, 182 n. 29
Legacy, 28, 29; see also 'The Legacy'
Lévi-Strauss, Claude, 5
library,
British Museum, 33
Cambridge University, 29, 39
London Library, 168 n. 22
the Women's Library, 38, 39; Fawcett
Library Appeal, 47–8
literary market, see marketplace
Lloyd George, David (1863–1945), 20
London, 19, 20, 21, 24, 26, 33, 52, 58,
61, 111, 112, 118, 169 n. 7
Bond Street, 22, 52, 55
Loti, Pierre (1850–1923), Ramunchto,
136, 139
Lukács, Georg (1885–1971), 17, 18

magazine publication, 10, 15, 128, 130,
132
'little magazines', 130
Majumdar, Robin, 12, 177 n. 42, 178
n. 52
Mansfield, Katherine (1888–1923), 128,
138
'Carnation', 184 n. 47
'Prelude', 180 n. 5
'The Little Governess', 170 n. 12
Marcus, Laura, 10, 19, 98–9
marketplace
consumer, 13, 15, 16, 50, 52, 54, 55,
57, 58, 61, 62, 129, 140
literary, 1, 7, 8, 9–10, 13, 14, 16, 18,
19, 21–2, 25, 27, 32, 34, 35, 48,
109, 110, 111, 112, 113, 130, 131,
137–8, 140–1, 163, 167 n. 14,
n. 15, 165 n. 1, n. 2
masculine economy, 62, 86, 157–8;
see also Cixous and individual
works
Mauss, Marcel (1872–1950), 2, 3–4, 5, 7,
40, 127, 148, 151, 153, 154
hau, 3
McNeillie, Andrew, 12
Meese, Elizabeth, 65
metaphor, 31–33, 34, 37, 66, 104, 105,
172 n. 35, 178 n. 56
and creativity, 95
and gift, 64–66, 67, 71, 74, 85, 88, 89,
109, 142
and homoeroticism, 71, 72, 93, 109,
143, 176 n. 38
and marriage, 28, 80, 172 n. 35
monetary, 20, 28, 32–3, 40, 66
modernist writing
aesthetics, 7, 11, 13, 15, 16, 17, 22,
28, 30, 31–2; see also 'Woolf and
modernist experimentalism'
and the gift economy, 141
and the market, 141
monetary economy, see capitalism
money, 8, 9, 10, 19, 20, 40–1, 42, 48,
140–1, 165–6 n. 10, 173 n. 11
women and, 14–5, 28, 29, 31
Woolf and, 13–4, 16, 25, 29, 51, 109,
142, 166 n. 14, n. 1
Morrell, Lady Ottoline (1873–1938),
156, 182 n. 28

Index 197

Nava, Mica, 75, 112, 172 n. 29

Osteen, Mark, 2, 3, 62–3, 154, 163, 175
    n. 19

pacifism, 18, 39
patriarchy, 2, 5, 6, 13, 15, 18, 28, 50,
    87–8, 131–2, 166 n. 10, 178 n. 57
    and war, 85, 86, 87, 178 n. 54
    see also individual works
peace, 37, 45, 46, 49
politics, 1, 6, 7, 8, 9, 11, 13, 15, 18, 19,
    27, 30, 34, 36, 37, 38, 40, 50, 90,
    95, 129, 140, 152, 157, 160, 168
    n. 21, 174 n. 18; *see also* 'Why Art
    Today Follows Politics'
post-war period, 3, 7, 16, 30, 60, 86–7,
    100, 101
Pound, Ezra (1885–1972), 140, 141, 173
    n. 11

Rainey, Lawrence, 1, 130, 140–1
Raitt, Suzanne, 109, 176 n. 38
readers/reading, 1, 9, 11, 13, 15, 17, 21,
    25, 31, 35, 39, 47, 110, 132, 161;
    see also individual works
realism, 17, 21, 22
    'cheapness' of, 138
    limitations of, 53
Reed, Christopher, 15
Rosenbaum, S.P., 29–30, 31, 32
Rosenberg, Beth Carole and Jeanne
    Dubino, 12, 17
Rosenfeld, Natania, 82
Rubin, Gayle, 5–6, 56, 65, 90, 135,
    140, 151
    women as exchange partners, 56, 65

Sackville-West, Vita (1892–1962)
    exchange of gifts, 108–9, 142
    Knole and the Sackvilles, 142, 176
        n. 37, 38
    Orchard and Vineyard, 142–3
    Passenger to Teheran, 176 n. 38
    peaches, 142
    relationship with Woolf, 176 n. 33,
        35, 36, 108, 142
    Seducers in Ecuador, 108
    The Land, 176 n. 37, 177 n. 47, 178
        n. 50

Sapphism, 50, 109, 131; *see also*
    homoerotic desire
Sarker, Sonita, 41
Sarton, May (1912–1995), 48
Scott, Bonnie Kime, 100
sexuality, *see* homoerotic desire and
    under individual works
Shakespeare, William (1564–1616), 122
    Judith, 33
    The Tempest, 140; *see also* 'In the
        Orchard'
shopping, 13, 15–6, 20, 22, 37–8, 52;
    see also individual works
short story
    as a commodity, 137–8
    form/genre, 128–9, 132, 154, 155
    and generosity, 129, 132; *see also*
        individual works
    and the literary market, 129, 130–2, 138
    modernist, 128, 129
    subversiveness of, 128, 129, 132
Simmel, Georg (1858–1918), 2, 62, 154
Skrbic, Nena, 132
Smith, Patricia Juliana, 59
    'lesbian panic', 66–7, 134–5
Smyth, Ethel (1858–1944), 18
Snaith, Anna, 47–8
Sproles, Karyn Z., 142
Staveley, Alice, 9, 131, 133–4, 139
Stephen, Leslie (1832–1904), 8, 165–6
    n. 10, 167 n. 14, 168 n. 22
Still, Judith, 61, 163, 184 n. 46
subjectivity, 17, 22, 26, 61, 64, 65, 66,
    67, 84, 139, 176 n. 38; *see also*
    'identity'

textual generosity, 6, 11, 16, 31–2, 46,
    48, 161–2; *see also* individual
    works
Todd, Dorothy, 8, 15, 166 n. 12
Tratner, Michael, 16, 23–4, 92, 95, 96,
    99, 126, 171 n. 27
Trotter, David, 181 n. 16

Victorian period, 88, 91, 102–3, 110–11,
    122
Vogue, 8, 10, 15

war, 18, 19, 29, 37, 39, 40, 41, 43, 47,
    48, 51, 60, 85, 86–7, 178 n. 54

198 *Index*

Wicke, Jennifer, 16
Winston, Janet 149, 173 n. 4 and 5
women
  as commodities, 19, 22, 23, 133, 134,
    138, *see also individual works*
  economic position of, 13, 50, 39, 40,
    41, 42, 43, 44
  and gifts, 29, 30, 56, 86, 109
  as objects of exchange, 5, 56, 58, 59,
    134–5, 174 n. 17: *see also*
    individual works
  and professions, 12, 14, 28, 30, 31, 38,
    42, 44, 47: *see also* 'Professions
    for Women'
  and writing, 8, 16, 19, 27, 28, 30–1,
    32, 33, 43–4, 85
Women's Co-operative Guild, 7, 175 n. 20
Workers' Educational Association, 7
working-class characters; *see* individual
    works
writing as commodity, 19, 22, 24–5, 31,
    41, 177 n. 46, 181 n. 15; *see also*
    marketplace (literary); women and
    writing; individual works
Woolf, Leonard (1880–1969), 36
  The Barbarians at the Gate, 178 n. 54
  and Labour Party, 51
  'Three Jews', 131
Woolf, Virginia (1882–1941)
  attitude to the literary market, 109,
    131–2, 138; *see also marketplace*
    (literary); women and writing;
    individual works
  as essayist, 12–3, 14, 16, 17–8, 32, 36, 48
  and modernist experimentalism, 6, 10,
    13, 17, 30, 31, 110, 128, 132, 138,
    139, 155, 177 n. 40, 180 n. 14
  as novelist, 87
Woolf, Virginia (works)
  'Anon', 124, 127, 179 n. 60
  'An Unwritten Novel', 131
  A Room of One's Own, 13, 14, 15, 18,
    27, **28–34**, 44, 46, 49
  and audience/reader, 28, 30, 31,
    32, 33
  homoerotic possibility in, 30–1
  legacy in, 29
  literary experimentalism, 30, 32, 33
  market in, 15, 32
  Mary Carmichael in, 30–1, 32

money in, 28, 32–3
reading in, 3
'A Woman's College from Outside',
  134, **143–7**
  class in, 142, 143
  clock in, 145
  gambling in, 146
  gift: as gift, 142; gift in, 142, 143, 146
  goddess figure in, 143
  higher education in, 143, 144
  homoerotic desires in, 143, 146
  and *Jacob's Room*, 143
  laughter in, 145
  and *Mrs Dalloway*, 147, 146
  patriarchy in, 143, 144, 145
Between the Acts, 86, **115–27**
  and 'Anon', 127
  and the reader, 116, 117, 127, 136
  audience in, 122–3, 125, 127, 178–9
    n. 58, 179 notes 62, 66
  class in, 178 n. 54
  creativity in, 117, 119, 126
  Empire in, 119–20, 122
  Miss La Trobe in, 119–121, 124,
    125, 126
  pageant in, 118–24: comedy of, 120,
    121; as counter to war, 126–7;
    'failure of', 124–5, 127; as fertility
    ritual, 126; as gift, 123, 124, 127;
    as inspiration, 125, 126
  patriarchy in, 120, 122, 124, 178
    n. 54
  'present time' in, 122–3
  Victorian period in, 122
  working-class characters in: Eliza
    Clarke, 121–2; Budge/Hammond,
    122
'Gypsy, the Mongrel', 131
'How Should One Read a Book?', 15, 25
'In the Orchard', 134, **135–40**
  and 'A Woman's College from
    Outside', 142
  class in, 135, 137, 139, 142
  patriarchy in, 135, 137, 139, 140
  tea-taking in, 139
  textual generosity in, 139
  The Tempest (allusion to), 140
  women as commodity in, 136,
    137–8, 139, 140: economic
    position of, 137

Index 199

Jacob's Room, 141
'Kew Gardens', 9, 131, **133–4**, 139, 180 n. 12
patriarchy in, 134, 139
tea-taking in, 134
women as commodities in, 133, 134
'Lappin and Lappinova', 131
'Modern Fiction', 15, 21
'Modern Novels', 21
'Moments of Being: "Slater's Pins Have No Points"', 131, 134
collecting in, 149–50, 154
commodities in, 148, 150, 152
flower in, 152–3
gift in, 147, 148, 151, 153–4: artistic (musical), 148, 151; imagination (stories) 151–2, 155; and market 147–8, 148–9, 150–1
homoerotic desires in, 147–8, 149, 150, 153, 157
jouisssance in, 155
patriarchy in, 149, 152, 154
reader and, 155
shopping in, 148, 150
textual generosity, 148, 155
women as objects of exchange in, 152: and economic position, 149, 152
'Mr Bennett and Mrs Brown', 7
Mrs Dalloway, 16, 50, **57–83**
class in, 68, 70, 76, 82, 84
feminine economy in, 64, 71, 82
flowers in, 62, 68, 70–1, 72, 73, 74: roses, 77–8, 79–80
gifts in, 62, 63–4, 73, 74–5: corrupted gifts, 76, 81, 82–3; disruptive gifts, 63, 69, 80, 82; and homoeroticism, 65, 66, 69; kiss as gift, 62, 63, 64–7, 68, 69; social gift, 63
homoerotic desire in, 51, 62, 63, 64, 67, 68, 71, 73, 75, 76, 80, 82, 84, 170 n. 15, 170–1 n. 18, 172 n. 35, 174 n. 16, n. 17, 174 n. 19
homophobia in, 64, 74
jouisssance in, 63, 71
masculine economy in, 62, 72, 77, 78
party in, 80–1, 82, 83
patriarchy in, 64, 65, 68, 69, 78, 80, 82, 83

pseudo-gifts in, 62, 63, 67, 68, 77, 78
shopping in, 70, 73, 75, 80
spirit of the gift, 63, 69
women as objects of exchange, 68, 77, 78, 83, 84
'Mrs Dalloway in Bond Street', 50, 51, **52–62**
class in, 52, 57, 58, 59, 60, 61
feminine economy in, 54, 56
gifts in, 53, 55–6, 57: disruptive gifts, 56–7; women as gift givers, 61, 65
gloves in, 55, 58–9, 60
homoerotic desire, 54, 55, 57, 58, 59–60, 61
'lesbian panic' in, 59
masculine economy, 52, 55, 57, 58
patriarchy in, 57, 59, 169–70 n. 11
shopping in, 52, 54, 55, 61
women as objects of exchange in, 56, 65, 169–70 n. 11
Orlando, **110–115**
and creativity and, 112–3, 114–5
and gift, 108, 109, 110, 114
homoerotic desire in, 111, 113, 114–5
ideas for, 107–8
jouissance, 115
literary market, 110, 111, 112, 113
patriarchy in, 112
Sackville-West and, 108
shopping, 111, 112
writing as commodity, 111, 112, 115
'Oxford Street Tide', 15, 18, 21, 22, 25, 84, 167 n. 12
'Professions for Women', 38, 44
'Reviewing', 13, 14, **35**
'A Sketch of the Past', 139
'Solid Objects', 131, 132–3: collecting in, 133
'Street Haunting: A London Adventure', 13, 15, 18, **19–27**, 28, 40, 48, 166 n. 5
books in, 19, 24, 25, 27
capitalism in, 22–3, 24, 25
class in, 48, 167 n. 9
commodity culture in, 23, 26
modernist aesthetics in, 21–2

200 *Index*

Woolf, Virginia (works) (*cont.*)
shopping in, 20, 21, 22, 23, 25, 26, 27
'The Docks of London', 23, 167 n. 9
'The Hours', 50, 51, 70, 75, 138
'The Legacy', 131, **155–161**
class in, 158
gift: threshold gift in, 158, 159, 160; pseudo-gifts in, 157
homoerotic possibilities in, 157, 161
masculine economy in, 157, 158, 159
patriarchy in, 157, 161
reading as capitalist exchange in, 160
suicide in, 156, 157
Woolf's death and, 156
'The Mark on the Wall', 131, 132
To the Lighthouse, **86–107**
and capitalism, 88, 91, 97
class in, 88–9, 90, 92, 95, 96, 97, 98, 99, 106–7, 172–3 n. 2, n. 5, n. 6, 175 n. 24
creativity in, 87, 89, 92–3, 94, 95–6, 97, 98–100, 101, 106, 107
fertility myths, 89, 90, 91, 94–5, 101
gift: gift cycle, 88–90, 91, 93, 97, 100, 102, 105, 106; spirit of the gift, 89, 90, 102, 105; women and, 88, 89, 90–1, 91–2, 97, 98, 103–4, 174–5 n. 19
goddess figure in, 88, 90, 91, 93, 94, 173 n. 9

homoerotic desire, 93, 94, 97, 102, 103
jouissance, 99
patriarchy in, 89, 90–1, 104, 173 n. 9, 174 n. 17
temporal frame, 86–7, 89–90
threshold gift, 87, 90, 107
tripartite structure, 87, 89
war, 86–7, 88, 95, 96, 97–8, 101
women as objects of exchange, 87–8, 91, 104
and Woolf's experience, 87, 90, 107–8
working-class women in, 87, 100, 101–2: Mrs McNab, 95, 96–7, 97–9, 101–2, 103, 106, 175 n. 22
'Thoughts on Peace in an Air raid', 18, **37–8**, 40, 49, 118
Three Guineas, 13, 14, 15, 19, 28–9, 38, **39–48**, 49
capitalism in, 39–40
education in, 39, 43, 44–5, 47
gift in, 40, 42–3, 44, 45–6, 47–8
letters in, 39, 45–7
literary market in, 34, 41
money in, 28–9, 39, 40–1, 42, 43
professions in, 41–2, 43, 44, 47: and 'Professions for Women', 44
war in, 39, 40, 47
'Why Art Today Follows Politics', 13, **36–7**

Zwerdling, Alex, 7, 11, 179 n. 66